IN MEMORY OF TIMES TO COME

ASAO Studies in Pacific Anthropology

General Editor: Rupert Stasch, Department of Social Anthropology, University of Cambridge

The Association for Social Anthropology in Oceania (ASAO) is an international organization dedicated to studies of Pacific cultures, societies, and histories. This series publishes monographs and thematic collections on topics of global and comparative significance, grounded in anthropological fieldwork in Pacific locations.

Recent volumes:

For a full volume listing, please see the series page on our website:
https://www.berghahnbooks.com/series/asao

In Memory of Times to Come

Ironies of History in Southeastern Papua New Guinea

Melissa Demian

berghahn
NEW YORK · OXFORD
www.berghahnbooks.com

First published in 2021 by

Berghahn Books

www.berghahnbooks.com

© 2021, 2024 Melissa Demian
First paperback edition published in 2024

Library of Congress Cataloging-in-Publication Data

A C.I.P. cataloging record is available from the Library of Congress
Library of Congress Cataloging in Publication Control Number: 2021015524

British Library Cataloguing in Publication Data

A catalogue record for this book is available from the British Library

ISBN 978-1-80073-116-5 hardback
ISBN 978-1-80539-136-4 paperback
ISBN 978-1-80539-405-1 epub
ISBN 978-1-80073-117-2 web pdf

https://doi.org/10.3167/9781800731165

In memory of Ellis Avery

Contents

Illustrations

Figures

Map

Table

Acknowledgments 🍀

Any ethnography is ultimately composed of all the people whose ideas, support, criticism, hospitality, and goodwill contributed both to the fieldwork on which the ethnography is based and to the creative processes brought to bear on the writing of it. As this particular ethnography has had a longer gestation than most, it follows accordingly that there are a great many people to thank for standing behind this book in one capacity or another over the years.

In 1996 and 1997 my hosts in Leileiyafa were Saunia Beliliso and May Roguwe, along with their daughters Agula, Cecily, and Noiali (all of whom are now grown with children of their own). This family and I, thrown together as hosts and guest more or less by accident, were engaged for fourteen months in a sometimes joyous, sometimes difficult, often absurd project of learning by the seats of our pants just how challenging the ethnographic enterprise is. For their good grace in embarking on a relationship with a total stranger dropped into their household willy-nilly, I will be always be grateful. Many thanks also go to Kiukiuna Yokotali for her work as my field assistant during this time, and to Matilda Pilacapio for making it all possible in the first place. To Leileiyafa's one-time village court magistrate, Elia Seromai, I owe particular thanks for initiating what would unexpectedly become an ongoing interest in how Papua New Guineans negotiate their relationship with a sometimes baffling but always fascinating legal system. For this, my debt to him and his family is incalculable.

In 1999 and 2000 I moved the site of my fieldwork to Isuisu and the hospitality of local-level government councillor Mamari Eseroma, his wife Baigayo, and their children Hannie, Eliot, Sarah, Marie, Ben, and Sharon. Ken Ah Chee offered his services as dinghy operator extraordinaire, and Margaret Sunday worked as my field assistant in this period; we all shared as much laughter as we did taped interview material, for which I am so appreciative. Together they introduced me to life on the coast and showed unstinting generosity with their time and energy in helping with shorter but more structured periods of fieldwork during this first stay with them and continually afterward. I hope these words can serve as some sort of reassurance that the relationship between Mamari's family and myself is an ongoing one with a future. To "auntie" Sunema Bagita in Alotau I extend the same promise.

In Alotau in the mid-1990s I was also shown hospitality by Allan Jones and by Ken and Lisa Schultz, and in 2008 by Jeff and Sylvia Kinch. Chris Abel and Murray Abel both welcomed in different ways the newest foreigner to be interested in the part of Milne Bay Province with which their family has had such a long and distinguished history. In the late 1990s I was frequently hosted on Samarai by Andrew Margetts and Anna Keusen (later Margetts), to whom I am grateful for many stimulating discussions and congenial dinners. David and the late Ann Hall, as well as Ian Poole, also acted as part of my wider Samarai support network during that time.

In Port Moresby I have been at various points either hosted or otherwise supported by the late Dr. Lawrence Kalinoe, Her Excellency Winnie Kiap, Dr. Andrew Moutu, Sebastian Haraha, Olinda Bunena, colleagues at the University of Papua New Guinea, all the staff and tenants at Haus Ruth, and the entire Suau congregation that was until a few years ago based in the Ela United Church. My gratitude is extended to all these good and hardworking people for making life in a difficult city that much less difficult.

Without the enormous package of Buhutu and Suau language material that Russell E. Cooper of the Summer Institute of Linguistics sent me back in 1996, and ongoing support thereafter, I would have been up the Sagarai River without a paddle.

My entire life as a scholar has been shaped for the better by teachers. My education was bookended by two Cambridges, and the most profound effects on my development as an anthropologist are attributable to each end, starting with my teachers at Cambridge Friends School in Massachusetts who were committed to introducing their pupils to the gift that is human diversity well over a decade before "multiculturalism" became a fashionable concept. And eight years later at the University of Cambridge I had the incomparable good fortune to work with Marilyn Strathern, whose gifts to my understanding of what anthropology is and might become will always be, appropriately, immeasurable. If she perhaps suspected this book might never see the light of day, all I can offer in mitigation is that I never forgot her exhortation to keep going.

There have been any number of colleagues whom I also count as friends and who have, over the years and in one way or another, affected the production, shape, and flavor of this book. I would like to express particular gratitude to Debbora Battaglia, Tony Crook, Karen Sykes, Stuart Kirsch, Matt Tomlinson, Lissant Bolton, Judith Bovensiepen, Noreen Galante, Sari Wastell, Paige West, Carly Schuster, and John Cox. Within my personal circle of friends, Talya Leodari and Ellis Avery shared at various points in our student and adult lives the pleasures and pains of academic writing, and writing more generally. Those conversations with Ellis are the memory of her that I will cherish for the rest of my life. But especial thanks must go to the following people for sustaining my work on this book in the moments when I simply could not see my own way forward with it: Ilana Gershon, Joe D'Andrea, and, like a hero shooting out of the sky in the last ten minutes of a film when all seems lost, Sarah Perrault.

Finally, at its heart this book bears the indelible imprint of the person who instilled in me a lifelong curiosity about experiences radically different from my own, and about the dazzling variety of futures available to the human imagination: my father, Dennis Livingston. Science fiction kept us connected at times when very little else did, thereby creating the foundation not only of an intellectual orientation to the world but an affective one. Kinship is established in all sorts of unexpected ways. So while I may not have become the intergalactic explorer he imagined at my birth in the early 1970s, I hope this comes close enough.

Introduction

On Anthropology and History in the Pacific

Some people no longer feel global but wish they could. There are parts of the world in which globalization is regarded as having already concluded after being introduced decades ago, leaving in its wake people who live in anticipation of a time when they might once again be connected to the rest of the world in ways that they find productive and satisfying. Between the late nineteenth century and the end of World War II, Suau people on the coast of southeastern Papua New Guinea (PNG) experienced educational, travel, and wage labor opportunities that were among the first of their kind available to a Melanesian population—and that no longer exist. In the decades following the war, the connections with the United Kingdom, Australia, and the United States to which they had grown accustomed gradually disappeared, leaving them with a sense of isolation that, arguably, they had never experienced before. In other words, Suau people briefly resided in a regional metropole within a global periphery, and furthermore, this occurred by means of their deliberate shedding of practices and relationships that they felt would not lead to fruitful relationships with the new regional powers. Suau frequently say that they have lost or "forgotten" their *kastom*, or a repertoire of practices and moral orientations associated with a way of life that people are imagined to have led before their encounters with Europeans. While the claim is a rhetorical one, it also points to a sophisticated and agentive positioning of themselves in history, in relation both to other Papua New Guineans and to foreigners.

This is not a simple tale of an indigenous people overrun by forces beyond their control; that story has been told already, in dozens of settings, and in any combination of scholarly, artistic, and political forms of expression. Instead, this book offers a consideration of how a people's temporal orientations and historical consciousness have constituted the basis for their decisions to engage with foreign others in particular ways since the end of the nineteenth century. These memory practices inspire them not only to memorialize a past that is regarded as superior to the present dispensation but also to employ remembering, forgetting, and ironic reflection as techniques for creating a space in which they can exercise mastery over their own future.

This book is based on a somewhat patchwork twenty-year ethnographic relationship with Suau-speaking peoples in Milne Bay Province, PNG, that gave rise to the foregoing problems—or *pilipili* as Suau would call them, a term referencing the entanglement of a fishing or pig-hunting net, or the construction of a string bag gone awry. I refer to Suau "peoples" deliberately, for as I will discuss further in chapter 1, the boundaries of who belongs definitively to a Suau *ethnos* are not at all clear. Their entanglements with a series of foreign guests, visitors, and colonizers, and the sense they have made of these relationships as a mode of historical consciousness, form the backbone of the book. Suau relationships with others over time would not make much sense, however, without my also providing some key accounts of the social world inhabited by many Suau. Many, but not all: this is a book about Suau people living on their ancestral land at the southeasternmost mainland extremity of the island of New Guinea and practicing a mixed economy of swidden horticulture, fishing, hunting, and small livestock husbandry, alongside cash cropping and wage labor. A long history of Suau uptake of formal education (see chapter 3) means that many Suau people also live in towns and cities across PNG, working in various white-collar sectors, but this is not their book. At least, not explicitly, acknowledging the extent to which people and resources now flow between urban and rural populations in PNG.

This book is about memory practices, and a sense of history framed by the perspective of a rural Papua New Guinean population, who for a time were not a *remote* population but became one through the loss of a colonial infrastructure and the entangled relationships that went with it. In this book I ask, what would a theory of change look like if it were not solely informed by the modernist orientations of European and North American concepts but devised in conversation with these concepts? Is there a way to talk about the experience of change that does not draw upon the "modern constitution" (Latour 1993: 13) of designating opposed categories—say the traditional versus the new, although Latour is more concerned with nature versus society—in order to then contrast them as antitheses or recombine them as hybrids, depending on which version of the modernist game one is playing. For Latour, the separation of categories, which he termed purification, is precisely what causes hybrids between these categories to proliferate in the background, as it were, and continually take moderns by surprise—such as when a Suau person declares, "Our *kastom* is Christian." Latour's modern constitution is the always-incomplete project of acknowledging one category of action while keeping the categories from which it has been distinguished out of view. "Who is to write the full constitution?" he asks, and then answers himself with tongue at least halfway in cheek: "As far as foreign collectives are concerned, anthropology has been pretty good at tackling everything at once" (1993: 13). His compliment to anthropology refers to the ethnographic tendency to gleefully disregard what "ought," for the moderns, to be distinct domains and put mythological culture heroes and postcolonial court systems in the same book, as I have done in this one. The problem is, his compliment is not quite accurate: anthropologists can be as captive to the allure of modernist distinctions as anyone else.

"That the idiom of the modern can be used over and over again," as Brenner (1998: 88) has noted, "attests to its enduring power as a signifier of historical transformation." So for example, the Papua New Guinean (and arguably pan-Melanesian) category of *kastom* might appear at first blush to look something like the standard modernist division of a temporal or cultural break between an era identified as "traditional" and one identified as "modern." Particularly when Papua New Guineans like my interlocutors on the Suau Coast deploy language that appears to map onto these divisions (such as terms that could be translated as "time immemorial" versus "nowadays") and claims about having forgotten *kastom* entirely (see chapter 2), it is tempting to say that they are experiencing a modernist disjuncture of not only a break with history but also a rejection of it.

In order to resist that temptation, I ask not only where the category of modernity is coming from in accounts of this kind but also where the category of history itself enters the picture, and how these categories continue to be applied to analyses of the experiences of once-colonized people. This book will consistently point toward a number of capacious nouns that do adjacent kinds of intellectual work: history, modernity, even culture or tradition as they appear at times to ride alongside *kastom*. The central objective of this book is to show how the work that Suau people have been doing since the end of the nineteenth century is a mode of relationship building by means of imagining others as social analysts like themselves. By "work" I mean the hospitality shown toward missionaries and other agents of colonial expansion that Suau people hold up as the defining factor in their own social genius. This social and analytical generosity later proved troublesome when the colonial world contracted. It forms the irony at the heart of Suau memory work: the skillful efforts to meet foreign others on their own terms are precisely what has stranded the Suau Coast and its people in a state of seeming to be stuck in time as well as space. The language they deployed with their ethnographer, when I first gave myself this role and became their guest in the mid-1990s, was again the language of hospitable reaching out to the other in terms intelligible to that other. It was the very terms of history, modernity, and all the rest that Suau people used, and that enabled a connection to become established. This does not mean that my Suau friends were deceiving me, or themselves: it means that they were demonstrating their skill as social analysts of our relationship.

Even in contexts like that of Papua New Guinea, where the project of co-lonialism was on its last legs even as it got underway in the early twentieth century, Papua New Guineans learned rapidly what it meant to engage with others who presumed an asymmetrical relationship with them from the very outset, in which the possibility of coevalness was denied (Fabian 1983). It is even debatable whether Europeans were able to conceive of anything like a re-lationship with Papua New Guineans at all. Particularly for Suau people, who were early on the scene of the colonial encounter in comparison with most other Papua New Guineans, the relationship presumed by Europeans even be-fore the commencement of missionization was one in which no such identity as "Suau" even existed; there were only "natives" or "savages" or simply "can-nibals," as most Pacific Islanders were (and arguably still are) categorized in the fevered European imagination. Suau people learned in that encounter that not only did their elaborate local and regional complexes of identification by lineage, clan, and dialect not matter to the foreigners they were hosting, but *nothing* about them mattered other than their occupation of a space now usu-ally identified under the rubric of the indigenous.

This rubric has its uses, especially in those legal and political spheres where colonized people never stopped being colonized and were forcibly dis-possessed of their land—I am describing, of course, Australia, Aotearoa New Zealand, and the Americas, as well as less obvious "Fourth World" settings across Asia and Africa (Ryser et al. 2017). But even in the western Pacific, where the project of imperial expansion almost literally ran out of steam, the analytical methods and tropes that European social scientists had brought with them from elsewhere in their experience traveled almost seamlessly. This means that one can ask, with Simpson (2007), how "anthropological analyses of indigeneity may still occupy the 'salvage' and 'documentary' slot for analy-sis, an elaboration of object that results from the endurance of categories that emerged in moments of colonial contact, many of which still reign supreme. In those moments, people left their own spaces of self-definition and became 'Indigenous'" (2007: 69). Once people have relinquished even a modicum of their sovereignty over defining themselves as ever having had an identity other than the one created in the process of colonization, even as deliberately as my Suau friends say they did, they form a new set of attachments to a raft of exog-enous categories, some of which will be assimilated to the needs of the current era, and some of which will remain backgrounded in an uneasy relationship with this era—as in, say, the category of *kastom*. "And so it is that concepts have teeth and teeth that bite through time" (2007: 69), Simpson warns us. A number of these mordacious concepts have dogged the anthropology of Mela-nesia for years if not decades, unmooring our ethnographic sensitivities from the categories to which our interlocutors are trying to call our attention and setting us adrift in a doldrums of our own creation.

Anthropology's Modernism Fetish, or, "What Do Melanesians Want?"

It may seem awkward to attribute to the anthropology of Melanesia a question patterned on the one Freud famously once asked about women (Jones 1955: 421). The problem is one both of uncertainty even in the face of experience—Freud couched his query in a statement about how long he had treated women patients—and of experience of persons who, for whatever reason, appear to resist intelligibility. Freud's remark is these days played for laughs, or held up as a data point in the many failures of a profession that was resoundingly masculinist in its formative years. But Freud knew what his failures were; he documented them almost obsessively. He also documented a range of possible human responses to failure, or the threat of failure. These will return to my narrative shortly, but for now, I invoke his formulation as a kind of question that has also, arguably, plagued the anthropology of the western Pacific, because the answer since at least the early 1990s seems repeatedly to have been: modernity.

"To 'modernize,'" Sahlins (1992) remarked, "the people must first learn to hate what they already have, what they have always considered their well-being. Beyond that, they have to despise what they are, to hold their own existence in contempt—and want, then, to be someone else" (1992: 24). Sahlins's project at the time was concerned with showing how the enthusiasm for particular manufactured trade goods by Pacific Islanders was not a way of rejecting themselves but of becoming more emphatic versions of themselves, at least insofar as these trade goods became a means of magnifying particular Pacific systems of prestige and political-cosmological hierarchy—Fijian chiefs and Hawaiian kings, for example. And indeed, his account of these systems becoming supported rather than undermined by trade goods, so that trade goods become enveloped by an already existing "cultural logic," is appealing, but it also immediately raises troubling questions. One asks what happens to those corners of culture that are on the other side of prestige, hierarchy, and power. Is that as far as cultural logic gets us, and what of nonpowerful persons and groups when a system of power relations is remade into a more extreme version of itself? But my more pertinent question for the purposes of this book is: Can we track what anthropologists of the Pacific have used as their signifier for modernity and ask what this modernity is that so easily lends itself to repeated manifestation as the temporal form of greatest concern to the anthropologist? For Sahlins in the 1990s, modernity was trade goods and the system of market capitalism that brought these goods to the Pacific. But this is not the only form taken by modernity in the accounts of anthropologists.

Christianity is another popular exemplar of modernity, as it appears to give rise to extreme self-reflexivity, such as that described by Robbins (2004a) for

Urapmin people in the Western Province of Papua New Guinea. For Robbins, the practice of self-discipline and the expiatory revelation of sin, which are the hallmarks of certain varieties of evangelical Protestantism, offered to Urapmin a vertiginous opportunity to experiment with the kind of epoch-breaking division that appears to signify a modernist reorientation to the world. "What troubles the Urapmin," he writes, "is . . . to some extent an outcome of their very success in reproducing the traditional grounds of their lives: their families, their gardens, their hunting territories. What troubles them is trying to live with the culture that supplies those grounds and another culture, a Christian one, at the same time" (2004a: 314). Although Urapmin people may fairly be said to have evangelized themselves, and were never subject to the kind of sustained missionary project that people on the Suau Coast were, they nonetheless—in Robbins's account—somehow adopted along with Christianity the epochal divisions of the modern constitution. The very notion of two cultures—one newer and one older, one of which is in tension with the other—are components of the modern constitution. In order to imagine themselves as having to hold two cultures in tension or balance with each other, they would have first to imagine that being Urapmin and being Christian are somehow different projects.

These anthropological accounts of autosurveillance in the face of historical processes is a common trope, and a compelling one. Anthropology has been generating this trope for Melanesia since at least the middle of the twentieth century, with exemplars such as Mead's (1956) account of the "transformation" of Manus Island following World War II and Worsley's (1957) attempt to make sense of a type of Melanesian response to colonialism that had become categorized as "cargo cults" by suggesting they were protonationalist movements. But it did not stop there, and it continues in the present century with Sillitoe's (2000) account of Melanesian "misunderstandings" of development projects leading to violence, LiPuma's (2000) argument that certain Melanesian worlds have been encompassed by a modernity that is then reinterpreted through a Sahlins-esque cultural logic, and Knauft's (2002) notion of "recessive agency" to describe what was, for him, a baffling affective stance in response to introduced institutions such as schools and churches in a remote part of Papua New Guinea. Anthropologists have continually grappled with the question of why Melanesian peoples engage with their histories in the ways that they do. Too often, however, these boil down to questions of how Melanesians respond to—or in less charitable terms that are often just below the surface of these accounts, cope with—variations on the theme of modernity that is continually conceived as the same "package" of artifacts, both tangible and systemic in nature, introduced from elsewhere by means of colonialism and its aftermath. Even Knauft's hedging with the notion of "alternative modernity" leaves the category of the modern assigned to the standard collection of institutions, bureaucracies, religious practices and orientations, and technologies to which Euro-Americans have always assigned it. Each iteration of the modern may be locally inflected, such that "Western practices encode Western epistemology and notions of subjectivity and . . . these interact with local categories and concepts of knowledge to generate new and mediated forms" (LiPuma 2000: 185), but suggesting even a mediated form of social and cultural practice is to claim a disruption of whatever forms came before. We are still dealing with a Melanesian modernity, in other words, and while there is certainly a great deal of theoretical mileage to be got from this notion, the troubling issue remains: modernity is not a Melanesian category, but a European and North American one, and a mode that Europeans and North Americans have been very fond of using to explain our own histories to ourselves for a very long time.

The problem with using this modernist narrative—a break, and then a re-combination, of cultural elements and social systems—in its various guises to explain recent Melanesian history is that each time we do this, anthropologists of Melanesia commit the same self-defeating act, our own version of "hating what we already have" to employ Sahlins's turn of phrase. He also noted this tendency among anthropologists toward the end of the last century, in the discipline's shift from breathless empiricist naïveté to postcolonial, postmodern melancholy (Sahlins 1993: 6). That theme, of a melancholic anthropology, has more recently returned in the form of an ethnographic relationship in which the dream of reciprocity between anthropologist and hosts is shown to be just that, an unattainable condition that produces dysphoria in the wake of its revelation as fantasy (High 2011). High focuses on Freud's theory of melancholy and anxiety as affective responses to the return of the repressed, the acknowledgment of a sense of failure to avert troubling events. This is doubtless a fruitful avenue for ethnographers to consider, but I am more interested here in a different facet of Freud: the fetish, and how that has produced certain ethnographic fixations.

Whatever else a fetish meant for Freud, he regarded it as a product of a sense of loss or threat of loss and a need to avert the gaze from this threat and fixate it elsewhere, on an object or body part that is not the "actual" or "proper" object of sexuality. That the loss for Freud, somewhat inevitably, came down to castration is not especially important; the point for my purposes was his use of the fetish concept to distinguish a response to repression (*Verdrängung*) from a response to disavowal (*Verleugnung*) (Freud 1950: 199). It is the latter affective state that generates the fetish, wherein the need for disavowal requires a new object of attention and of overwhelming presence. In this view, the fetish is "a fixed power to repeat an original event of singular synthesis or ordering" (Pietz 1985: 10) that becomes concentrated in the object of the fetish. My concern here is that the "original event of singular synthesis" for many anthropologists is modernity itself, the category by which we cannot help but imbue power to the ideas of "before" and "after" and observe processes of historical transformation occurring in astoundingly consistent ways across multiple contexts.

Englund and Leach (2000) observed the consolidation of this preoccupation in anthropology two decades ago, and it shows no sign of abating. Whether or not the modernity fetish is an eruption of sociological ideas into anthropology, as Englund and Leach suggested, is no longer the issue. The issue is what this now almost inescapable framework has done to the way anthropologists think about history, especially when that history appears to be presented in very stark terms of before and after. My argument is that the modernity fetish has overwhelmed these terms and assimilated them to itself, before we have even had a chance to consider what people might actually be saying about their own memory practices. By suggesting that modernity and its trappings present people in Melanesia with a set of challenges by which they are continually flummoxed and to which they continually struggle to adapt, anthropologists have essentially made the statement that the ethnography of this part of the world has nothing to offer the rest of the field or to adjacent fields in the social sciences and humanities. While people in Nigeria, Venezuela, Romania, or Kazakhstan are apparently getting on with the business of life in a world of flows and connections, anthropology has consistently portrayed people in Papua New Guinea and other localities of the western Pacific as trapped by their own beguilement with modernity.

One way to imagine the modernism fetish is as a disavowal of the possibility of talking about history and change in any other way. Disavowal does appear in the way that many Suau people talk about the loss or forgetting of *kastom*, but my project is to demonstrate that Suau values of hospitable curiosity are at least in part what has led the production of a narrative that *seems* intelligible as one about modernity—because it is the narrative that their guests expect of them. As a periodic guest and *dimdim* (as white foreigners are known throughout Milne Bay Province) on the Suau Coast, I have had ongoing questions about how much of that narrative was produced for my benefit. This book is an attempt to tread a path between taking seriously the way my Suau friends and interlocutors spoke about their own history, and eschewing modernist narratives such as a break in history, a combining of cultures, or a loss of authenticity, in favor of what a Suau historiography might look like. The *might* here is important: this is after all a book written by a non-Suau person for a largely non-Suau audience. It is nonetheless an effort to use what I learned on the Suau Coast about history to reflect on the way anthropologists talk about history in any of the places where we might be working.

I hope Suau readers will look on this effort with the same generosity of spirit with which their parents, cousins, aunts, uncles, and grandparents have welcomed its author over the years and shared what knowledge they thought it was appropriate for her to hear. And they very explicitly did not share everything; see chapter 6 for a consideration of what the refusal to share certain kinds of knowledge with certain kinds of persons means for this ethnography in particular and for the ethnographic endeavor in general. What I have made out of the knowledge I was permitted to share is borne out of a long relationship with the Suau Coast, beginning in 1996–97, with repeat visits of varying length in 1999–2000, 2008, 2013, 2014, and 2015. I hope the relationship continues, whatever the shortcomings of this book. It is an attempt to ask, following the lead of Teresia Teaiwa (2006: 75), "how change in the Pacific gets collapsed with previously formed ways of knowing, how change in the Pacific gets incorporated into familiar models." Asking this question, after an engagement of nearly twenty years with a particular place and the people of that place, means not only that the ethnographer in this instance was able to see how a place changed over time but also that what I was able to learn from my Suau friends also changed with time. By this I mean not only that what they deemed knowable for me changed but also that what people indicated to me as signs of change was itself a shifting ground.

The seed of this book was planted when I was a young woman: the term in Suau is *hasala*, connoting the naïveté and inexperience with which I initiated this relationship. Twenty years later, it has become a project that combines two particular streams of experience. One is all the things my Suau friends have told me over the years, and the other is the potholed road of an academic career in an era when the old trajectory of the scholar who lands a permanent job straight out of her PhD, and then stays in that job forever, has receded into myth. This book was written at multiple universities in three countries. It reflects the generosity not only of my Suau hosts but also of my academic ones in all those environments. I hope to have produced, as a result, something a little different from the sort of ethnography developed out of a doctoral dissertation after which the ethnographer then walks away from the community that hosted him, never to return. The calcified "ethnographic present" that has not been updated for decades is not without theoretical interest, but only when it is presented in a clear-eyed manner as history and not as anyone's current lived experience. And let us be honest: this book also documents a series of moments in the engagement between an ethnographer and her host communities, and it too will enter the ethnographic record as history. It is an experiment in communicating a Suau sense of ironic nostalgia that only the ironic nostalgia of middle age has truly made possible. In the mid-1990s, when Suau people told me in the same breath that they had lost multiple meaningful modes of action—glossed as *kastom*—and that they themselves were responsible for that loss due to the hospitality they had shown colonial others, I was baffled. Some of that bafflement will be evident in the chapters that follow. But bafflement and perplexity are themselves modes of knowledge formation and are, I submit, preferable to the overweening confidence of the one-time or occasional visitor who claims to have grasped the entire cosmological or ontological system of their hosts, which I would characterize as reproducing some of the oldest colonial tropes of anthropology itself. "We need to draw on all our maps of understanding," Linda Tuhiwai Smith (2008: 136) exhorts the researcher willing to embrace the inevitability of making partial knowledge claims in a world of scholarship still plagued by the inequities of colonial relations. If this book is a line on a map, it is one shaped by the very particular relationships between a researcher and the people who taught her that a place is also a history and a life also a landscape (chapter 4).

Pacific Theories of Space/Time

Over a decade ago, the geographer Doreen Massey warned us that

> conceiving of space as a static slice through time, as representation, as a closed system and so forth are all ways of taming it. They enable us to ignore its real import: the coeval multiplicity of other trajectories and the necessary outward-lookingness of a spatialized subjectivity. . . . Conceptualizing space as open, multiple and relational, unfinished and always becoming, is a prerequisite for history to be open and thus a prerequisite, too, for the possibility of politics. (Massey 2005: 59)

If this sounds a little abstruse, it is worth setting Massey's observations alongside those of Smith (2012), who has noted that the "classical" post-Enlightenment notion of space as an empty void to be filled is also the conception of space that makes colonial domination and appropriation possible. An empty, timeless space is one that can be occupied with whatever notions and categories one likes, whether the grand-scale legal fiction of *terra nullius* that was used to justify the invasion and settlement of Australia or the philosophical conceits projected by scholars upon our subjects of study.

But space conceived as "multiple and relational, unfinished and always becoming" is something else entirely. It is a space filled with people's memories, dreams, fears, aspirations, and intentions for, with, and through each other. And it is a space filled with care: an element that also points to the temporality of this filled-up space. Ka'ili (2005) offers a discussion of the Tongan concept of *vā*, or space-in-between, which is a first step to understanding a number of Pacific knowledge practices wherein space is replete with relationships between persons, between things, and between persons and things. This kind of space, argues Ka'ili, is operational regardless of distance and must be looked after whether the persons holding it between them are located on neighboring islands or in different countries at opposite ends of the Pacific Ocean. And it is in the looking after or nurturing of this space, not only between contemporary actors but also over time, that provides Tongans with the intergenerational knowledge that enables them to know how to act even with persons they have never met before. As long as an intergenerational connection can be established, the caretaking potential of *vā* is activated. Or as Gershon (2007: 474) has put it, "Ethnographers of the Pacific have long known that the Pacific is not just a sea of islands, but also a sea of families."

This is not a rhetorical statement but a methodological and an ethical one. Like Kaʻili, Gershon is engaged in asking how imagining the Pacific as made up of familial relationships conducted over vast distances affects both an ethnographic sense of scale and one of obligation. How Pacific peoples maintain their relationships across space and over time reverberates back on their own identities, conceived here not only as a political formation but also as the basis for an actual, everyday ability to flourish in the world. Rooney (2017b) has written evocatively of the constantly shifting identities of migrants to Papua New Guinea's capital of Port Moresby, the ways these identities can be both a lifeline in a prohibitively expensive city and a source of continual pressure from family "back home," where "home" may signify a part of the country they have never lived in. Whether exercised between island nations or between the country and the city, Pacific peoples' claims both to their own identity and to each other's are claims to the circulation of care, of information—and of ignorance. "While ignorance is normally portrayed by scholars in terms of cultural loss, there is a more nuanced possibility—that judicious knowing and not knowing are strategies for navigating the many claims that people can make on each other" (Gershon 2007: 489). Navigation will appear again shortly, in a literal sense: but here it stands for the constantly shifting orientation to relationships made by Pacific peoples as they manage the flow of knowledge and care between themselves, and in so doing, generate a temporal and affective rhythm of relationships across distances long and short, and between persons with connections of many possible kinds.

The philosophical and ethnographic consequences for failing to attend to and care for these relations-over-time are profound. "The anthropology of the Pacific that I encounter," writes Māhina (1999: 44), "promotes a world of cultural symbols dissociated from historical realities and as a direct consequence implies a control of the subjects of its research." Here Māhina is discussing how anthropology is taught to Pacific Islands students, but his concerns are reflected elsewhere in the activist literature coming from Pacific scholars who have long been calling attention to the way that colonial epistemologies—space is a void to be filled, and time is only happening if a heroic figure, usually white and male, is there to witness and alter it irrevocably—have shaped an entire discipline's understanding of the Pacific region, and even its boundaries and characteristics as a region (1999: 53). In an effort to recover the ways in which Pacific peoples themselves designate the spaces they inhabit and move between—qualities of the sea, of the land, and of how people interact with land and sea—Māhina asks for nothing less than a Pacific realism, a way of apprehending and communicating a Pacific history that is static neither in space nor in time, but perpetually present and dynamic for those who continue to make it.

So many intellectual traditions, after all, stem from what is conceived as mobile, whether in a literal or a philosophical sense, and what is conceived as stationary. Consider, for example, the following account of the Carolinian seafaring concept of *etak* from Diaz:

> Typically translated as "moving islands," *etak* is the technique for calculating distance traveled, or position at sea by triangulating the speed of the islands of departure and destination with that of a third reference island. This is accomplished, furthermore, by plotting these islands' courses in the celestial sky, which in effect serves as a veritable map for the world below. A map and time piece, a way of negotiating emplotment in time/space—or more precisely, a way of conceptualizing time/space in order to fix one's place—*etak* was a critical technological development . . . that permitted humans to traverse over 2/3rds of the globe's southern hemisphere millennia before Europeans ventured from eyesight of their shores.
>
> In theory and practice, it works like this: first, you steer toward the stars that mark the island of your destination. While doing so, you back sight your island of departure until you can no longer see it. At the same time, you calculate the rate at which a third island, off to the side, moves from beneath the stars where it sat when you left your island of departure, toward the stars under which it should sit if you were standing in the island of your destination.
>
> Let me simplify: you get on your canoe and you follow the stars in the direction where lies your destination island. As your island of departure recedes from view, you pay attention to a third island, as it is said to move along another prescribed star course . . . for the navigator, the canoe remains stationary and the islands zip by. (Diaz 2011: 25–26)

As a navigational technique and a conceptualization of the subject in time and space, *etak* also suggests a certain ethnographic sensibility. Diaz goes on to point out that not only do islands move, they also *expand* as the navigator descries her location through observations of wave patterns, the presence of particular dwellers on the seascape (fish, birds, turtles, marine mammals), and the smell of prevailing winds and currents. The multisensory nature of Micronesian navigation holds the subject still while the world moves past him or rushes out to greet him. There is a Pacific realism in this version of subjectivity, but also the "unfinished and always becoming" nature of space in the philosophy implied by social geography. Because while the perspective of the subject in this formulation might appear to be one of stillness, it is also constantly shifting and expanding as well, as she employs all her embodied capacities to render intelligible the signs and entities that the world is sending to meet her.

Sometimes those signs demand particular modes of action, or at least affect, with regard to the past. Tengan (2005) defines the Hawaiian concept of *kuleana* as "responsibility, right, claim, authority" (2005: 252), most particularly in terms of caring for the ancestors correctly, and notes that "*Kuleana* also chooses us rather than the other way around" (2005: 252). The past is watching, in other words; it has interests and even demands to which people of the present have the privilege of responding; like an island receding into the distance, it may be lost to view but remains a vital and vitalizing part of the landscape, and seascape, of contemporary human action. Tengan identifies much of this action in the Pacific as struggle, and identifies ethnography as an activity indelibly inflected by this struggle. But it is not the kind of struggle to cope with modernity mentioned in the previous section; rather, it is struggle in the political-spatial sense of a history whose outcome is still unfolding. Or as Tengan puts it, "When ethnography is conducted in a community engaged in struggles over land, identity and history, struggle characterizes all facets of the ethnographic project" (2005: 250). I take his words to indicate not only the overt political struggles of still-colonized peoples in the Pacific, from Hawai'i to New Caledonia to Guam, but also those everyday struggles of self-determination undertaken by every Pacific population that has confronted the asymmetrical relationships of colonialism at any point in its ancestral reckoning—which is to say, all of them.

What does this somewhat breathless inventory of Pacific philosophies of care, navigation in space and time, and ancestral responsibility indicate for the current demands of Pacific ethnography? We must attend to an orientation to time that frames it as a body of privileges and duties, an orientation to space that frames it as change and movement expanding outward to the subject, and an orientation to other persons, living and dead, that demands they be cared for once they have been acknowledged as part of the subject's field of responsibility. This is not just a Pacific philosophy but quite specifically a Pacific *ethics* of responding to the expansiveness of the world with a reciprocal expansiveness.

This is a particular challenge now that scholars in, from, and of the Pacific are at pains to justify our field of study in terms of its "relevance" to the human endeavor elsewhere on the global stage. If history is a category that has been captured and nearly monopolized by metropolitan scholarship, it can be very difficult indeed either to insert into that category conceptions of time and space that have become muted or refracted over the course of the colonial project or to formulate a decolonized scholarship that seeks to re-privilege these conceptions. And sometimes, even in the identification of a region (in this case, say, the Pacific, or even more arbitrary regional designations such as "Melanesia"), we become our own worst enemies and disconnect it by means of insisting on a kind of cultural or social uniqueness that becomes incommensurable with ideas being generated elsewhere in the world.

Teresia Teaiwa (2006) once remarked on how, a century after the Pacific had generated some of the most enduring theoretical frameworks in anthropology, a contemporary interest in the ongoing questions, problems, and solutions offered up by Pacific peoples must now be analogized to comparable issues elsewhere in order to be considered timely. I suggest, along with West (2016: 28), that this state of affairs has come about precisely because of the lapidary focus by anthropologists of the Pacific on microregionalism and the uniqueness of Pacific societies. This focus has produced both a body of ethnographically rich and theoretically imaginative literature, and also a certain insularity of the variety that does not necessarily expand outward and affect scholarship on other national and regional contexts. It is not enough to say that Christianity in the Solomon Islands is like Christianity in Tanzania, or that consumption practices in Samoa are comparable to those of Thailand. Such analogies, as Teaiwa observed, somehow only serve to underscore the movement of Pacific scholarship toward the margins of anthropology rather than drawing other places in.

But the Pacific generally and Melanesia in particular—of course I will say this, because Melanesia has expanded outward and demanded the attention of this ethnographer for over two decades—belong back at the center of discussions about colonial histories and their continuing presence in the multiplicitous contemporary of people's lives. It belongs there precisely because the interest in difference across Melanesia is an interest in connection to other people and other places. As Hukula (2017) has shown for urban Papua New Guinea, Melanesian people have no trouble imagining "recognition of a multiple sense of place" (2017: 165), particularly when people from different places come to embody and care for connections over time, through sharing food, worship, and the cumulation of everyday acts of coliving in the swiftly growing metropoles of Melanesia, where everyone can be identified as being simultaneously of the city and of a distant ancestral ground. The interest in others is not about imitating what a group of people deemed more powerful or more connected are doing, and never has been. This interest stems from difference itself as a fundamental social and aesthetic value in Melanesia: you cannot make flourishing gardens, children, churches, neighborhoods, or anything else considered vital to the human endeavor if all you have are people just like yourself to make them with.

Toward a Melanesian Theory of Change

For the Pacific to reassume its place at the table of debates in anthropological theory and practice, it is critical to begin to release the categories that European, North American, and Australian scholarship have been importing into the regional ethnography since at least the end of World War II. As useful as they have been to think with, most of these categories continue to reflect the colonial-philosophical traditions that gave rise to them rather than the various Pacific contexts to which they have been applied. This book is a still-incomplete endeavor to release them, but the incompleteness is rather the point. Ethnography is always about finding the gaps, impositions, and errors in one's own knowledge claims, as well as querying the bases for the knowledge claims of others. But my opening gambit here is actually quite a simple one: even though a number of the tropes invoked by my hosts, interlocutors, and friends on the Suau Coast of Papua New Guinea look familiar, and seem to be part of transnational narratives around the loss of authenticity in the pursuit of the project of modernity, what if that is not what has happened at all? What if Suau people have been trying to articulate to their ethnographer a Melanesian theory of historical change in terms she will understand but with meanings quite different from what those terms appear to signify?

Melanesian peoples have always had their own categories, after all, some of them well known in the anthropological canon. These have included value as a function of social relationships and political efficacy (Munn 1986), the concealment of knowledge or living beings in order to make them potent and abundant (Gillison 1980; Biersack 1982; Bercovitch 1994), the flow of agency between persons both living and dead (Schieffelin 1976), and the aesthetics of gardens and their products as evidence of the positive or efficacious state of relations among persons (Young 1971; Coupaye 2013). Perhaps the most critical category underwriting all of these is that of land, which in no part of the Pacific is reducible to a mere geographical territory but is a space filled with relationships, which can be both productive and contested in nature (de Coppet 1985; Tuwere 2002; Biersack 1999; Black 2011; Rooney 2017a). As the foregoing discussion of space and time in Pacific cosmologies indicates, land concentrates both of these categories at a physical point—the ground on which people live and make their livelihoods—but that physical point also contains an ever-ramifying field of spiritual and temporal potentialities. Land in Melanesia, as elsewhere in the Pacific, is never a generic or generalizable category: it always has a specific identity, divisible incrementally into even more specific subidentities that also lend people their own categories of identification, which might include clans and lineages or the social categories of men and women, chiefs and commoners, junior and senior siblings, initiated and uninitiated persons, ancestors and descendants. The mobilization of land either legally, in terms of registering it to pave the way for alienation and other forms of exclusion (Strong 2006), or literally, in terms of removing its resources for export around the world (K. Teaiwa 2014), is one of the most powerful and recurring modes in which Pacific peoples have found themselves required to reflect upon their status as indigenes or autochthones, in the original sense of being substantively related to the ground itself.

Despite a longstanding anthropological appreciation of these modes of thinking about the world—through land, through powers of growth and health and wealth, and through the ongoing relationship between the temporal and spiritual worlds—we, and I include myself in this indictment of my discipline, still struggle to avoid projecting a set of notions about history, and who has power over history, that stem from a set of profoundly Euro-American concerns. A classic example is the early—and apparently never-ending—concern of anthropologists with the concept of cargo cults, the term thrown onto any Melanesian collective activity that includes some combination of spiritual, political, and economic elements that foreigners have tended to find baffling and in need of explanation. For the Marxist Worsley, the explanation was about political and economic inequities and an incomplete or rearranged Melanesian understanding of these. For Wagner (1981), the explanation was one of reflecting the Europeans' concept of culture itself back to them, but again, as if through a funhouse mirror: an ethnographic counterdistortion, deliberate or otherwise, of what Europeans might have thought they were telling Melanesians about themselves. For Lindstrom (1993), the explanation was a comparable act of communication: all right, you have told us that your airplanes, phonographs, and refrigerators are the most important things in the world to you, so we will communicate with you through the medium of these things. Along with other "second generation" theorists of the phenomenon (e.g. Lattas 1992; Dalton 2004), Lindstrom suggested that cargo movements are the commodity fetishism of the colonizers reflected back at them.

In other words, there has been a long history of anthropologists speculating as to how Melanesians might be trying to establish relationships with foreign others in a way those others would understand. This book, too, belongs to that intellectual tradition. At the same time, it is an attempt to discern what categories arising from a Melanesian milieu generally and a Suau one specifically might be the actual framework upon which the categories I thought were familiar—tradition, loss, epochal transformation—had been stretched. For example, it has taken several years and no small degree of effort to release the category of "the Massim" as a convenient shorthand to describe the cultural sensibilities of my Suau friends. This term, a corruption of the name of the island of Misima (Young 1983a), originally entered into the anthropological consciousness courtesy of its use by Haddon (1894: 94) and became mapped onto the region that is now Milne Bay Province, along with an identification of this region as a culture area. But the original designation of the region by Haddon had largely been racial, not cultural, in accordance with the obsession with "racial types" that characterized the ethnology of his era. Nonetheless, the term was adopted with enthusiasm by later generations of anthropologists to describe what seemed to be a regional cultural complex of long-distance ceremonial exchange relationships and elaborate mortuary rituals. It was also adopted by Milne Bay elites as a shorthand for what they felt was the cultural distinctiveness of the province, and it has most recently been enshrined and materialized in the form of the Massim Museum and Cultural Centre in the provincial capital of Alotau. Notwithstanding the adoption of the "Massim" designation by many contemporary people in Milne Bay to describe their corner of Papua New Guinea, this book will attempt as far as possible to eschew this Victorian imaginary in favor of the local complexities of identity that are a feature of the Suau Coast, and which will be elaborated in more detail in chapter 1.

But the term will never entirely be released by the ethnography of this region, and for good reason, which is that "things that come from exotic places are always evidence of people's local capacities to draw them in" (Strathern 1992: 251). Expansion again: the world becomes knowable through the exogenous elements of it that reach outward to communicate something. The embracing by some people in Milne Bay Province of the term "Massim" to describe themselves is one example among many of what Strathern noted is a tendency among Papua New Guinean peoples to draw out of foreign others what they recognize as fundamental human capacities—and then to reflect those capacities back to the foreigners in order to instantiate a relationship. This reflection is a process of witnesses meeting difference at a moment or point of incomprehension, discovering what capacities are held inside the bearers of difference that the witnesses can recognize in themselves, eliciting from these foreign others the capacity that the witnesses know to be a feature of human agency, and making that capacity a foundation for a relationship. Or as Strathern put it in the context of a first encounter between Papua New Guinean Highlanders from Mount Hagen and Australian gold prospectors in the 1930s, the Australians "now appeared not as spirit analogues of Hagen men, but as transformations of them—not divided from 'us' as 'others,' but 'ourselves' in another form" (1992: 250).

It is this mode of recognition that will appear repeatedly throughout this book, whether in Suau interactions with Victorian missionaries or the contemporary government of PNG. But Strathern's model for interactions between Papua New Guineans and foreign others leaves open the question of structural asymmetries between parties in the act of recognizing a relation, and so the other element that will appear in my account is the repeated failure or refusal of non-Suau agents to recognize the relationship in anything remotely approaching a reciprocal manner.[1] It is this element that I am describing as the irony of Suau history, this unrequited nature of the Suau success at finding an element of themselves in the various waves of foreigners to visit them. Or to put it even more baldly: while people all along the Suau Coast still celebrate annually the arrival of James Chalmers, the Scottish missionary who converted them to Christianity in the late nineteenth century, I am fairly certain I could visit Chalmers's home village of Ardrishaig on the west coast of Scotland and not find a single person who knows where the Suau Coast even is—and perhaps not even Papua New Guinea at that. Only certain features of the colonial era were a two-way street, and a sustained, good-faith interest in the lives of colonized peoples on the part of those engaged in the colonial project was not frequently one of them.

Exploring a Suau theory of how this state of affairs came about is a process of asking how each seemingly familiar category may signal a Suau appropriation of a colonial category to demonstrate that, indeed, Suau people and their non-Suau interlocutors already shared common capacities. *Kastom* is a prime example of this: it looks like an English word, and certainly in elite Papua New Guinean contexts, such as the chambers of judges and the conferences and seminars at which its nature and future are debated, it can take on contours that at times look like a straightforward analogue to law or to culture (Demian 2015). In neighboring Vanuatu, similar analogues appear to economy (Rousseau and Taylor 2012). But as soon as one is discussing this concept with people who are no longer connected to their local metropoles, the areas of life signified by a term like *kastom* are constantly shifting. Of course, the term does not only refer to what people have lost, but to any number of everyday practices and affective modes to which people still have recourse. These practices may "actually" have existed for a very large portion of Suau history, or they may not have, but that is not the point. The point is that they are associated with a Suau deep time. If, as Greenhouse observes, "in so-called timeless societies, the principal relevance of time is to divide the matrix of significance from the lived-in world" (Greenhouse 1996: 87), then the "matrix of significance" to which *kastom* appeals is perpetually at one remove from everyday life, even as it is called into people's lives to infuse them with awareness that another time exists alongside this one. Greenhouse continues: "In such contexts, agency is highly concentrated in the indeterminate point of transformation (I will not say 'moment') when the lived-in world could be distinguished from some other; such transformations are the subject of myths, but (as we shall see) events, too, can be transformative in this sense" (1996: 87).

If *kastom* is one such way that Suau people have found to describe transformative points in their history, where history is understood both as the distant past and as the ethnographic present of this book, it is an extremely effective descriptor that allows them to demonstrate to foreign others, including the ethnographer, what they have discovered in these others that is also a component of their own historical sensibility.

"We Will Never See Your Place"

The trajectories of anthropology have shifted too, and our own sense of locating the proper identity of anthropologists is as contingent on whom we are engaging with, and on what terms, as the identity of my Suau friends. What once seemed to me the daring decision to live and conduct fieldwork on the relatively cosmopolitan mainland of a province famed for its unique ("authentic") island cultures has, in the intervening years, become not only not so radical but also rather unfashionable. The first hint of a problem was brought to my attention over a decade ago, at a job interview of all things. My interviewers opened the discussion with the following observation: "So you do quite *traditional* anthropology, don't you?" The categories that had haunted me as a graduate student, from "the Massim" onward, were evidently still haunting these colleagues as well, and the Malinowskian fantasy of an insular idyll had somehow jumped out at them from my curriculum vitae. I attempted to point out that while, yes, I was working largely in rural Papua New Guinea, I was also developing a specialist focus on the country's legal system and how that played out in relations between the rural population and the Papua New Guinean state. In the event, I did not get that job. I am however grateful to those colleagues for asking such an irritating question, as it has obviously stayed with me all this time. It has stayed with me precisely because it alerted me to a concern emerging in anthropology at the beginning of the present century that rather intriguingly parallels a concern voiced by my friends in Papua New Guinea: what, exactly, do we mean when we claim for ourselves, or accuse others, of doing something "traditional?" By this I mean, what relationship, not only to people in our past but also to those in our future—our children, our students, and so on—are we imagining, and how do we imagine ourselves to be mobilizing both those past and future potentials?

For people staking their claim to identity formation in a history they say is now lost to them, the affective orientation to time may be described as an ironic one. I take my cue from Fernandez and Huber (2001), who note of irony that

> it is a potential consequence of all practice, arising as it does in the space between the world as planned or promised and the world as achieved or received. Yet the problematic of unrequitement in which irony flourishes has a positive as well as negative pole. Belief may be lost for good as well as bad reasons. And the loss, whether justified or not, may excite the moral imagination to explore routes to a better way of life. (2001: 262)

Irony may be a "potential consequence of all practice," but its consequences are magnified in practices that carry a high degree of social risk—say, in recognizing relationships with others who turn out not, in the long run, to recognize a reciprocal relationship with you, generating the "problematic of unrequitement" described by Fernandez and Huber. The historical encounters between Suau people and colonial others are described by contemporary Suau as having been filled with a potential that was never realized. The overwhelming majority of foreigners to arrive at the southeastern tip of Papua New Guinea never had any intention of staying there. In colonial, missionary, and military accounts of the region, Suau people and their coastal home are only ever a backdrop against which the aspirations and fears of foreign actors are played out; "the native" is a largely generic figure to be managed as efficiently as possible in the interests of empire. It is this disjuncture, between the world Suau people say they expected when they embraced foreigners and their presumed interests and the world that actually transpired when those foreigners turned out to be not so interested in Suau people after all, that I am calling ironic. As Fernandez and Huber suggest, this gap or disjuncture tends to be filled in with moral significance. More often than not, my Suau interlocutors have held themselves responsible both for failing to hold the attention of the foreign other and for failing to maintain what might be called their own cultural patrimony, presumed to be flourishing before relations with foreigners got underway in earnest. It remains to be seen whether this claiming of responsibility for the loss of connections, either to their own past or to an anticipated future, might provoke a positive movement toward some revised or entirely new version of that future. The Suau Coast of my acquaintance still gives the impression of a place in which the future has been placed on hold—or to be more precise, a future whose contours are recognizable to a foreigner.

It was not always thus. In the first half of the twentieth century, Suau people were already experiencing what they now reflect back upon as a golden age of experimenting with translocal connections. The London Missionary Society and its maverick offspring, the Kwato Extension Association, had been making converts since the 1870s, and the Kwato mission at the eastern extremity of the Suau language area also saw as part of its project, radically for the era, vocational education of young men and women who had come up through the mission school. The descendants of those educated at Kwato continue to be disproportionately represented in the political, educational, and business life of the province and of Papua New Guinea more widely. The location of the district headquarters at the eastern end of the coast on Samarai, with the island of Kwato and its pioneering mission next door, meant not only that Suau people had access to a world of unprecedented opportunities for education, work, and travel but that that world had come to them and appeared ready to stay with them. But it did not stay, as the cataclysm of World War II took with it not only the soldiers but also the missionaries and planters, as well as much of the colonial infrastructure to support them.

The midcentury colonial preoccupation with "race suicide" (Williams 1933: 5) is a telling one. Well-meaning foreigners like the government anthropologist F. E. Williams were worried about Suau people becoming caricatures of Europeans, whereas by their own account, Suau were intensively exploring the possibilities that relations with Europeans might offer them. These are not at all the same sort of project. I will make the claim that Suau had no intention of becoming like Europeans or like anyone else: they were interested in becoming like themselves, as they imagined themselves standing in relation to a relatively new and almost unfathomably different category of others. This experiment would later be construed by Suau people of my acquaintance as an entirely new epoch in the history of a region that is well established in the anthropological canon as always having enjoyed long-distance relations of both trade and ceremonial exchange. In other words, if Suau were reasonably mobile before the colonial era—in the strictest physical sense of mobility— then they were extraordinarily mobile during the era of colonialism. And the mobility intensified further during World War II, when entire villages were emptied of able-bodied men who went to work as manual laborers for Australian and American troops stationed around Milne Bay. Older Suau recalling this era were always careful to emphasize two points to me: that American soldiers were more generous than Australian ones, and that the racial hierarchy they had been taught in the mission schools and plantations was called into question by the revelation that some Americans were dark-skinned like them. While the generosity of American soldiers is a consistent trope in the war remembrances of many Pacific Islands populations (Lindstrom and White 1989), it does appear to have been the case that American servicemen, unschooled in the particular colonial relationship Australia was striving to maintain in then-Territories of Papua and New Guinea during the war, routinely flouted the sumptuary ordinances and other rules against "fraternizing" with Papua New Guineans that were enforced on Australian troops (Riseman 2012: 128). Certainly this wartime memorialization of Americans worked in my own favor as an American visitor to Milne Bay Province, despite the constant reminders that my own national point of origin had become subsumed in the local geopolitical power structure that persists in the present day: "Ah, you're American, yes, I know about America! Now, what part of Australia is that in?"

The war also saw an intensification of infrastructure, with perforated steel planking being used to build everything from runways to pontoon bridges to temporary roads. But the operative word here is "temporary." After the war, the missionaries who had been evacuated never came back. A fall in world copra prices meant that the coconut plantations were also becoming less lucrative as enterprises, so that by the 1960s, only a single planter, Rex Goodwin, remained on the Suau Coast. And in 1969 the district headquarters were moved to Alotau, a minimum of a day's travel by boat from most parts of the Suau region, effectively erasing the south coast of the province as a regional metropole. By the time I began doing fieldwork in the region in 1996, the dominant narrative in the villages where I worked was one of inexplicable loss.

This loss took two forms. One was the form that I have tried to encapsulate in the concept of *kastom*. This is the term in Tok Pisin for any number of practices, relationships, and material forms associated with a domain of ancestral or temporal depth. But it is absolutely critical to bear in mind that not everyone means the same thing when they speak of *kastom*. One person might be talking about the old songs and dances forbidden by the missionaries; another person might be talking about the use of shell valuables instead of money for marriage and funeral transactions; another person might be talking about appropriate behavior between brothers and sisters. And people are profoundly ambivalent about many of these things—someone might in one breath speak of the power or danger that is gone from a cave where a culture hero is said to have lived in ancient times, and in the next breath deplore the fact that high school students in the present era have left graffiti all over it. Also there are differences of gender and generation: men and women tend to speak of different forms that *kastom* might have taken, and older people say that *kastom* is all finished while younger people say it is still around, and making it hard for them to conduct their romantic lives in the way that they would like.

So far, so paradigmatic: whatever *kastom* is or might have been, this appears to be a straightforward tale of colonial dispossession. But the second form that loss has taken for many Suau people is the loss of all the connections of infrastructure, and of educational, economic, and social opportunities that presented themselves in various forms beginning with missionization, proceeding through the buildup to the war, and culminating at Papua New Guinea's independence in 1975—an event that is viewed as a positive development by no Suau person I have ever discussed it with. The Papua New Guinean state simply has not been able to deliver what the colonial or military enterprises did: mobility. Here I am not just talking about physical mobility, but a mobility of the imagination. The new national identity offered by the creation of an independent state was one that proposed to unite the country in a fairly standard discourse of national similarity, as against the difference of the Australians and earlier colonizers. But similarity is, I am proposing, an aesthetic that is counter to the ideals of mobility and multiplicity in the minds of many people I have worked with over the years, not just in Suau but in other parts of Papua New Guinea as well.

And the interest in maintaining connections over long stretches of time and space with others is of course not just a Papua New Guinean concern. It is one found throughout the Pacific, as McDougall (2016) notes, in pervasive ideologies of incorporating the foreigner into the ground of home. "Diversity," she writes, "is not the automatic result of historical isolation from interactions with other people. Diversity is valued, cultivated, and made possible by translocal relationships and ongoing engagements with strangers" (2016: 27). She goes on to indicate the myriad ways in which relationships with foreign others, and eventual inclusion of those others into your own group (while simultaneously maintaining their distinctiveness as others), is a fundamental component of Pacific sociality. It is one that has given rise to networks of ceremonial exchange, trade, marriage, and ritual, as well as warfare and conquest, over vast distances across the Pacific Ocean and its landmasses, for millennia. But as McDougall also notes, the inversion of this phenomenon is also possible, wherein kin may be turned into non-kin, and this is taken as a sign of the correct ordering of relationships gone awry.

That correct ordering is often what Melanesian peoples say they have lost in the aftermath of the colonial era. Much of the anthropological and political discourse on Papua New Guinea is that its people have relinquished many of the economic, spiritual, and moral systems that were once their own and replaced them with those of the colonizers. I am suggesting that while a great deal of this loss is of course a function of colonialism, other elements of it are, in fact, a fundamental component of a Pacific sociality in which the stranger, after having been greeted with caution and perhaps even violence, becomes adopted, incorporated, or otherwise engaged in a flow of things, ideas, and practices with the hosts.

The problem here is that under the conditions of colonialism, Europeans had no interest in a relationship of mutualism or exchange. From seemingly trivial appropriations and dislocations of cultural artifacts (hula, tattooing) to invasion and destruction on a grand scale (settler colonies, nuclear testing, world war), the effects wrought by Europe, the United States, and Australia represented—and continue to represent—an asymmetrical relationship that was unprecedented in kind for most Pacific societies. Toward the end of the nineteenth century, Suau people in what is now Papua New Guinea embarked upon a relationship that they may have hoped would constitute an ongoing flow of exchange that never eventuated. They converted to Christianity with a speed even missionaries found remarkable (chapter 3). They seized educational and wage labor opportunities with both hands. And then a century later, the foreigners had almost all gone, and the Papua New Guinean state has never been able to replace or replicate the promise of that initial relationship.

Certainly during field trips in 1999 and 2008 my Suau friends gave me the impression of having gotten themselves stuck. The era of physical and educational mobility was behind them, and people were casting about for what, in the uncertainty of the postindependence era, might provide the next set of fruitful connections. Oil palm was introduced in the late 1980s, and it continues to be planted throughout the lowland areas of the province at a truly alarming rate: each time I have visited, the descent of the short flight from Port Moresby into Alotau reveals less forest and more oil palm. Vanilla was introduced more recently as a less land-intensive cash crop, but its uptake seems to have been patchy at best, and the families I know who planted it enthusiastically in the early years of this century had not actually found a buyer for their mature pods by 2008. The built-in supply chain that had been a feature of colonial cash cropping could not be replicated in the postcolony.

The religious makeup of the region has also shifted since independence, with evangelical churches reconverting many Suau people, especially young men and women who are drawn to the replacement of older forms of hierarchy and authority by the relationship between an individual and Jesus, by the energetic and emotionally satisfying form of their services, and by the opportunity to travel up and down the coast as "prayer warriors" without the oversight of kin and in the company of other young men and women. Some Catholic churches have also appeared in the Suau hinterland, offering yet another option in the free-for-all of Christianities that PNG has become in the century since the Victorian missionary organizations carefully carved up the new Melanesian territories among themselves.

But again, it is not enough to talk solely about the kind of mobility that just moves people up and down the coast between prayer meetings and village markets. In a context like Papua New Guinea, which never became a settler state, and this part of Papua New Guinea, which has not experienced the kinds of wholescale landscape alteration and ecological destruction seen by mining communities elsewhere in the country, I have the luxury of asking what people "really" mean when they talk about what they have lost. They still have their land, in other words, and their livelihoods; this is not a dispossessed population. But when people speak with relish and nostalgia about a past filled with opportunities to interact with missionaries, planters, government agents, and soldiers, they are not just talking about the material opportunities offered, although those cannot be dismissed either. They are talking about an immediate world populated with others who were not connected to them by ceremonial trade partnerships, marriage connections, totemic affiliations, and other relational forms that might or might not be placed under the rubric of *kastom*. The others of the Suau "golden age," from the late nineteenth century to the end of World War II, were *so* different that entirely new ways of forming or discovering relationships with them had to be found. And because those others expressed no interest in communicating or otherwise dealing with Suau people in any way that might be intelligible to them, the novelty of working out what these various kinds of others—Europeans and Australians, Polynesian missionaries, Chinese entrepreneurs, African American soldiers, and so on—wanted from them formed a central part of the Suau creative endeavor for the better part of a century.

It is that satisfaction that has been lost: the satisfaction of having worked out what someone else wants, how you can stand in relation to someone whose motivations and desires are really a closed book, but in whom you have chosen to recognize the potential for a productive future. A cliché I became weary of hearing from my Suau friends was, "You have come all this way to our place, and we will never see your place." I took it for a very long time to be a matter-of-fact statement about the disparities in our comparative wealth, in that I could travel to PNG, and most of them could not travel to the United States or United Kingdom or wherever I happened to be living at the time. And it is of course an issue of comparative wealth, but it is more than that. Each time I was asked to attend to the structural immobility of my friends and hosts, I was also being asked to attend to what seeing "my place" might mean for them. My place is filled with other people like me, and maybe other people not like me, with whom other sorts of relationships might be imagined. The act of seeing itself is also critical as a component of what lends veracity to the retelling of an experience for many Suau people. To have seen the place where a person is from is to render them that much more knowable, because people and their places are mutually constitutive (chapter 4).

I have argued elsewhere (Demian 2015) that Suau, in common with most if not all Papua New Guineans, find their creative satisfaction in the differences between people, in mixing languages, spiritual practices, the orders of the state and the local, and so on, to see what sorts of fruitful or vitalizing relations might eventuate from all this mixing. This will be a theme that appears periodically throughout my consideration of how Suau people conceive of Suau history, which then informs what an ideal Suau future might look like. A nontrivial component of the current dissatisfaction with having been left behind by successive colonial others is that they are now left with just each other. The high value placed on seeking relationships elsewhere is encapsulated vividly in the Suau proverb, "You squeeze your finger until it bleeds, then you marry nearby [literally, inside ourselves]" (*nimam we hihi 'osi'osina, boto tawasola boyauda*). At first blush this appears to be a straightforward exhortation in favor of exogamy. But as the young man who first told me the proverb went on to explain, it was about the social and personal risks of marrying the "girl next door." Your family would know everything about her already, and her family would know everything about you. All your personal foibles, and hers, would be up for examination. Neither party to the marriage would have anything to discover for themselves. It would surely be doomed. Better, he said, to marry a young woman from elsewhere in Milne Bay, or even better still, from another part of PNG entirely.

In this young bachelor's explanation of the proverb lies a signpost to the importance that Suau people place on constructing a satisfying life for oneself by forming relationships with incompletely known others. And as Harrison (2000) has demonstrated, this fascination for trading in difference—often quite literally, with the purchasing of other groups' songs, spirit cults, and ritual systems—almost certainly precedes contact with Europeans and appears to have been a longstanding feature of many Papua New Guinean societies. For someone like myself, who does such "traditional anthropology," it is salutary to be reminded of what I have always felt was the foundational principle of anthropology as a discipline: it is difference, not similarity, that mobilizes the human imagination. But for my Suau friends, this is not just a clever intellectual project: it is one that has animated their reflections on their own lives and the world around them for over a century. It is not just the absence of infrastructure that has caused them to feel stuck. It is the absence of others to express any sort of interest in them, or in engaging with them. The problem, in other words, is not that my friends and consultants in Suau are "still" living in small villages, or "still" engaging in swidden horticulture as their primary mode of subsistence, or whatever the objection to "traditional anthropology" might be. The problem is that they know it is possible for their world to attract the attention of others with whom they might conduct fruitful relations—because it happened once before, and was sustained for several generations. So they know it is possible. The question vexing them now is how they might make it happen again, to realize a future that will be filled with others to mobilize their imaginations anew.

Note

1. Here I retain an intellectual debt to Worsley (1957), who first alerted me to both the uniqueness of Melanesian responses to colonialism and the equally critical fact that one of the things Melanesians were responding to was precisely the disinterest of colonizers in engaging with them as equals—or even as humans.

🎵 1

Naming, Loss, and Waiting

"Suau" as a Historical Category

This year, between Samarai and Mullen's Harbour, the recruiting has been heavier than ever, more than one in every two natives being employed. . . . The craving for excitement has certainly got into the blood of the "Suau," and he finds signing-on the best field for fulfillment. He does not realize, of course, the inevitable reaction, personally. Tribally, he has no ambition, and cares not for posterity. Which is all very well if the one purpose of the Government was to escort him, one by one, to his last resting place.
> —1925 report by Assistant Resident Magistrate R. A. Vivian,
> Milne Bay District, Territory of Papua

I notice that you do not seem to be working with "a people."
> —1996 letter to the author early in her first period of fieldwork,
> from her PhD supervisor

This chapter is offered in the way of setting the scene for the more specific topics, historical and contemporary, that will follow in subsequent chapters. Because this book was researched and written over a very long period of time, I invite the reader to adopt a kind of dual vision for the material to follow, in the manner of the double exposures that sometimes occurred back when we used cameras with actual film in them. For readers unfamiliar with this phenomenon: a double exposure occurs when the film is not advanced between exposures, either accidentally or deliberately, so that two exposures at different times happen to the same frame of film, creating one image superimposed on the other. This filmic artifice creates an illusion of, among other things, events and objects at different points in time appearing as though they occurred simultaneously and in the same space. Much of this chapter, and this book, creates the same effect. It is important to bear this in mind as I describe the sites where most of my research took place. All of these places exist as multiple versions of themselves. Take, for example, this passage from my own 2015 field journal, describing a road journey that would have been inconceivable when I first visited the hinterland of the Suau Coast.

We pass through villages that I once hiked through to reach the road to Alotau: Siasiada, Sinalili, Tautili. All unrecognizable to me now as they have become completely enveloped by oil palm. Some have become quite suburban in character, with sports ovals, covered markets, schoolchildren walking home for lunch in their neat uniforms. Regardless of my feelings about it, oil palm has created something like town life outside of Alotau for the first time since the demise of Samarai.

We crest the hill at the hamlet of Labapaʻana (the name refers to a former cash crop: "laba" is a vernacularization of rubber) and descend into Leileiyafa. The speed with which we rattle through the village I spent 14 months in nearly 20 years ago leaves me somewhat breathless. I should stop and greet old acquaintances—but we've already left it behind.

In this journal entry, a village where I once lived flashed by in the blink of an eye. During that first period of doctoral fieldwork in Leileiyafa, I sometimes felt so isolated that I became trapped, ensnared by my own romantic notions—fetishes, even—of what fieldwork was supposed to look like. Nowadays, not only is Leileiyafa no longer isolated, its location on the new road to the coast threatens to make it just one more place for the visitor to glimpse from a truck window as it recedes in the distance.

The temporal layering in the foregoing paragraphs is a theme that will appear again throughout this book, both as a reflection of the long-term character of the research that produced it and as an attempt to reflect on how my hosts, friends, and interlocutors may also be regarding the passage of time in their place. The descriptions of place that follow, then, should again be taken as a double or multiple exposure: parts of these descriptions belong unequivocally in the past, while other parts may have the ring of familiarity to a contemporary reader.

Two Villages

Leileiyafa[1] (pandanus sleeping mats) and Isuisu (nose/coastal point/canoe prow) are located on the southern mainland of Milne Bay Province, at the westernmost edge of what Seligman (1910) designated as the Southern Massim cultural region. The languages of this region are all closely related members of the Papuan Tip branch of the Western Oceanic languages (Lynch, Ross, and Crowley 2002). The Eastern Suau dialect was used as a mission language in the late nineteenth and early twentieth centuries, giving it an outsized regional footprint, but most people in Milne Bay can speak or at least understand several neighboring languages on top of their own vernacular. The early British missionary presence in the province also meant that English was established as a lingua franca, to the almost complete exclusion of Tok Pisin and Hiri Motu, which were being used elsewhere in PNG as linguae francae.

When I first began working in Milne Bay in the 1990s, hardly anyone in the province spoke Tok Pisin, and indeed speaking it was considered a sign of poor education or incomplete cosmopolitan attainment. There has historically been a certain degree of chauvinism among Milne Bay people, who gleefully reproduce the old colonial denigration of Tok Pisin, which in reality is a creole, as "broken English."[2] My fieldwork was perforce conducted initially in English and then, as my competence in local languages grew, a mix of English and two dialects of the Suau cluster. These days, with the influx of Papua New Guineans from other parts of the country to the provincial capital of Alotau and its adjacent oil palm plantations, Tok Pisin is heard much more often, but still largely in the urban setting and other contexts of ethnic mixing. It has been adopted by many younger Milne Bay people as a marker of urban sophistication, in a neat reversal of its formerly denigrated status. It is also increasingly becoming a pragmatic necessity. "We never used to speak Tok Pisin here," a truck driver from the Trobriand Islands said to me in 2014, "but now we all do! You have to, otherwise you can't talk to people from anywhere else."

I lived in Leileiyafa for fourteen months between 1996 and 1997 and in Isuisu for six months between 1999 and 2000. I visited both villages for several weeks during a return trip to Papua New Guinea in 2008 and spent a month at a time in Isuisu in 2014 and 2015. This book represents, without question, a specific set of ethnographic moments in the history of the Suau Coast and in a particular ethnographer's relationship with some of the people living there. There are some aspects of life in Suau I can claim to know quite well by now—the system of land tenure and inheritance, for example—and others about which I know very little, and in fact am not permitted to know anything about, as I discuss further in chapter 6. I mention this to signal to the reader, both Suau and non-Suau, that the absences are there. Given that any account can only ever be partial, I am able to offer what has emerged from this particular relationship at the moment in our respective life histories that my hosts and I occupied at the time.

Leileiyafa lies between the Momore Mountains to its south and east and the estuary of Mullins Harbour to its north. Before it opens into Mullins Harbour, the Sagarai River's long valley between the Momore and Pini mountain ranges is home to a series of Buhutu-speaking villages as well as an extensive tract of oil palm plantations, run in the 1990s by the United Kingdom–based Commonwealth Development Corporation (CDC) and now by a number of private owners, some of them local to Milne Bay Province, others based elsewhere in Papua New Guinea but owned by large Malaysian oil palm companies.

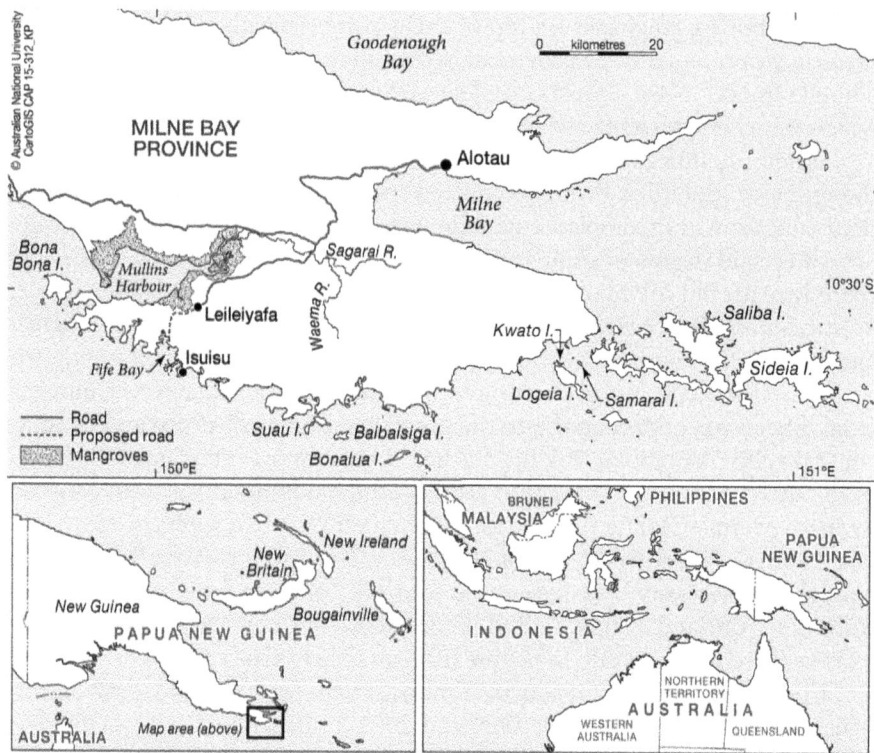

Map 1.1. Map of Milne Bay Province and the Suau Coast. Commissioned from CartoGIS Services, Australian National University.

At the end of this chain of villages is Leileiyafa, whose administrative identity is as ambiguous as the linguistic one I will describe later in this chapter. It falls under the administration of the Suau local level government council in Fife Bay (on the coast) and belongs to the Dahuni Circuit of the United Church (on Mullins Harbour), but most children attend school elsewhere entirely, either further inland at Siasiada or down on the coast at Saga'aho or Savaia. Market activities in the village involve the selling of mud crabs (*Scylla serrata*) at the oil palm villages of the Sagarai Valley or at the large market in Alotau—mostly a women's pursuit—or small-scale coconut and cocoa cultivation, the products of which will also be sold in Alotau. The latter is primarily engaged in by young men under the auspices of their parents. These young men may also go to work as oil palm harvesters or as drivers and "offsides" of the public motor vehicles (PMVs)—flatbed trucks with canvas covers and wooden benches for passengers—that ply the road between Alotau, the oil palm plantations, and Leileiyafa. This road did not exist when I lived in Leileiyafa in the 1990s; as mentioned in the introduction to this chapter, the village at that time was permeated by a far more isolated and enclosed atmosphere than it is now. To reach Alotau, one had to either take a dinghy into Mullins Harbour and up the Sagarai to the old CDC wharf at Tamonau to catch a PMV from there or walk inland for several hours to where the road stopped at Tautili and hope an energetic PMV driver might be going that far. Both options entailed nearly a day's travel. Since the building of the road, with Alotau now only two hours away by PMV, Leileiyafa has become a minor local metropole in a way that it was not when I did my doctoral fieldwork there.

Isuisu is a coastal village one bay eastward from the local level government council seat at Fife Bay but solidly at the western end of the Suau Coast, where the Daui dialect of Suau is spoken. Its church belongs to the Fife Bay Circuit, and most children from Isuisu also attend primary school at Fife Bay. Since 2012 they have also had the option of attending high school up to grade ten at the newly established James Chalmers Memorial High School, which occupies the former site of a United Church seminary, Lawes Bible College.[3] Isuisu women, and a few men, take garden produce, fish, and baked goods to the twice-weekly market at Fife Bay to sell to schoolteachers, council officials, health center workers, and villagers from the surrounding hamlets. Isuisu is flanked by an old copra plantation that was run until the 1960s by an Australian, Rex Goodwin, who married an Isuisu woman and bequeathed both his first and last names to the local naming repertoire. Copra is still produced at Isuisu whenever good market prices justify the effort involved, although young men can earn just as much in a shorter period of time by diving for trochus (*Tectus niloticus*) shells to sell to traders in Alotau. Some of these shells are destined for souvenir shops; most will eventually be made into mother-of-pearl buttons for clothing. The bulk of the monetary wealth in Isuisu comes from remittances from kin working in Alotau, Port Moresby, or other Papua New Guinean towns.

All travel between coastal Suau villages is by foot or by boat, either a swift if slightly hazardous fiberglass dinghy with an outboard motor or the sturdier but slower wooden-planked workboats that chug with diesel engines up and down the coast, taking copra bags to Alotau and bringing in canteen goods on the return trip. There is also the new road from Alotau to Leileiyafa, which was being extended to Fife Bay at the time of writing, but there are no roads running along the coast itself. Older coastal people speak nostalgically of the roads that at one time connected the LMS mission station at Fife Bay with the copra plantations along the coast; since the end of World War II these have reverted to bush. These days a Suau woman taking her produce to market or an anthropologist longing for a hot shower and a cold beer can take a dinghy from one of the western coastal villages up into Mullins Harbour, spend the night at Leileiyafa, and get on a PMV at 4:00 A.M. in order to be in Alotau when the market opens. My own memory of this journey, undertaken countless times, is sharpened by smells: the marine funk of the crabs in their coconut-frond baskets, the metallic tang of the betel nut chewed by my friends (and myself), and the intimate fertilizer stench of mile after mile of oil palm plantations. In 2014, I was attempting this journey when our PMV broke down in the middle of one such plantation, and its hapless passengers were left to find lifts on other passing vehicles. Another PMV stopped to pick some of us up, and I was given pride of place in the cab of the truck, wedged between the driver and his offside. After a few kilometers the previously laconic driver said to me, "So, you decided to come back, ah?" To my shame I did not recognize him, but I said yes, I had been back a few times, and when had I met him before? He said, "You stayed in Leileiyafa when I was a little boy."

Time passes. Little boys grow into enterprising young men. The ethnographer had forgotten a face, but her host community had not.

Aidobudi? or, Locating the Visitor in a Field of Relationships

Late afternoon and early evening tend to be the times when travelers arrive in a village on the Suau Coast, especially if they are coming on foot rather than by boat. If someone is sitting in a window or on the ladder of a house, those inside will ask that person, *aidobudi?*—who's that, which people are they? A satisfactory answer will contain the name of someone known to the asker and then the generic term *edi pele*, connoting something along the lines of "and their people/and those guys." The name of a village of origin would never suffice; a personal name must be supplied. *Margaret edi pele. Weni edi pele.* When you ask who someone is, you are not asking what village or matrilineage they belong to. Their names will tell you that. You are asking instead how you know them, how to respond to their arrival in your place.

In this sense it was perhaps fitting that for the first few months of my residence in Leileiyafa in 1996 I did not know with whom I was living. That is, I had no name for them as "a people," and I was not entirely sure how to locate them in the rich ethnographic tradition of Milne Bay Province. The south coast of the province's mainland seemed to be an ethnographic void, not because nothing has been written about it but because anthropologists and other visitors seem only ever to have been passing through, never staying for any appreciable period of time.[4] The south coast was a stopping-off point en route to other places that were more congenial to the twentieth-century anthropological imagination: the islands. Mailu to the west; Logea, Saliba, Sideia, and Basilaki to the east; beyond them, the islands of the Engineer Group and the Louisiade Archipelago. And to their north, the Trobriands, looming disproportionately large in the anthropological imagination ever since Bronisław Malinowski's foundation myth of having invented ethnographic fieldwork there by virtue of getting stuck due to the onset of World War I. The romance of isolation is often a trap, albeit a trap inside of which interesting things can sometimes happen.

But because no anthropologist ever *stayed* on the south coast, I had no readily available designation for the region or its people, any more than they knew how to locate me, an unmarried young woman (*hasala*; the male equivalent is *hewali*) with access to the kinds of resources normally associated with (male) Korean logging surveyors and (male, married) American Bible translators. The bafflement was mutual, but its terms were very different. For my hosts during those first months, the problem was one of determining who had sent me there, who was my "boss," who directed my agenda. For me, the problem was an academic one of classification. Who were these people, anyway? As a doctoral student at the beginning of my relationship with them in the 1990s, I was initially hung up on the categories I had inherited from the literature I read in preparation for fieldwork in Milne Bay. They shared certain structural features with their island neighbors, such as matrilineal descent and a language belonging to the vast Austronesian family (Bellwood et al. 2006), but was that sufficient to lump them into the same "culture area?" They did not even seem to have a name for themselves, instantly muddying the relationship between the ethnographic descriptions I had come prepared with and the reality of the people I was trying to get to know. When I asked, interlocutors in Leileiyafa would say, "Mostly we are *somo* people, but we have some *safa* and *saha* as well." At first I thought these were names for ethnic groups. Soon I learned that they were dialect designations, indexed by the word for "what" in each dialect referred to (Cooper 1975: 232). Thus the experience of the anthropologist Michael Young, working in this hinterland region on a social impact study for the introduction of oil palm in the early 1980s, who recorded in his field notes the following language lesson:

> Questioning Bune in Borowai after hearing the word SOMO so often, and knowing already that it is the name of the language/dialect . . .
> Me: What does somo mean?
> B: Somo means what.
> Me: Yes, what does somo mean?
> Pause
> B: Somo means what.
> Pause
> Me: Yes?
> B: What.

> I give up. Then later I get Francis to ask and get the same answer . . .
> F: What does somo mean?
> B: Somo means what.

Me: What?
B: Yes.
Me: Somo means "what"?
B: Yes, "what."
F & me: Oh, "what"!
(Young 1981b: 27)

I must have had an almost identical conversation not long after my initial arrival in Leileiyafa. But even after I had worked out that *somo* meant "what" and that it, along with *safa* and *saha*, served as dialect markers, I still had no idea which language group they belonged to, having been told very little by my contact in Alotau, the provincial capital, who had first extended the invitation to work in Leileiyafa. The self-representation of my hosts repeatedly failed to map neatly onto the categories that I had carried to Papua New Guinea in my novice ethnographer's toolkit.

Part of the issue was, as I eventually learned, Leileiyafa itself. The village is a crossroads of the south coast. Like Mullins Harbour on which it lies, where the Sagarai River opens into a broad, shallow, and mangrove-dense estuary before making its way into the sea, it is a place of mixing. Lineages that have called it home for as far back as their oral histories reach live shoulder to shoulder with lineages relocated down from the mountains by Mr. R. A. Vivian, known locally as "Misibibi," and other members of the Australian colonial administration in the early part of the twentieth century. Women from Bona Bona Island and from coastal villages marry into Leileiyafa, as do women from Milne Bay proper and its hinterland, bringing their lineage names with them. It was therefore little wonder that people were circumspect when I pressed them to tell me who they were. One of the defining features of being a person from Leileiyafa was emplacing oneself in a series of relationships to other places and other people. Also, an answer that left anyone out would be impolitic in mixed company, and almost all company was mixed company. This too was a defining feature not only of Leileiyafa but also of the coastal village of Isuisu that I later made my fieldwork base: on the coast people could point to ancestral connections both recent and deep among the Milne Bay islands, in the more distant Autonomous Region of Bougainville, in Australia, and in China. More to the point, my desire to answer the question "who were these people" was eminently an ethnographer's problem, a hangover from the historical categories invented by my own discipline and by the ethnonyms of the Bible translators for whom I was so frequently misrecognized. That was not the problem of my hosts in Leileiyafa. Their problem lay in determining what persons—particular, named persons, not funding bodies or academic institutions—stood behind me and the work I professed to be doing. Knowing where I stood in relation to these unknown (or presumed) persons would help them to determine where they stood in relation to me. Had I been sent by one of the Bible translation organizations? Was there not already someone doing that? Had I been sent by their kinswoman from town, with whom relations were unreliable at best? Why should they help me in that case? When I insisted repeatedly that my "boss" (*tanuwaga*) was a senior anthropologist in the United Kingdom, no one seemed satisfied. They had no points of reference for this person. The last anthropologist to visit their area had been Young, and he had stayed further up the Sagarai River from Leileiyafa. Not until my "boss" actually visited me in the field, a year into my first period of residence in the area, was the question resolved. "Is she English?" May, one of my hosts, asked me as we took my PhD supervisor back up the Sagarai in a dinghy. "I think she's English, because of her long nose." On hearing a translation of this observation about her physiognomy, my "boss" told me to inform May that it was in fact a Welsh Methodist nose.

After my first funeral in Leileiyafa (see chapter 2), there was no longer any doubt in my mind that I was working in a society that featured at least some of the characteristics that have long captivated anthropologists about a region of Papua New Guinea still, somewhat problematically, referred to as "the Massim." But even this comparison raises issues of the categories to which Milne Bay societies are still being assigned. As discussed in the introduction, by the late twentieth century "the Massim" had become so canonical that it was a term on which I continued to hang my own analyses of what I was seeing for years, until the discipline of anthropology itself began to critique its own century-old preoccupation with "culture areas," and I began to develop a certain rage against "the Massim" and the grass-skirts-and-Kula mode of anthropology the term appeared to index.[5] It had come to signify the Euro-American preoccupation with islands as sites of sublime isolation, dots to be connected by the imperial project and imprinted with a thousand European fantasies of seduction and domination (Hau'ofa 1993; T. Teaiwa 1999; Na'puti and Bevacqua 2015). The legacy of "the Massim" seemed to be of a piece with "the insularism that straightjackets modern, colonial, and anticolonial definitions of 'islandness' and 'island culture'" (Diaz 2011: 28), and it is long past time to let it go.

Releasing the term also opened the door to an appreciation that Suau people have always inhabited a world of connection, mixing with people both familiar and unfamiliar to them, as when Mailu Islanders with whom they share no common language sail eastward up the coast to buy betel nut from them during the dry season between November and January. And it is precisely that mixing, I argue, that Suau people find so stimulating in their search for connections that will prove fruitful to them and extend that fruitfulness into the future.

But anthropologists struggle to be entirely free from problems of identification, which is why, eventually, I came to refer to people living in Leileiyafa
and in Isuisu, the coastal village where I later stayed and worked, as Suau. This
solution to my naming problem will satisfy very few people other than myself.
Most of those living on the Suau Coast reserve the Suau appellation for coastal
(*gabogabo*, sea; or *gelegele*, sand/beach) dwellers, while those in the hinterland—including estuarine villages like Leileiyafa—are called by coastal people
Yaleba, a term roughly translatable as "rustics" or, less charitably, "bumpkins."
Almost no one in the hinterland uses this term themselves, with the occasional
exception of people from the southern half of Milne Bay itself, in order to
distinguish their dialect of the Tawala language from that of the northern half.
Further up the Sagarai Valley from Leileiyafa, people call themselves Huhu or
Buhutu. But in Leileiyafa itself, at the transition zone between hinterland and
coast, people can only say that they are mixed: *somo, safa,* and *saha*. Everyone
more or less understands everyone else while at the same time poking fun at
everyone else's dialect. When I first went to stay in Isuisu and told my hosts
that there was a snake in the latrine, they fell about laughing. Much put out, I
told them to go see for themselves. No, they said, they believed me. It was just
that I had used the inland word for snake, *weso*, instead of the coastal word,
mota. "You know how to talk like them, and we don't," said Baigayo, wiping
tears from her eyes. "You're a real Yaleba woman." After several months in
Isuisu I ran into some Leileiyafa women at a United Church Women's Fellowship fundraising event in Fife Bay. I had only been talking to them for a few
moments when one of them said sadly, "You changed your language already."
It was true. I had grown tired of people laughing at my Yaleba words and
pronunciation and had adopted a more coastal "tune," as English-speaking
Milne Bay people like to refer to the difference between their closely related
languages.[6]

Why are coastal people Suau but inland people are not? They understand
each other's dialects, most of the time, and follow almost identical procedures
for marrying and burying. They are thoroughly intermarried with one another,
particularly since the mass relocations of the early twentieth century. Inland
lineages call themselves by coastal place names, and vice versa. But the distinction is adamantly maintained. Those on the eastern half of the coast, known
locally as Duiduisae, maintain furthermore that they are the real Suau people.
This is in part because Suau Island itself is there, where the London Missionary
Society landed in the 1870s, and in part because the mid-twentieth-century
translation of the New Testament, still in use today, was made in their dialect.[7]
As in many cases where the religious privileging of a dialect raises it to the status of a language, Eastern Suau people came to be regarded as speakers of the
"true" or "real" (*moisa*) form of the language, while speakers of other dialects
were, in a word, bumpkins. I have even heard non-Eastern Suau people adopt

the Eastern Suau dialect at public meetings where they wanted to appear more cosmopolitan but could not quite manage English. In Isuisu, where the Daui dialect of the western half of the coast is spoken, it is not uncommon to hear Eastern Suau spoken by in-married wives and, significantly, their children. This painstaking assertion of multiple linguistic and even cultural identities goes almost completely unnoticed outside the Suau Coast. In the provincial capital of Alotau and elsewhere in the province, anyone speaking any of these dialects (with the occasional exception of Buhutu) is generally referred to as "Suau." Worse still, elsewhere in Papua New Guinea people from the Suau Coast are collectively referred to as "Samarai," the name of the tiny island at the eastern extremity of the coast where the colonial district headquarters were located until 1969, when they were moved to Alotau on the mainland. Rather like the shifting boundaries of the term "Yankee,"[8] who qualifies as "Suau" depends on whom you ask. But I worked at the western end of the coast, Duiduileu, and still call them Suau. I even call Leileiyafa people Suau, primarily because I have nothing else satisfactory to call them.[9] My decision to set local distinctions aside in the name of clarity may offend some Suau readers of this book, to whom I offer my apologies, while at the same time reserving the outsider's prerogative not to recognize all insider distinctions at all times. Category errors, whether deliberate or accidental, are a perennial feature of relations between guests and hosts: May certainly neither knew nor cared that my PhD supervisor, pigeonholed as English, actually regarded herself as Welsh, a category that has no meaning in Papua New Guinea. For my part, I was impressed that May had discerned any ethnic distinctions between *dimdims*, as white people are called throughout Milne Bay, at all.[10] And so for the sake of argument, this book is a book claiming as its subjects some people called Suau people and some times called Suau history.

"The Way the Whole Country Will Someday Be"

All this is just to say that the problem with which I initially started, that of finding a name for the people who hosted me, was one that would replicate itself in different forms over the next several years. Who were these people? Would it be acceptable to call them all Suau? Did they really care by what ethnonym they were identified, or was this only and ever a problem for anthropologists trying to stake claims to knowledge of "a place" and "a people" for themselves? And why did I not want to be a Yaleba woman, anyway? I maintain that these are not merely academic conundrums; to the contrary, one of the most ubiquitous tropes of the early twenty-first century is implicated in the questions I asked of my Suau friends and which they asked of me, and of each other. In 1925, Assistant Resident Magistrate Vivian was concerned that the enthusiasm for contract labor threatened to wipe out all trace of an identity, ethnic or otherwise, for the people living closest to the coconut and rubber plantations of the southern coast. He attributed their enthusiasm to a lack of ambition, a disregard for posterity. Eight years after Vivian's report, the government anthropologist F. E. Williams made a brief visit to the Suau Coast in order to determine why, in the estimation of the local colonial authorities, the population of the coast had suffered from rapid decline in recent years. Like Vivian, Williams opined that Suau people displayed alarmingly little regard for their own future as a "race," which in the early twentieth century was a term that arguably included within its parameters the current category of "culture." But unlike Vivian, Williams saw the enthusiasm for working on the plantations as an effect rather than a cause of low morale among the local populace, who had been deprived by missionization and colonization of such stimulating activities as warfare. While praising the missions for their "civilizing" work, he went so far as to suggest that their introduction of soccer and cricket superseded religion in effectiveness as a substitute for former activities: "For the present, indeed, one is tempted, even at the risk of irreverence, to suggest 'Less Christ and more cricket'" (Williams 1933: 49). While reasserting the necessity of the colonial project, including elements such as "pacification"—as the suppression of warfare was called—and the introduction of wage labor, Williams also speculated that rapid social and cultural change could result in such a depressed condition among Suau people that they would die out rather than proceed into a future that held nothing for them other than Christianity and copra.

The predictions of Vivian and Williams were couched in idioms that now ring as not only paternalistic but also bizarrely mistaken—indeed, the demographics of the Suau Coast are these days so robust and so youthful that my friends there invariably articulate their predicament by using the English expression "population explosion." But I would ask the reader to attend to the way these older concerns for the future of "Suau-dom" resonate quite closely with contemporary debates about the seemingly inevitable "culture loss" that will accompany globalization, or worse, has done so already. Just as the monoculture of cash cropping threatens the diversity of local subsistence crops, there is imagined to be a human monoculture, a "McWorld," that will lay waste to the diversity of forms of human expression and social structure. Anthropologists, historians, and other scholars ought to have something to say about this discourse, which in its more unhinged versions is thrown up as a possible source of future wars, and even in its more benign versions is certainly the source of preservationist intentions scarcely distinguishable in their paternalism from those of Mr. Vivian nearly a century ago. If we are to take seriously the potential effects of globalization on human diversity, then instances such as the one offered by the Suau Coast are instructive. While I have no way of verifying this suspicion, it seemed increasingly apparent to me during my visits to the Suau Coast that the reason no anthropologist ever stayed there was not only because the Suau region lacked the reassuring boundedness and romance of an island population but also because Suau people were themselves insufficiently "cultural." Or to put it more succinctly, when a Suau friend once asked me why his beautiful coastal home had such trouble attracting tourists, I replied under the influence of a sour mood, "Your women wear clothes." The remark was not only born of cynicism, however; the "trademark" image of Milne Bay promoted across Papua New Guinea and indeed internationally is of bare-breasted, grass-skirted Trobriand Islands women. And it is not only tourists who have a reputation for spurning the familiar in favor of the exotic and the titillating:

> On Friday, 12.11, in the morning I observed the interesting ceremony of payment, with *Sinesaramonamona* [an old-fashioned Suau woman's name]; then I went to sit with the pigs in the house of the *tanawagana* [a lineage head or steward]; very bored by what went on. In the afternoon, went again, hoping there would be a ceremonial slaughtering of the pigs. Actually it seems there is no such thing. (Malinowski 1967: 51–52)

Thus Malinowski summed up his disappointing visit to the village of Isudau at the western end of the Suau Coast in 1914. Like nearly every anthropologist to follow him to what would later become Milne Bay Province, the Suau-speaking region was a place to pass through on the way to more interesting places. When the above field diary entry was recorded, Malinowski was dutifully following the historic (and still extant) trade routes from Mailu Island in Central Province up the Suau Coast to the colonial headquarters at Samarai, stopping along the way at villages with mission stations where he could have reasonably comfortable accommodation and fellow Europeans to talk to. On the way back to Mailu he was afforded more of a spectacle in Silosilo to the west of Isudau, where he commissioned the performance of a *damolea* dance. He also witnessed the ritual attack of pig-givers upon their humiliated affines, although neither he nor his missionary hosts were apparently aware that this was an expected component of the proceedings and not a random outbreak of violence (see chapter 2). Apart from these moments of excitement, however, the anthropologist's brief sojourn along the south coast went unremarked. A year later he had embarked on fieldwork in the Trobriand Islands, and the pattern for anthropology in "the Massim" was established for nearly the entirety of the twentieth century. The mainland, with its rapidly converting people and its burgeoning plantation economy, was to be eschewed in favor of the more isolated, and hence more culturally "authentic," islands.

Whatever other virtues the Suau Coast may be able to claim, this kind of "authenticity," in the romantic and almost totally imaginary sense of a

population affected only lightly by the twin projects of colonialism and capitalism, is not one of them. Suau people have been avowedly Christian since
the landing, at Suau Island in 1877, of the London Missionary Society in the
form of the Reverend James Chalmers along with his wife and Polynesian co-
missionaries. Suau people have, almost from the moment of Chalmers's arrival,
enthusiastically sent their children to be educated and to seek jobs in their
local metropoles of Samarai, Alotau, and Port Moresby. They enjoyed close
proximity to the district headquarters at Samarai, with its infrastructural links
to Australia and the United Kingdom, for nearly a century. They have worked
on rubber and copra plantations in the 1920s and 1930s, as domestic laborers
for Australian and American soldiers during World War II, at gold and copper
mines in the 1970s, and on oil palm plantations and logging projects from
the 1990s to the time of writing this book. For the last 140 years, then, Suau
have participated in every single phase of European religious, economic, and
political expansion into the Pacific, and they have not only accommodated it
but also embraced it.

Suau are of course not alone in having had this sort of experience during
the colonial era, but their response to that era is noteworthy. A Papua New
Guinean colleague from Port Moresby remarked to me once, "Those Suau and
Tolai people—the way they are now is the way the whole country will someday
be" (L. Kalinoe pers. comm. 1999). I found his mentioning of Suau and Tolai
in the same breath remarkable. Compared strictly as language groups, there
are roughly nine times as many Tolai-speakers as there are Suau.[11] But more
importantly, the Tolai people of East New Britain Province are renowned for
their resolute maintenance of the very kinds of practices—songs, dances, ritual
societies, the use of shell wealth for important payments—that Suau system-
atically discarded both during the colonial era and after, in spite of Tolai having been German subjects for as long as Suau were British ones. In addition,
Tolai living on the Gazelle Peninsula of New Britain were subject to one of
the earliest and most extensive land appropriations in the colonial history of
Papua New Guinea, when the German administration built its headquarters
at Rabaul.

Both Tolai and Suau experienced some of the first experiments of their
respective colonial regimes in initiating a plantation economy, in both cases
driven primarily by copra. But thereafter the histories of the two groups di-
verge. Tolai had far more land alienated for plantations than Suau did, land that
now forms much of the township area for Rabaul and neighboring Kokopo.
During World War II, New Britain was invaded and occupied by the Japanese
in 1942, while a subsequent invasion attempt in Milne Bay was successfully
repulsed by the Allies later the same year.

It is therefore striking that despite successive waves of occupation by Ger-
mans, Australians, Japanese, and then Australians again, Tolai people could

reasonably be held up as standing for everything Suau people threw under the bus: the outward manifestations—in the form of ritual societies, costumed song and dance performances, and exchanges of shell wealth—of their culture. While these are now maintained by the more self-consciously conservative strata of Tolai society (Martin 2013), they are again, critically for my own project, regarded by outsiders as bastions of cultural preservationism. For Suau, the distant Tolai and the more geographically accessible Trobriand Islanders represent everything they regard themselves as having lacked the foresight to do: maintain something called, throughout Papua New Guinea and Melanesia more generally, their *kastom*. But the shifting ground of what *kastom* might actually refer to is an ongoing matter of debate for Suau people, and it has informed much of the twenty-year relationship between this group of people and this particular ethnographer. What Suau *kastom* is presumed to have been at one time, how that was released into the past, and what it is presumed to be now serve to bracket my understanding not only of Suau history but also of the anthropological endeavor itself. The stance of humility, and even shame, adopted by many Suau with regard to their own dealings with foreigners over the last century and a half is, for me, a challenge to anthropological knowledge claims—to who people are, at a minimum, and the profoundly relational nature of who they are. If a category like *kastom*, which has become a defining feature of ethnic identity in the Papua New Guinean postcolony, can be lost and then recovered again in a new if diminished form, what can the ethnographer do but adopt an analogous humility to her own claims of understanding what has happened in the interim?

Loss

There are precedents for anthropological considerations of losses in the face of rapid political and economic change. In the 1960s, for example, anthropologists and others were busy declaring the death of matrilineal kinship in the wake of capitalism's onslaught (Gough 1961). Since that time matriliny, the kinship system in which ancestral descent and inheritance of property are traced through maternal lines, has proved itself to be rather more resilient than expected (see chapter 5), while it is also important to note the ways in which matrilineal peoples have adapted their inheritance system to life in the market economy. Now that it is not just a form of social organization but entire cultures that are held to be at stake, it behooves anthropologists to pay attention to those cases of people who, rather than anticipating the loss of their culture, say that they have already experienced it. But in contrast to the by now common narrative of "Fourth World" peoples dispossessed by settler states, or other indigenous populations whose ways of life are threatened by the depredations of global capital, I consider what it might mean to claim the loss of cultural or social aspects without necessarily asserting that someone else has taken them away. Rather, loss may be claimed as the failure of a relationship to deliver on expectations. In his analysis of the particular circumstances leading to particular claims of loss, Kirsch (2001) importantly drew attention to the difference between loss as a form of property claim and loss as a form of grief. In both instances, loss is a function of social relations in a state of disruptive transformation. But, Kirsch asks,

> What are the kinds of things or relations that can be lost, and what are the contexts in which loss is implicated? The notion of loss appears to have two primary registers. It may refer to possession—to the objects or property for which one might claim rights or ownership. Loss in this guise implies value and property relations; it may therefore be possible to gain new understandings of property by examining re- sponses to loss. In other contexts, however, such as the intimate losses associated with grief, loss may be improperly referenced to property relations, as one does not necessarily hold comparable rights to per- sons as to things. (2001: 168–69)

I wish to propose here that there is yet another register for claims to loss, one sharing common attributes of the two described by Kirsch. It is of course not only property to which people ascribe value but also social relations them- selves and the potential for a common flourishing held latent within them. Their value is at once moral, aesthetic, and material, all acting upon each other in an ideal of world formation, where "the world" is understood as a process of relationships being recognized and their potential for positive effects released. The loss of such relationships, or the failure of their potential to be realized, can produce a narrative of grieving analogous to the loss of persons them- selves and demand analogous techniques for reorganizing the social world around the loss. It is this narrative that forms the thematic heart of the book. If relations with others may be mourned, the moral question contained in the process of mourning is: Why did those others withdraw, and why did the re- lationship fail?

Here I draw inspiration from Ferguson's (1999) work on processes of dis- connection throughout the decolonizing world. Although his focus was on the deindustrialization of Zambia following the copper boom of the mid- twentieth century, Ferguson set the tone for ethnographies of historical decline throughout the postcolony. If sub-Saharan Africa represented the first waves of both hope in the moment of independence and the subsequent dashing of hope as the process of "development" failed to deliver either economic pros- perity or political stability, then the nations of the western Pacific, including Papua New Guinea, may fairly be said to represent the last waves of this disappointment. Late to the colonial game and late emerging from it, Papua New Guinea was on the receiving end of such piecemeal and haphazard efforts at "development" that it could in no way be said to have even approached the experiments in industrialization that, say, Africa or the Indian subcontinent did. Foreign interests engaged with Melanesia just long enough to convert souls, make money, and fight wars—and no longer. As each of these enterprises concluded, the foreigners withdrew, their attention already elsewhere.

Ferguson is careful to note the affective inflection of relations between colonized peoples who experienced rapid withdrawal of foreign persons and foreign capital and the ways in which this differs from never having felt connected at all. "Just as being hung up on is not the same thing as never having had a phone," he writes, "the economic and social disconnection that Zambians experience today is quite distinct from a simple lack of connection. Disconnection . . . implies an active relation, and the state of having been disconnected requires to be understood as the product of specific *structures and processes of disconnection*" (1999: 238, emphasis in original). For Zambia in the 1990s, this meant the withdrawal of global capital from the country's copper mining industry. For Papua New Guinea in the 1970s and onward, it meant the withdrawal of colonial capital and its replacement by deterritorialized capital, which has by now become almost entirely dissociated from moral narratives of "development" and focused in laser-like fashion on extractive industries such as timber and mining—including, with some irony, the mining of copper, which has given rise to narratives of cataclysmic environmental loss described by anthropologists such as Kirsch.

But some populations in Papua New Guinea attempted in good faith and in the spirit of experimentation with new economic opportunities to sustain the relationships that colonialism appeared to offer them. The attempts of Suau people to accommodate themselves to colonial capital, and their sense of loss at its withdrawal, underline a distinction that Minnegal (2009) has identified as the difference between "waiting on" and "waiting for" another party to act in relation to oneself. The two modes of waiting index different types of relationship. To wait *on* another implies a mutuality of attention and regard. "In waiting on 'others' one confers on them agency and subjectivity equivalent to one's own, recognizing the need to wait for them to reveal themselves rather than presuming to know what they are" (2009: 92). By contrast, waiting *for* another subordinates one's own perspective to that other, acknowledging that one cannot act in an efficacious manner until they do. This type of waiting "emerges in any context where a division of labor exists within production sequences" (2009: 95), so that those consuming or receiving must wait for those on the producing or transmitting side of the relationship to act. I would also draw out Minnegal's implication, based on her description of waiting *on*, that waiting *for* another also means that one does not have to be knowable or even intelligible to the other who produces or transmits information about the state of the relationship. This implication is helpful to understanding the colonial relationship in general and absolutely critical to understanding colonialism as Suau people in particular encountered it.

Take, for example, the fact that the fabled Mr. Vivian omitted from his considerations the possible ramifications of having relocated dozens of families from the Suau hinterland down to the coast, where they would be competing with already resident lineages for garden land—and now land on which to plant oil palm, the cash crop that has rapidly replaced copra since its introduction to the province in the 1980s. He furthermore did not know, and arguably could not know because his job was to manage Papua New Guineans rather than to know them, what a concern for "posterity" might look like for Suau people. Suau are deeply concerned about posterity, and they are also concerned about loss. Perhaps unsurprisingly, their concerns have led them to take different actions from those anticipated or prescribed by witnesses to the processes of loss they have undergone over the past 140 years. Loss has never been accidental on the Suau Coast, nor has it been the inexorable byproduct of mission, plantation, military, and colonial administration. To assume otherwise is to deny the possibility that Suau people themselves exercised any agency in their losses. And if commentators on this process are to speak seriously of agency, we are necessarily speaking of relationships between Suau and all the people who passed along their coast during the nineteenth and twentieth centuries, people with whom Suau had to negotiate and of whom they had any number of expectations of their own.

Many of my interlocutors initially did not call themselves Suau, nor did they call themselves anything else in the fixed sense of an ethnonym, as their sense of who they were was a contingent set of relationships operating simultaneously at various scales of experience: the linguistic, the geographical, the provincial, the national, and, by virtue of their Christian faith, the international. Yet they were keen to discuss those aspects of their always-shifting identity, which they felt they had lost or were about to lose. They were also happy to cite, in appropriate contexts, their differences from people from other parts of Milne Bay or other provinces of Papua New Guinea. During a general election, they would call my attention to how peaceful and civilized they were, unlike those bellicose Highlanders who would start a fight over every ballot result. During a village court hearing, a magistrate would chastise a disputant asking for too large a bridewealth settlement, reminding him that payments of that size belonged to Central Province, not Milne Bay (Demian 2003: 108). They would compare themselves favorably both to uppity Trobriand Islanders and to those from rough and parochial Fergusson Island, "the Highlanders of Milne Bay" according to a popular cliché used in the province. Coastal men would say that inlanders did not conduct their funerals properly, and coastal women who had married inland would hint darkly at the love magic their husbands must have used to win them, since what coastal woman in her right mind would leave behind the white sands and teeming reefs of home?

But these chauvinisms were largely cosmetic, in the sense that they served as immediate index points, like assessing someone's dialect, to who and where they were. Like the terms for "up" (*sae*) and "down" (*dobi*), which in Suau can be used to index "eastward" and "westward" when referring to coastal directionality, emplacing persons is a process of determining where they are now, and where they are going, both literally and figuratively. Sitting on the beach at Isuisu on a calm night, my host family and I might hear the outboard motor of a dinghy making its way along the coast. We would pause in our conversation and listen intently. *I saema, e i dobima?* someone could ask: is it coming up here or down here? That is, is the dinghy traveling from west to east, toward Suau Island, Samarai, and Alotau, or from east to west, toward Fife Bay, Bona Bona Island, Mullins Harbour, and even Port Moresby? Contained in the trajectory of the dinghy might also be the identity of its passengers and even the reason for their journey, be it pastoral, medical, business, or familial. Does the dinghy have a diesel engine, with its note so distinctive from that of a petrol-oil-mix engine? Then it's cousin Ken, coming to deliver visitors and perhaps pick up the anthropologist to take her to another village.

Remembering and Forgetting

The spatial and temporal relationship between the past and the present in Suau is laden with assessments of value and references to the effects of European contact. Remembered, significant events are those that made an impact on the social and physical landscape, giving rise to a distinct (because unprecedented) "time" (*huya*) from which generations are loosely dated. They are sometimes referred to as *senis huyadi*, "times of change," which incorporates the Tok Pisin word for "change." The novelty of these "times" ensures their place in the temporal imagination, but they are only bounded at their commencement; that is, one does not end when the next one begins, but rather its ramifications are felt continuously by descending generations. The overall effect is a cumulative one, with history conceived almost as a sedimentary layering of past disruptions, introductions, and innovations.

The first of these disruptions reported to me was the arrival of James Chalmers ("Tamate") of the London Missionary Society on the Suau Coast in the 1870s, who has acquired something of a legendary status.[12] Coastal people in particular see themselves as his spiritual descendants, in deliberate contrast to the people of faraway Goaribari in Western Province, who are said to have eaten Chalmers as well as his boots (as the story, told repeatedly and with

considerable relish, goes). The Buhutu area, on the other hand, was not vigorously or methodically evangelized for another sixty years or so. By this time
the Kwato Extension Association, a mission founded by Charles and Beatrice
Abel which had grown out of the LMS and acquired a pastoral character of its
own (Abel 1969), was beginning to extend its activities from the coast to the
hinterland. Elders in Leileiyafa recall the arrival of one of the Abels' sons to
try to abolish sorcery; they cannot, however, remember whether it was Cecil
or Russell Abel. Indeed, all Abels of this historical period are more or less collapsed into one Abel ("Misiebo," i.e. Mr. Abel), an agent of radical change who
appeared on the coast in the late nineteenth century and in the Sagarai Valley
in the 1930s. Aside from the discouragement of sorcery, other practices such
as disinterment of the dead and placement of their bones in caves, full-body
tattooing of preadolescent girls, and presumably cannibalism were also done
away with in the period between Misiebo's arrival and World War II. Whether
or not these institutions "suddenly" died out is irrelevant to the local understanding of history; they are *perceived* as having done so. Misiebo and Kwato
heralded the advent of a new era.[13]

World War II, designated as *hiyala ana huya* (the time of the battle), was
the next significant temporal landmark for older people on the Suau Coast.
Hundres of men were recruited to work as domestic laborers for American
and Australian soldiers stationed on Milne Bay; old women remember villages
entirely bereft of able-bodied men and can describe the different sounds of
Japanese and American airplane engines. The shortage of men during the war
was followed by further upheavals in its aftermath, as patrol officers relocated
entire villages in order to make them more accessible and had walking tracks
made to link up the reinvented villages. Roughly half of the current population
of Leileiyafa attribute their presence there to this postwar resettlement, and in
fact, it looms much larger in the local imagination than the war itself. People
who must walk several kilometers to reach their ancestral lands are reminded
of it every time they go to their gardens.

The history of the relationship between Suau and exogenous agents of
transformation has been, in sum, a sequence proceeding from the religious
to the military to the economic. I do not mean to imply that these influences
were each in operation to the exclusion of the others, but to present the character of the twentieth century on the Suau Coast as it was presented to me.
The absence of locally generated events is glaring. Even Papua New Guinea's
independence in 1975, its reinvention as a state, is glossed over because it had
no appreciable effect (or, if my overwhelmingly disappointed interlocutors
are to be believed, a negative effect) on the local flow of events and relationships. That people would only tell me their history as a function of relations
with outsiders suggests a conception of time and history—a narrative of the
passage of time—as propelled by shifts in these relations. To adopt a phys-

ics metaphor, the "energy" of time is latent in unchanging relationships between people and groups of people, but it becomes kinetic when crises arise in these relationships. By crises I mean to suggest not cataclysmic events but stresses in the social field, something akin to "epoch" in Wagner's (1986) sense of time-as-perception rather than time-as-perceived. These crises or epochs (arguably analogous to *huya*) mark turning points in the relations between Suau and *dimdims*, Suau and other Papua New Guineans, and among Suau themselves. The colonial and postcolonial experience has supplied a series of such turning points over many decades in Suau, producing as it went an entirely new domain of relationships. These were the relationships described to me in the respective encounters of mission, war, and cash cropping with the Suau cultural imaginary.

Much has been lost as a consequence of these encounters, as Suau people will be the first to note. My own presence in Leileiyafa was a direct result of this sense of loss. I was first brought there by Matilda Pilacapio, an activist from Alotau with maternal roots in Leileiyafa (and paternal roots in the Philippines), whose intention was that I should engage in some form of salvage ethnography before residents of the village became irretrievably Westernized. Matilda's synecdoche for all things authentic to this region was "the matrilineal kinship," a phrase she repeated often and which she insisted was what I would be studying. This phrase came to take on a dual significance the more I came to know both Matilda and Leileiyafa. There was obviously some concrete concern on her part that land registration in the Suau region was being "corrupted" by the patrifilial sensibilities of both Euro-American jurisprudence and other Papua New Guinean societies, which recognize inheritance largely or exclusively from fathers to sons. But in addition to this was perhaps a reference to the past, a desire to forge some sense of continuity to countervail the sense of disruption I heard voiced frequently by educated people in Milne Bay. In a move of perfect irony, Matilda's solution was to achieve this by means of initiating a relationship between Leileiyafa and a *dimdim*.[14]

I cannot say whether this account will be precisely what Matilda had in mind when she invited me to work in Leileiyafa. While it probably is not, I often found her to be unexpectedly generous toward anthropological knowledge practices. Perhaps this is not so surprising in a province of Papua New Guinea that has seen so many anthropologists for so many years. Where my interests and Matilda's do appear to converge is on the passage of time in the Suau area, what has been remembered and what forgotten. I want to foreground the contentious nature of these two activities, because it is sometimes unclear whether they have been engaged in intentionally or unintentionally. When a linguist talking to a coastal man about traditional housebuilding and ornamentation styles in the 1960s is told, "The Queen doesn't want us to build those houses any more" (R. Cooper pers. comm. 1996), and I am told in the 1990s that

"We used to know how to do those things, but we forgot," what has occurred in the intervening decades? Forgetting in this case has entailed not simply a "loss" of knowledge but a disavowal of its relevance to the present dispensation. That there has been a tremendous rejection of institutions ranging from songs and dances to exchange relationships with the Milne Bay islands in the past century is not under dispute. But the process by which these institutions were deemed obsolete cannot, I feel, be attributed simply to the proximity of Suau to the one-time center of *dimdim* activities on Samarai, or to the efforts of mission and government. Forgetting has been as much an indigenous as an exogenous project, and while it was without question accelerated by the colonial encounter, we need to ask why that encounter was interpreted in such a way that it seemed necessary or desirable to eject so much information from collective memory.

The answer lies, I suspect, somewhere in the process by which relationships are replicated over time in Suau. The introduction of an entirely new field of relationships (with *dimdims* and their institutions) may have been seen as "replacing" many of those that formerly constituted the social world. Replacement, as I will show in the next chapter, is not a way of denying the passage of time but of ensuring its progress, and it is conceived very much as a process embodied in human beings and their dealings with one another. New people on the Suau social horizon had to be accommodated somehow by their cosmology, and it may be that they accomplished this by "replacing" the ancestors and their ways with some new heroes, such as Tamate and Misiebo, and theirs. How could they benefit from the new relationships otherwise?

In chapter 3 I discuss at more length the nature of the new culture heroes and their legacy on the Suau Coast. In anticipation of that chapter I will simply note here that while Chalmers/Tamate is widely regarded as the instigator of transformation, Abel/Misiebo made the actual commitment to stay in Milne Bay with his family and embark on an experiment in mission life that had no equivalent in the Pacific at the time. Suau people demonstrated their desire to be integrated into this extended family of *dimdim* relationships by accepting and adapting themselves to *dimdim* social forms, or Suau interpretations of those forms. This may be speculation but, to me, it offers a more meaningful way of regarding the wholesale forgetting professed by my Suau friends than the apocalyptic pronouncements of cultural death that pervade much well-meaning popular literature on the continuing struggles of the postcolony. Rather, death and its elaborations may be the very vehicles that enabled Suau people to embrace the altered shape of things.

In chapter 2, I will use death and mortuary practices as a starting point for approaching what a Suau theory of change might look like. This is key to locating Suau in the wider context of Austronesian ethnography, but it is also about the intimacy of loss and the elaboration of that loss throughout a community.

The reproduction of people is initiated at birth, an event whose celebration is largely confined to the immediate family; but social reproduction on the Suau Coast is completed at death, an event implicating every person who ever had a relationship with the deceased. Thinking about change begins with that moment of completion, when a human life recedes into the distance, and the living must carry on with their care of relationships over space and time. This includes care for the dead.

Death is a completion rather than an ending: this is why I can place a chapter about mortuary ritual toward the beginning of this book. It is in fact the most logical way to proceed for the purposes of my narrative, even if doing so is something of a conceit, in that the aim is to show how the temporal mode of the funeral sequence is one way of looking at how people approach change. History is another such mode. But history is never a straightforward matter of the effects of the past on the present. That can only be apprehended through the way people think about time itself, and the movement of people through time. The mortuary sequence is where this philosophy of time in Suau is at its most evident, its most "concentrated" in the work people do to complete the lives of those they have lost. The sedimentation of history described at the beginning of this chapter is not simply an automatic outcome of time passing; it is the deliberate, effortful orientation to movement through time that people adopt in their work for the dead.

Notes

1. On commercial maps of Milne Bay Province the name of this village is more likely to be rendered as "Leileiafa" or "Leileiaha." I am following the Buhutu orthography developed by Russell E. Cooper of the Summer Institute of Linguistics in collaboration with his local consultants, as Buhutu is the strongest influence on the Leileiyafa dialect.
2. Milne Bay people will also fling this insult at people who use English vocabulary with an Oceanic syntax, although this habit is also embraced with ironic affection with uniquely Milne Bay expressions, such as "That one how?" featured on t-shirts in shops in Alotau. The expression might be roughly translatable into English as "WTF?"
3. Students from anywhere in the Suau region who wish to complete their secondary education and are fortunate enough to pass the entrance exams that are designed to winnow out students competing for the limited places available generally do so at one of the two high schools in Alotau. This pattern is repeated throughout Papua New Guinea, where decades of noninvestment in the education system means there is a chronic shortage of secondary school places relative to the number of young people who could potentially fill them.
4. Seligman 1910 and Malinowski 1922 both contain brief descriptions of this area, and two reports by government anthropologists (Armstrong 1921; Williams 1933) cover particular ethnographic topics as they related to administrative issues of the time. More recently, Lepowsky 1993 and Mallett 2003 refer to trade routes historically connecting the islands with the southern coast of the mainland.

5. Kula is the most commonly recognized name for the complex of interisland transactions in high-prestige shell valuables and subsidiary trade goods that originally captivated Malinowski's attention during his stay in the Trobriand Islands. It then became something of an ethnographic and analytical preoccupation, not to say a fetish, that seemed to encompass all things authentically and uniquely "Massim" for several generations of anthropologists working in Milne Bay thereafter. Its status as an object of fascination for foreigners, and for Trobrianders interested in capitalizing on the fascination of foreigners, shows no sign of abating anytime soon.

6. The majority of languages spoken in Milne Bay Province are members of the Western Oceanic branch of the Austronesian language family, and as such they share many morphological and syntactical features. Exceptions are the mountainous Agaun region abutting Central and Oro Provinces, and the island of Rossel (Yela), where non-Austronesian languages are spoken. It is not uncommon for a Milne Bay person to speak between three and five of the languages of the province, especially those that are closely related to each other. Sometimes they do this by cheating, as when Suau people jokingly turn all their glottal stops into /k/ to mimic the sound of neighboring Saliba.

7. The earliest version of this translation to my knowledge is the Gospel of John (*Ioane ena Evanelia*), translated by Charles W. Abel in 1915 and held at the Cambridge University Library. The New Testament currently in use throughout the Suau language cluster was translated by Russell Abel and Benoma Dagoela (Abel 2013) and first published in 1962 by the Bible Society of Papua New Guinea.

8. For example: to anyone outside the United States, all Americans are Yankees. Within the United States, only people from the northeast (north of the Mason-Dixon Line) are Yankees. In New England, where I grew up, only people who are white, Protestant, and able to trace their ancestry to the original colonies really get to call themselves Yankees. I am therefore a Yankee to everyone everywhere except in my hometown of Boston.

9. I would like to think my strategy is comparable to Tsing's (1993) adoption of the geographical term "Meratus" to refer to the Dayak population with whom she worked in South Kalimantan, Indonesia, in preference to a local derogatory term for this population. While the specific problem I am trying to avoid—hyperdifferentiation at the local level—is different from Tsing's, the general ethnographic issue of what to call "a people" who do not ordinarily identify themselves as "a people" remains consistent between Tsing's account and my own, as well as those of many other anthropologists.

10. *Dimdim* is a term unique to Milne Bay Province, and may have been an archaic name in several of its languages for the ancestral realm, for a reef system at the eastern extremity of the province, or for both. Either way, the foreignness of Europeans is indexed by the term, and it can refer either to Europeans themselves or to the countries they come from, with some parallels to what Europeans might call the First World. Whether the term also refers to non-European foreigners is debatable; I have seen friends from Milne Bay flummoxed by the question of whether Asian people are *dimdims*, or whether a British mathematics teacher of African descent was a *dimdim*. This category is, in other words, as unstable as any other ethnonym in Papua New Guinea.

11. See https://www.ethnologue.com/18/language/ksd which puts the population of people speaking Tolai as a first language at roughly 100,000. This is an enormous language group by Papua New Guinean standards.

12. I met a young woman in Fife Bay who, because she was born in 1972, had been named Century in honor of the centenary of Chalmers's arrival. She bore this weighty appellation with admirable grace and humor. On a return visit to Leileiyafa in 1999, I learned that my friend Angela had named her young son Doulos because the mission ship MV *Doulos* had visited Milne Bay Province the year he was born. While the naming of children to commemorate historical events or persons is somewhat uncommon, it is consonant with the practice of naming them after living relatives to serve as their "memory."

13. Kwato no longer holds the spiritual monopoly it once did in Suau. Most villages on the coast are now United Church ("United Church is the mother and Kwato is the daughter," as my host in Leileiyafa, a deacon, explained their relationship); some Buhutu villages are Kwato and others United Church; there are even a few small congregations of Buhutu Catholics. More recently there have been re-conversions of villages near the mouth of Mullins Harbour to various Pentecostal sects, much to the consternation of the "older" churches and their followers.

14. See Kirsch (2004b) for a similar phenomenon among Yonggom people, residents of the Ok Tedi River, which has seen massive ecological degradation as a result of its proximity to the Ok Tedi gold and copper mine. Kirsch evocatively terms his study an "ethnography of loss," which is arguably what I was brought to Leileiyafa to undertake. But there is, I believe, a subtle difference in Kirsch's agenda and that of Matilda, who was keen that I should record the *kastom* of Leileiyafa before it "disappeared." Kirsch, on the other hand, has generated an account of transformations in Yonggom social life and the reckoning of time as a result of ecological loss—something that has not (yet) occurred on such a devastating scale in the Suau region.

🌼 2
Death, *Kastom*, and
the Work of Forgetting

Who else can I call Polo? Who will I call Polo tomorrow? You left a
wound in my heart yesterday that will never heal. When I scolded
you, you never talked back to me or picked up a stick to hit me, so I
knew you respected me more than anyone else. You never used to visit
me but you visited every day this week, and now I know the reason.
—Lani, at the side of her brother Polo the day after his death

I concluded the previous chapter with the statement that death is a completion. This may seem a counterintuitive claim to make, especially in the wake
of deaths that are premature, where the life that has ended should by rights
have included more years or even decades of flourishing. But that is precisely
the point: because most deaths feel like unfinished business, the business of
the living is to find a way to finish it. Whether "it" is the intimacy and depth
of their own grief, or the still-ramifying relationships between the person who
has died, their family, and the community, those left behind by a death must
find their way into a future without the one they have lost.

A chapter about the process of leaving behind the dead serves two purposes in this book. One is straightforwardly ethnographic: the mortuary
sequences observed by Suau people situate them in a wider regional complex of similarly elaborate (and in places far more elaborate) observances.
Why does this matter? Because noting the similarities of practice between
Suau on the mainland and neighboring groups of people throughout Milne
Bay Province, whether mainland or insular, serve to suggest some of the
long-distance connections throughout the region through a very deep history of trade, intermarriage, and warfare. Some other aspects of this history
will be elaborated further in the chapters to follow, particularly chapter 4.
The primary point of this chapter, however, is to note how death and its
accompanying processes of finishing and forgetting are themselves an orientation to history.

If funerary work is also the work of social reproduction, then I would like
to offer a consideration of what people do upon the death of a person in their

social field, in terms not only of the techniques they have at their disposal but of how those techniques enable a particular orientation to inhabiting time itself. As Schram (2007) has shown for a closely related language group in Milne Bay, this very aspect of funerary ritual can become a subject of ongoing debate and "engineering" attempts by local pastors in much the same way that nineteenth-century missionaries saw their work as that of remaking society itself (see chapter 3). Schram notes that "the power of mortuary ritual will often be called upon to provide legitimation of a particular kind of order. The converse could also be said to be true: that efforts to change the culture—by colonial governments, missionaries, and other agents with interests in making indigenous people pursue new goals instead of that of their own collective well-being—have to attack the sources of legitimate social reproduction in order to gain legitimacy for themselves" (2007: 187).

This point is key to understanding how funeral work is crucial to what a Suau theory of change might look like. The theory is embedded in the work itself, and in the way processes for "forgetting" and "finishing" the dead help the living to continue persisting in a flow of relations through time from which a person is now missing. It is also, I argue, a way of thinking about forms of social reproduction as epochal markers. The idea that changing the nature of funerary work can change the nature of society itself is a compelling suggestion of the relationship between this work and people's orientation within their own unfolding history. Funerary work is the reorientation of relationships in time and so has the power to demand reflection on how human time is itself composed.

An Untimely Death

It was January of 2000, and I was preparing to leave Isuisu after six months' residence in the village, my second period of fieldwork on the Suau Coast. My hosts had borrowed a barbecue—in this context, a large metal plate on legs to position over the fire—and planned to have a little party for my departure. In the universal manner of all well-intentioned parties, this one was accompanied by misfortune. But the misfortune that preceded the party was worse than most: a young man, Kodema, died the day before. Rumor had it that he died falling from an areca (betel nut) palm he had climbed to acquire betel nut to sell at the barbecue. So the mood at the party was subdued, for some reasons that I felt I understood at the time—no one can feel celebratory in the wake of a young person's death—and some that I did not—rumors about the causes of his death were apparently already in circulation, although I did not hear them until afterward. But few people came, and among those who did, conversation either was absent or focused on when the *buga* or funeral feast for Kodema would be held, and who would be bringing what. The *buga* was held a week later.

At the *buga* the rumors proliferated, and they were now out in the open. I heard that Kodema had not fallen, he had jumped. He was angry with his family, the story went, and had declared that the next time he went into the bush, he was going for good. The palm he climbed was old, tall, and mangled by years of bush knife scarring: not a tree one would ordinarily risk climbing. So if it really was suicide and not an accident, I thought, this time they could not possibly pin the death on witchcraft. No, my friend Miriam told me, of course it was witchcraft. Because his feelings were no good, this made him especially vulnerable to the influence of witches, who would have planted in his mind the suggestion to jump.

It was an unusually lavish feast for an unmarried and childless man in his twenties. Kodema's elderly parents, Teoma and Tubufuyo, were held in high esteem, and their relations were scattered across the coast and its hinterland. Tubufuyo was among the last Suau men to maintain a polygynous marriage, although only one of his three wives was still living at the time of my residence in Isuisu. At the *buga*, his many affines bearing pigs shouted the names of the pigs' recipients and hurled mango branches (*gisowa*), signifying that they had brought a prestation of three pigs, and trying to lodge the branches in the roof thatch of the house in which Tubufuyo and Teoma sat in quiet and studied abasement. Teoma's attitude was appropriately grave, but it was also evident that she was pleased with the aggressive display of affinal generosity being wrought upon her house. She told me that it was because she had a lot of children who brought pigs, although more accurately she had a lot of married children whose affines brought pigs. She then said, almost as if she were warning me, "If you don't have children, there will be no pigs at your *buga*." She gave me a small polished pearl shell (*giniuba*) of the kind that would once have been distributed to affines at Suau funerals, possibly to press home her point, possibly to ensure I would never forget that day or that conversation. It worked, of course.

Then Tubufuyo told me that none of the *buga* I had seen at Leileiyafa would have been done properly. "Buhutu people don't know *kastom*," he said dismissively. "They've forgotten." Somewhat to my surprise, a Leileiyafa man who was present nodded in agreement when I glanced at him to catch his reaction to this pronouncement. But I should not have been surprised: funerals on the Suau Coast are *par excellence* the technology of forgetting, and forgetting funerary work itself can, as noted above, become its own kind of metawork. In the weeks and interim events leading up to a *buga*, the task at hand for everyone who knew a person who has died is to remember to forget.

Death among the Anthropologists
of the Austronesian Culture Complex

Nearly every ethnography of a society speaking an Austronesian language, whether in Papua New Guinea or elsewhere, contains a chapter about death, mortuary rituals, or ancestral commemoration, and that chapter nearly always comes last. There are excellent reasons for the first aspect of what has become the canonical form of ethnography for this part of Papua New Guinea, but not for the second. As one colleague remarked felicitously when she relocated from doing fieldwork in the Eastern Highlands of Papua New Guinea to the province of New Ireland, "It was so interesting to go from a place where the most significant moment of social reproduction is marriage to a place where it's death" (P. West pers. comm. 2007). New Ireland, in common with Milne Bay societies, participates in a classically Austronesian preoccupation with death and the mortuary sequence as the unfolding of all the relations that constituted the life of the deceased, followed by their refolding or reorientation so that they no longer plague the lives of the living. Only upon death can the person become complete, a predicament that is often spoken of in idioms of "finishing" the dead or fixing them in place, both physically and metaphysically (Foster 1992; de Coppet 1982; Astuti 1995). Procedures for finishing and anchoring the dead assign them to the domain of the unchanging ancestors, whose very nature is defined in contradistinction to the changeability and dynamism of human lives in the process of being lived. "Working for the dead," Astuti (1995: 123) has observed of mortuary sequences in Madagascar at the western extremity of the Austronesian language family, "is another way of *separating* life from death."

The point however is that working for the dead does not only happen after death in many Austronesian societies. Ideally, it happens all the time and informs not only the character of time itself but also how people locate the temporal origins of particular practices. As this chapter will elucidate, how Suau people work for the dead is a fundamental component in their location of entire concepts in the category of time immemorial to which the dead also belong. The ancestors are an ever-present feature of the moral and indeed the physical landscape (see chapter 4), and their fixing into that landscape is an ongoing process. Or as de Coppet has observed of 'Are'are people in the Solomon Islands,

> In this part of Melanesia, what we may call subsistence or, in a more radical way, survival seems to be the main task of a society: it is achieved through the everlasting *work of mourning*. Everyday life, peace, fecundity and prosperity are entirely dependent upon the proper mourning of the dead. The harvest, the fish catch, seduction in

love, a successful journey through the forest or on the sea, the moving sound of Pan-pipe or slit-drum, the magnificence of the feasts, all depend on the constant flow of mourning work. (de Coppet 1982: 179, emphasis in original)

Although it may appear initially paradoxical to some readers, the point of all this work—much of it implicit rather than explicit, but evident in the way that so much of the health and well-being of the living appears bound up in their relations with the dead—is to forget the dead. I do not mean that the dead pass accidentally from people's everyday consciousness. What is meant here is that the work of mourning, which is also the work of finishing or forgetting, is "an act of *domination over death* . . . what is 'finished' is the mnemonic property of the person" (Battaglia 1993: 431, emphasis in original). In other words, a person whose memory is finished—complete—cannot vex the living with the incompleteness of relationships that point to an absence.

In light of this, and in light of its centrality to the issues of loss and forgetting on the Suau Coast, it is imperative that I do not leave death for last, as it were. No consideration of Suau social or cultural life makes sense without first dealing with Suau ways of death, that is to say, Suau ways of life and its fulfillment. These are, again, also ways of thinking about one's own place in history. While Suau people no longer practice the long-cycle mortuary sequences of the kind recorded by early observers of the region, the diminution of ritual has not, I argue, been accompanied by a diminution in meaning, function, affect, or any other of the putative "products" of ritual action. While some persons may occasionally be buried with a minimum of ritual activity or ceremonial exchange, these are usually distant relatives who have spent most of their lives in Port Moresby or other cities and only return home in their coffins. Even these benighted souls are given an abbreviated funeral feast. Hymns are sung, tea is drunk, and modest amounts of pork are distributed to those affines who have faithfully performed the work that they must carry out for the dead.

I want, therefore, to make it plain that this is primarily a chapter about mortuary practices, as in actions, and not grief. While grief—in the sense of emotion erupting from the insuperable pain of the loss of a person—does have a place in Suau funerals, it is as often as not something that leaks out from the interstices of the funeral process. When a friend from home wrote to me asking what Suau grief "looked like," I wrote back saying that it looked like Joshua brushing the grit from his wife's closed eyes while she lay in her coffin, a re-purposed canoe, before burial. The tenderness of this gesture struck me like a blow to the stomach, and it happened entirely outside of the promptings of ritual, between stages of the funerary sequence. Such intimacies of grief inhabit a space entirely outside the actions that people must undertake in the course of the mortuary process. While I do not feel at all equal to the task of conveying the depth of feeling that grips those left behind in the wake of a death, I will attempt to demonstrate the impact of death on the social environment of which I was very briefly a part, to show respect for the dead. In Noenoe's case, the relationships that made up this environment will unfold in the course of the telling—but the account begins with her at its center.

Noenoe's Death

Noenoe, a mother of seven in her mid- to late forties, became ill shortly before Christmas 1996. She and most of her immediate family moved into the barely functional aid post at Leileiyafa, where her sister's son (hence her classificatory son) was the medical officer at the time. She worsened over the following two weeks, and as time went on the residents of the village began visiting her with increasing frequency, in what I later learned is a standard practice of paying last respects. Periodically I would go to the aid post and beg her husband and sons to take her to the hospital at Alotau; each time they assured me they would do so the next day. They never did. The reasons for this are probably more numerous than I can know, but they must have included the distance to the hospital and the fact that they would have had to carry Noenoe part of the way on a bush track—this was long before the arrival of the road to Leileiyafa—followed by a dinghy and then a truck journey, the cost of inpatient admission (K20 per day in 1996–97), and last but perhaps most significant the widespread belief that biomedicine was ineffectual against sorcery.

On 6 January she asked to see her eldest son, Hamahewa, who had been avoiding the aid post since having an altercation with his father several days before. While someone went to fetch him, Noenoe lay down to rest, and another older woman placed some divinatory leaves under her pillow in the hope that they would induce Noenoe to say the name of the sorcerer who had caused her illness while she slept. She did not, but when she woke, Hamahewa had arrived. His grandmother Naomi, Noenoe's mother-in-law, immediately launched into an indictment of his irresponsible abandonment of his mother while she was sick. Hamahewa began to cry, and soon everyone in the aid post was crying as well. Whether they wept in response to Hamahewa's remorse or in anticipation of his mother's death, or both, I cannot say. There may have been little distinction between the two at that point.

Noenoe died that afternoon. The palpable tension that had persisted in the aid post for the previous several days was broken suddenly as the medical officer flew into a rage, Noenoe's daughters began to wail, and other women hastened to arrange Noenoe's limbs before rigor mortis set in. The threshold from everyday time to the time of mourning had palpably been crossed, and Noenoe's journey from living kinswoman to ancestor had begun. Young men from the lineage serving as funeral workers arrived within minutes to begin chopping firewood and building shelves for serving tea to the mourners. Children were sent with the news to other hamlets. And Hemisi, Noenoe's husband of some thirty years, could be heard from across the hamlet crying "Agu li'u!" (my broth), the new widow or widower's shorthand for everything given and fed to them by their spouse during the lifetime of the latter. It is understood that the broth from cooked food, whether vegetable or animal, is what makes a person fat (*tubu*), increasing their size, strength, and health. It is the "medium" for solid food, the substance that is produced by it and completes it. To cry for the loss of this long-term sustenance is a profound acknowledgment of the contribution a dead spouse has made to one's well-being by means of a causal chain in reverse: the fat of one's body, produced by broth, produced by work, performed by the dead spouse. Broth from cooked food, at the center of this chain, "points" in the direction of both the living and the dead partner in marriage, in that position making manifest the relationship between them. Food in general and broth in particular is a product that has as its referent both men's and women's work. A woman crying for broth mourns the end of gardens built and animals caught by her husband, while a man, like Hemisi, mourns the end of meals cooked by his wife.

Figure 2.1. Hemisi in mourning for his wife, Noenoe (Leileiyafa, 1997). He and his wife's sister Pinole, at the head of the coffin, requested that this photograph be taken. Photo by the author.

Villagers came for the rest of the day to weep (*tantan* L.; *doudou* D.) over Noenoe's body. That this was a matter of procedure became apparent when an older girl's parents scolded her for not crying in the presence of a laid-out body, and in the wake of later deaths, people en route to another hamlet would tell me matter-of-factly, "I'm going up there to cry." I am not suggesting, however, that because crying is obligatory it is not expressive of powerful emotion. People say that until they have wept for a dead person, their "feelings are bad" (*amnadi ti heyaya*) or that their "minds/hearts are bad" (*nuwadi ti heyaya*). But crying is a categorically *public* activity, done in the presence of, and often elicited by the crying of, other people, as when Hamahewa was upbraided by his grandmother. Crying alone does not constitute grief; crying in front of appropriate others does. This was strongly demonstrated when news reached one of my hosts in Leileiyafa, May, that her sister had died in the coastal village of Saga'aho, their place of origin. May sang and wept quietly as she packed her bag to leave for the long walk to the coast, but her husband Saunia chastised her for doing so, telling her to save her breath and wait until they got to Saga'aho. Even more striking was an incident after her return when, upon meeting an affine who had not gone to her sister's funeral, the two of them sat down in the middle of the path and cried. It was as though the sister's death had to be registered in a display of weeping but could only be done so in May's presence, for May was the junction through which her in-law was related to the dead woman and the death was refracted back by her to kinfolk in Leileiyafa who had been unable to weep at the funeral itself. Grief, in this case, travels along the paths of relationships and cannot manifest by itself, but must be passed between the grieving. Crying, the outward manifestation of grief, is what renders it visible, demonstrating that a unified experience is happening. To cry before someone else is to turn one's mind inside out.

The night after Noenoe died, the crying continued during the mourning vigil held outside of the aid post. Fires and kerosene lamps burned all night as attendees sang hymns and keened over Noenoe's body, generating a peculiar dissonance of moods. Outside the aid post people sang, chatted, chewed betel nut, and drank tea, while inside Noenoe's immediate family held their heads and wailed as though oblivious to the activity around them. The object of the vigil, I was told, was to "punish" those who came so that they would remember everything Noenoe had done for them during her lifetime. It was said that some people could even prolong the vigil by forestalling sunrise with magic spells, because when the cocks begin to crow in earnest, the vigil participants can go home and rest. This apparently was not done at the vigil for Noenoe, although Saunia did ask me later the following day, "Did the night seem very long to you?"

Noenoe's burial (*toletoletau*) happened the day following the vigil. Her body was taken initially to her own hamlet for a "visit," where her family picked a croton flower, placed it by her head, and addressed her through it to encourage her spirit (*yaluwa*) to follow them. At home her daughters combed her hair and dressed her in her Sunday finery. Finally she was put into an old canoe that had been converted into a coffin and covered with hibiscus flowers, wooden crosses, and a can of insecticide spray.[1] She was carried in the coffin to a meeting area near the aid post where her sister's son gave a eulogy and two deacons read from the Bible. The croton flower accompanied her on this short journey—"U lauma, ta lau," murmured the kinswoman carrying it: Come, let's all go. Finally, the coffin was carried up to the hamlet belonging to her lineage. Before interment, her small grandchildren were picked up and passed between adult family members over the open coffin to prevent her *yaluwa* from touching the children and making them ill. Then the coffin was placed in the grave dug by the funeral workers, who covered it with a pandanus sleeping mat before filling in the grave. Later the workers would build a miniature house over the grave, plant flowers around it (including the croton to which her *yaluwa* had been "attached"), and set a coconut on a post of the grave house to begin sprouting it. This would later be planted too as a memorial (*he'ihe'inoi*) to Noenoe.

The burial marks the beginning of *tautauwela'i*, a period of one to three days of deep mourning during which no work is permitted, especially the burning of new gardens or of weeds in established gardens.[2] Noenoe's was the first death I encountered on the Suau Coast, and I was not prepared for the way time seemed to slow down during this period. The weekly market was not held, nor were any soccer games played; church services were sparsely attended, and the whole place generally began to take on an aspect of neglect. Voices were subdued, words were few, visiting between houses and hamlets stopped almost entirely, kunai grass grew tall in the soccer field. Unaccustomed to this response to a death and unnerved by the death itself, I grew ferociously bored and, with few field notes to type up, read *Crime and Punishment*. Although the deep mourning period lasted only a few days, the ordinary pace of life did not fully resume in Leileiyafa until several weeks later. It felt as though the entire village had been removed to some other world where everything was quieter and slower and everyone suffused with regrets, and we only gradually emerged into the buzz and warmth of living people when not attending to the dead.

Noenoe's husband Hemisi also went into seclusion following her burial, covering his head with a black cloth and confining himself to the house of a senior affine, that is, a member of Noenoe's lineage. The period between a death and the funeral feast, the *buga*, that occurs roughly one week later is a hazardous one due to the possibility of contact with the dead person's *yaluwa*, thought to be particularly mobile and capricious during this time. Some accounts I was given of the *yaluwa*'s activities identified it as the source of mischief; others blamed witches (*'alawan*) for "wearing" the *yaluwa* as a sort of mask or glamour in order to frighten people. Whatever the agency of its movements, the *yaluwa* is regarded during this time as a more or less direct link to the consciousness of the dead person, but it may not be acting with his or her will.

The possibility of communication between the *yaluwa* and the living was most evident in the next stage of postmortem activities after Noenoe's death, the *fafabou*. This is a divination procedure claimed to be exclusive to Leileiyafa and intended primarily to discover the identity of the sorcerer (*aiyahan*) responsible for a death. But because the *yaluwa* is directly addressed during the divination, it can also be asked about a preferred location for the funeral feast and other auxiliary questions whose answers may serve as instructions or warnings to the family of the person who has died.

For Noenoe's *fafabou* we gathered three days after Noenoe's death in the local government councillor's house. A curl of hair cut from above Noenoe's ear (so the *yaluwa* could hear the questions asked of it) before burial was tied to a long, stout stick held at either end by two funeral workers, who stood back to back. Noenoe's sister Pinole sat at the midpoint of the stick, where the hair was tied; Elia, the village court magistrate at the time who was also a specialist in *fafabou*, sat on the other side to coach her. She began by asking, in Leileiyafa dialect, the names of villages where the sorcerer might live: "Sinalili sai ya golim? U tuhu, u tuhu!" (Was it Sinalili that speared you? Move, move!). She would then strike the stick with a branch of leaves, the identity of which no one would tell me. The stick should remain stationary if the answer is no and swing back and forth if the answer is yes. After determining that the village where the guilty party lived was Tautili, further up the Sagarai Valley, Pinole began to ask the names of sorcerers from Tautili. The stick swung at the mention of a particular senior man. Then she asked possible reasons for the murder. The stick indicated "yes" when asked about an insult or other verbal affront made by an elderly member of the same lineage as Noenoe. Since it is understood that a sorcerer will always take revenge on the entire family of a person at whom he is angry and will continue to kill them until caught, the most pressing task after the divination was for the local level government councillor to go and collect the named sorcerer as soon as possible for the inevitable village court hearing.

There still remained the question of where to hold the *buga* for Noenoe. Pinole spoke of all the fish and bush pigs they would catch for her (the stick swung vigorously) and then began to name hamlets in Leileiyafa where the feast might be held. It remained still until the aid post was named; this was typical, I was told afterward. Dead people usually want their funeral feast to be held in the place where they died.

As it turned out, the *buga* was not held at the aid post but at Noenoe's lineage hamlet (*siu*). This was where Hemisi had been confined after the burial, and Noenoe's family also felt they were more able to stage a decent feast there.

It was an impressive production: the hamlet had been transformed by the presence of a large tent made from plastic tarpaulins, shelves, and tables of corrugated iron on sapling legs, and large cooking fires were scattered everywhere. Under the tent a string band set up their battery-powered amplifiers to play all night for anyone who wanted to dance, primarily younger people and children. Others watched the dancing, cooked, ate, gossiped, and dozed as the night wore on. The festivities were punctuated by the arrival of pigs for distribution the next day; these were brought by groups of men from locations as close as other Leileiyafa hamlets and as distant as villages on the coast. The men sang *wowo*, arpeggiated tones on a descending minor scale, and sometimes blew conch shells as they approached, announcing their burden of another pig to be tied underneath the house where Hemisi was confined. Each new group of pig-bearers was fed by the family in mourning, ideally a large bowl each of garden or "real" food (taro and sweet potatoes, bananas, sago dumplings) and *dimdim* food (rice, tinned meat and fish, noodles), complementary categories that were invariably set up by my informants that demonstrated the industriousness in both garden and money-earning work of the *buga* hosts. At this point, it was the prerogative of the pig-bearing guests to harangue the feast-givers for every time they did not help their affines with something, every time they neglected them during sickness, every outstanding obligation that could be dredged up and paraded before them. People might become so worked up with scolding that they would dance and leap about and throw sticks, rocks, or mud at the houses of the people being scolded. The latter could not talk back or defend their houses, but were obliged to endure the abuse. When this was finished, the pig-bearers could sit down and eat. This last is a normative version of what might happen at a *buga*, however. What I saw of it at Noenoe's feast was very subdued, and it now only appears to happen with any regularity at coastal funerals, such as the one with which I opened this chapter.

The actual feast, in the sense of a great deal of food being consumed, did not occur until the next day after everyone had gone home to rest and bathe. Cooked garden food, rice, and pig meat were laid out on banana leaves on the makeshift tables for any who chose to attend, while all the live pigs that had been brought during the night (as well as that morning) were staked out in a long line. Next to some of the pigs were placed bundles of bananas, baskets of large sweet potatoes and taros, and ten-kilogram bags of rice.

These funeral gifts are called *anban* in hinterland dialects or *aibai* in most coastal ones. They serve as compensation for the funeral workers who are identified by their reception and consumption of such gifts (*tau'anban/ tau'aibai* depending on dialect: "funeral feast eaters"). *Tau'anban* are led by the *wolisau*, a senior man or woman of their lineage who ensures that mourning restrictions are observed by the widowed spouse and to whom extra pigs may later be given as the bereaved person comes out of mourning. *Tau'anban* are not the only people who consume a funeral feast; other guests and most members of the bereaved lineage or *ulutubu*—that is, descendants of a common ancestress—do as well, apart from the immediate members of the deceased person's family, who observe the abstentions of deep mourning. The lineage who have lost a member are the "owners" of the feast and entitled to some of the gifts it yields. But *tau'anban* are, for the aesthetic purposes of the feast, identified as those who will be fed by it, in recognition of the work they do for it. The vigorous activity of the *tau'anban*, their hard work and the feasting that follows, is contrasted with the relative immobility of the mourning kin of the dead (see Foster 1990 and Young 1989 for other examples of this sort of aesthetic opposition). This ideal of mourners disengaged from the activities of everyday life temporarily cocoons them in an alternative flow of time, one that could be argued either to imitate the status of the dead (nonproducing, nonconsuming) or to reject the processes of death and decay.

Tau'anban are affines of the bereaved lineage, associated through a "mirror image" marriage pattern wherein same-sex affines are related through marriage to same-sex siblings.[3] An example using women as the subject of the funeral and the recipient of the *anban* respectively might look like the configuration in figure 2.2, although the same pattern would hold if all the sexes were reversed.

This marriage may involve living people, or it might have taken place several generations before, with the relevant lineages still acting as *tau'anban* for one another. Noenoe's funeral proceedings were a case in point. All anyone could tell me was that people from the Mahimahina *ulutubu* served as *tau'anban* for people from the Siwe'oya *ulutubu* (of which Noenoe was a member) because of a marriage from "a long time ago." The division of funeral work, then, is not an *ad hoc* arrangement but enduring pairs of lineages who maintain this relationship to each other even after the specific marriage from which it originated has been forgotten. Such arrangements can be "spoiled," however, if members of lineages standing in a *tau'anban* relationship to one another intermarry. If this happens, the lineages involved cannot automatically assume their *tau'anban* status in the event of a death but must ask permission from the bereaved family to perform funeral work for them.

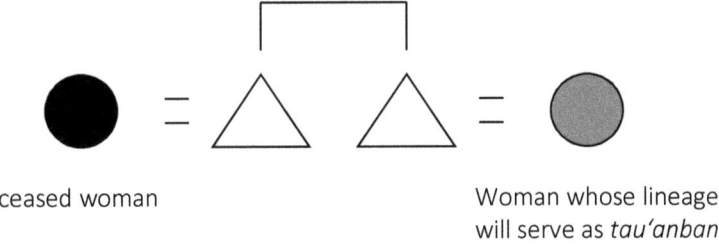

Deceased woman   Woman whose lineage
                                                                will serve as *tau'anban*

Figure 2.2. *Tau'anban* reckoning. Created by the author.

Affinity and consanguinity are thrown into sharp relief in the funeral process, because the two forms of relationship are recognized by means of the fact that they are exchanging pigs. This is a recursive definition: just as there are two significant categories of kin relationship, there are also two types of pig, which are in turn determined by the people who bring them. The pigs displayed at the hamlet where Noenoe's *buga* took place were classed either as *silia*, those brought by Noenoe's consanguines, or *ya'o* (or *eba*), those brought by her affines. These could not be eaten by any member of the groups bringing them and were to be exchanged with each other. Some were repayments of outstanding debts (*haga*) from previous funerals, while others generated new debts that could only be repaid at future funerals. Pigs in this environment are the most outward manifestation of the *tau'anban* relationship's trajectory through time, the display of pigs before an exchange constituting a living catalog of debts completed and initiated at each death in the participating lineages. These debts, or rather the pigs and auxiliary consumables used to pay them, may be the most visible form of distinction between "kinds" of kin.

They would also serve one more purpose before being given to their designated recipients. From the day of his wife's burial until the day of her *buga*, Hemisi had been sequestered in the house of a senior Siwe'oya man, dressed in dark clothing, and prohibited from eating pig or any other food classed as "greasy" (*momona*), ranging from store-bought powdered milk to unicornfish (*Naso* spp.; *itela* in Suau). The house to which he (as with any widow or widower) was confined was said to be "closed" (*guduna*), and in order to close it a pig could be briefly propped against the door while still tied to the pole used to carry it. "Ma'ena salai bili sa gudu," one woman told me at a later funeral where this was done: They are closing the room with a pig. In order to "open" (*so'e*) it again, two *ya'o* trussed up on stout poles were propped against the ladder of the house. Hemisi was led out of the house and onto the poles, where he climbed carefully over the pigs brought by the *tau'anban* and sat down next to the row of pigs for exchange. His action marked the *hamogululu*, or end of deep mourning for a widowed person. Hemisi could, if he chose, ease his dietary restrictions at this point or continue them for as long as he considered himself to be in mourning. The *hamogululu* would have had more significance at a time when strictures placed on the recently widowed were far more severe, which I will discuss shortly.

So the pigs brought to a funeral serve not only to open and close debt relationships but also to open the sequestration of the bereaved and begin the normalization of time and events following a death. At more elaborate coastal funerals a pig can even accompany the dead person on the way to the afterlife. For Kodema's funeral, with which this chapter opened, a *dahu* was created: two coconuts and two arecas felled to make a symbolic raft on which the young man's *yaluwa* would travel to the afterlife (or to Heaven, depending on whom I asked). A pig was slaughtered at the same time as *guligulibe'u*, a complement to the valuable trees sacrificed in the service of creating a new road for the dead.

On the night of the "party" phase of Noenoe's *buga*, I was speaking with a guest from a Buhutu village about the enormous level of activity focused solely on the execution of the funeral proceedings. For over a week, I noted, all garden work, all travel to other villages, all hunting and fishing, and all construction projects had had this evening as their object. He agreed with this assessment and then said, as if to reassure me, "After this the work is finished, and we can forget all about it." It was a casual remark, but one that pointed up the demarcation I perceived at this and subsequent funerals between "funeral time" and "real time." Even after Noenoe had been commemorated and her husband released from his confinement, village life continued to have a quality of suspended animation about it for nearly a month. Noenoe's family eventually moved out of the aid post and back to their own hamlet, but work on a new aid post, which had been interrupted by the death, was completely abandoned. After the intensification of activity to produce the events of Noenoe's funeral, it seemed there had to be a corresponding de-intensification. People's thoughts were still preoccupied with death, and it was during this time that I learned of what would have happened following a death "in olden times" (*huyahuya yai* or *beabeana*).[4] This part of the account will of necessity be rather distanced from its subject matter, as it was not related to me in connection with a specific death. People were comfortable speaking of how funerals used to be performed. As a body of discontinued activities, like a *yaluwa* confined to a gravesite, they presented no threat to those living in the contemporary world.

A notable difference between contemporary and former funeral practices was the distribution of *anban* in the form of shell wealth, now no longer used on the Suau Coast, although certainly used within living memory.[5] The bodies of the deceased themselves were the sites of wealth distribution, when wealth items such as *bagi* (red *Spondylus* shell strings), *ka'e* or *giniuba* (pearl shells), *wanepa* (shell septum ornaments), *gawiwila* (shell armlets), and *diliwa'u* (ceremonial greenstone axe blades) were laid on top of the corpse by lineage members, to be removed by the *tau'anban* just before burial (cf. Macintyre 1989 and Battaglia 1992 for analogous practices on Tubetube and Sabarl respectively). The corpse would then be buried in an upright sitting position on a sleeping mat. Widows and widowers would blacken their entire body with soot and cut their hair short to signify a state of mourning; in addition, a widow would wear a very long, black coconut-leaf skirt and a necklace of black seeds. Prior to the *buga* the widowed spouse (and often other relatives in mourning) would observe *udi*, a fasting regime intended to make the practitioner "hot/potent" (*gigiboli*) in order to attract many pigs to the upcoming funeral feast.

Table 2.1. Ideal schema of the funeral sequence.

Name of Activity	Description and Time Frame
Tantan/Doudou	Weeping over the dead; begins immediately after death and continues as all-night vigil
Toletoletau	Dressing and burial; the day following *tantan/doudou*
Tautauwelaʻi	Deep mourning for one to three days following burial, proscription on garden work
Fafabou (in some locales only)	Divination at end of *tautauwelaʻi* to ask deceased person his or her preferred location of funeral feast and cause of death
Buga	Funeral feast; approximately one week after death, but usually longer
Hamogululu	Widow or widower emerges from seclusion
Toleha, Aiwabosa, Tumioya[6]	Subsequent mortuary activities in former times, now discontinued.

At the *buga* for a married man, his widow would cut her black skirt to knee length, but she would still wear the black necklace and observe the dietary taboos (*aidabu*) of the bereaved. Roughly one year after the *buga*, a second commemorative feast called *toleha* would be held, at which the *tauʻanban* would give the widow a black-and-white skirt to wear. She could at this time resume eating pig, taro, and other proscribed foods, and she was also able to remarry. The *toleha* has by now almost certainly been discontinued, as no one I spoke to could remember having attended one more recently than twenty to thirty years ago.

I do not want to present funeral activities in this region, however, as a domain divided starkly between "what people did then" and "what they do now," despite the fact that most of my interlocutors did so. Working for the dead was precisely what provided the link between an ancestral epoch, from which practices identified as customary were presumed to emanate, and the present dispensation. The differences between how mourning was once conducted and how it is conducted now infused people's consideration of the current forms of mortuary observance with a moral reflection as well as a temporal one. More specifically, the funerals I attended over the course of my two longest and earliest periods of fieldwork differed substantially from one another in their varying adherence to what people identified as *kastom* as opposed to *misinale* ("missionary"; the distinction is theirs) practices. The restrictions on a widow or widower's movements in particular can shift significantly according to the social stature of the deceased spouse, the devotion of the relict spouse, and the strictness of the *wolisau*. My friend Margaret reported that her mother Tobe observed extremely strict mourning constraints following her husband's death in the early 1990s. Tobe did not so much as leave her hamlet in Isuisu until pigs had been killed for her husband's *wolisau*. Two were eventually killed to reopen the following roads: one so that she could go to the garden and the river and generally move about the village, and one so that she could board dinghies and travel to other villages. Margaret speculated that if her mother were in any shape to get on an airplane and travel that way, they would have to kill yet another pig.

In addition to the contemporary variations of regional and personal preference in funerary observances, not all accounts of *kastom* funerals that I was given agreed with one another. For example, the normative versions I was given of what was done with the dead "before" did not account for the ossuaries in limestone caves on the hillside shown to me by Cecily, a daughter of my hosts in Leileiyafa. Indeed, accounts of the region from a century or more ago (Abel 1898; Seligman 1910) point to a longstanding tradition of burial in the ground with a miniature house built over the grave, as is still practiced. Whether the ossuaries represented the practices of hinterland people and the house-graves those of coastal people, or whether both constituted stages of the burial-exhumation-reinterment practices recorded elsewhere in the province (Chowning 1989; Mallett 1998), I can only speculate. Photographic evidence in Beran (1996) and Armstrong's (1921) report suggest the latter was probably the case. In any event, the old cave burials, while acknowledged (and still tended) by people as their ancestors, are nonetheless anomalous in the face of what is presented as "customary" by both indigenous and exogenous accounts. Some people would say to me, "We used to bury our *bubus* [grandparents] in caves, but then the government told us to put them in the ground," while others would insist they had "always" buried them in the ground. Conflicting versions of the treatment of the dead in times past was only one of several histories of the Suau Coast that I found occasionally to be at odds with itself.

Another was the identification of funeral feasts other than the *buga*, which everyone was familiar with because it is still widely observed. Most people could either remember the *toleha* themselves or recount it from the stories of others. But another category of feast, identified variously as *soi* (Williams 1933) or *mata'asi* (Seligman 1910), was harder to place. *Mata'asi* was used by my Suau friends as a blanket term for any large, pig-inclusive feast, which older people told me used to occur frequently for the sole purpose of demonstrating competitive strength in exchanges. This kind of feasting "for its own sake" no longer happens, although it appears only to have been abandoned in the past thirty to forty years (Young 1981). While Williams did not connect *soi* with mortuary practices, Armstrong (1921) did, and Macintyre (1989) does so with a Tubetube feast of the same name.[7] In both cases, it was held infrequently at anywhere between five- to twenty-year intervals, and on a massive scale, commemorating in the case of Tubetube all the significant members of a given matrilineage who have died since their last *soi*. *Soi* was described by my older interlocutors as a formal distribution of pig meat at any large feast (such as a *mata'asi*) rather than a feast in its own right, and this may indeed have been the extent of the *soi* concept in the Suau region.

Event History and the Production of *Kastom*

It is appropriate to pause on this rather uncertain note. The uncertainty stems from the status of a category that has emerged sporadically throughout this chapter and will continue to do so throughout the chapters that follow. I want to pause to make this category explicit before proceeding further, because it appeared to be as much an organizing framework for my Suau interlocutors as it was for me. The knowledge or experience organized by this conceptual framework was, naturally, highly negotiable. Initially I found its invocation profoundly frustrating, because I assumed people were using it to withhold information from me. Over time I came to suspect that they were in fact using it to withhold information from themselves.

Whenever I wanted to know more about a practice or event that people felt unable or unwilling to explain, they invariably said, "It's our custom" (*mate ema kastom*) or something similar. Their use of the Tok Pisin term *kastom* was interesting in that it suggested there was no equivalent concept in Suau, since Milne Bay is the only province of Papua New Guinea where Tok Pisin is not widely spoken. As several writers (e.g. Foster 1992; Jolly 1994; Demian 2006b) have suggested, *kastom* can be framed as an artifact of historical processes throughout the Melanesian region, emerging from the particularities of the colonial encounter at a given site such that "the elaboration and reification of particular notions and/or practices is part of this process inasmuch as these notions and/or practices furnish the colonized with the means for explaining, resisting, or accepting their situation" (Foster 1992: 284). In this model, the emergence of *kastom* as a category of action occurs as a result of the discourse between indigenous and exogenous social systems, with *kastom* positioned opposite institutions introduced by colonialism. Foster's Tangan interlocutors in New Ireland, for instance, classified *kastom* in opposition to *bisnis*, or the encroachment of the market economy as represented by the copra industry, which they were unable to assimilate into the traditional economic sphere of wealth exchanges conducted at mortuary feasts and controlled by big men. Because this new economic activity operated outside the influence of traditional leaders and regardless of the relationships being realized in mortuary exchanges, it provided an antithetical construct (*bisnis*) against which to place *kastom*, which previously had "not existed." That is, with nothing against which to contrast it, *kastom* was not a meaningful category.

Tangans of the 1990s maintained that *kastom* is one of several domains of activity that must be undertaken separately but simultaneously, including *bisnis*, *lotu* (church), and gardening (A. Holding pers. comm. 1997). By contrast, *kastom* in Leileiyafa and Isuisu during the same period could almost be defined as "what is no longer (acknowledged to be) done" or "what has been forgotten." That is, everyone has some idea of the old funeral practices, but nobody follows them anymore.[8] The most common circumstances under which *kastom* was set up as a Tanga-style opposition by my interlocutors were against "missionary ways" (*misinale edi laulau*) of conducting funerals, and against money. At the coastal hamlet of Tadigala I was shown an heirloom valuable, a circular pig's tusk necklace (*kaipesi*) kept by a man there. When some young men who were present asked what he had paid for it, he said in a contemptuous tone, "Salai moho! Ige moni: kastom" (Only pigs! Not money: *kastom*). He also said that soldiers during the war had once tried to buy it from him and that he had set the price at A\$200 in order to dissuade them.

It took me some time to realize that the invocation of *kastom* was not simply avoidance of a difficult explanation but referral to a temporal mode in which a given practice or set of practices emanate from a particular historical location. It is shorthand for a pre-mission, pre-government, circumscribed span of time that is said to have been "forgotten," although its marks have been left on contemporary lived experience (Battaglia 1992: 5). A person may say of former funeral practices, "We forgot everything," and then give a detailed explanation of what they were. The point is not that *kastom* has vanished from memory but that its application or relevance to contemporary life has been diminished.

The context in which *kastom* is used also changes its specific point of reference, although in all cases it maintains a relationship to what was done "before." For activists and politicians in Alotau, it is synonymous with "culture" and refers to readily packageable performances of difference (songs, dances, housebuilding styles) that can be displayed at Independence Day celebrations and other public occasions. For a village court magistrate, it means that a fine imposed will be one of concrete and fixed value (pigs and feasting) rather than the abstract and fluctuating value of money. For the hosts of a foreign anthropologist, it explains and at least partially excuses the behavior of village boys waking her up at night. And for anyone talking about the cause of a death, it denotes sorcery.

My most painful encounter with this use of *kastom* occurred in the aftermath of the death of a very old woman to whom, in a misguided attempt to "save" her as she could not travel to hospital, I had given some of my supply of doxycycline. Two days later I was dispensing the same antibiotic to a young woman with a urinary tract infection. "You really know a lot about medicine," she commented as she watched me count out the tablets.

"No I don't," I replied with some bitterness. "I gave these to Nawabu and she still died."[9]

"But Melissa, this was *kastom*. It was *kastom* and there was nothing you could do," my friend insisted, obviously trying to comfort me. What she meant was that antibiotics, like any other form of biomedicine, were ineffectual against sorcery. Her attempt at consolation only made me feel worse, convinced I had just reinforced the local aversion to going to hospital.

The identification of sorcery with *kastom* in this case indicates sorcery's belonging to the domain of "before" (*huyahuya yai* or *beabeana*), a temporal mode impervious to the influences of mission and government. But sorcery, as an immutable relic in the conversations of my informants, appears to mediate between temporal registers in a way no other expression of *kastom* could. Because of its identification as a practice from "before," it suggests a threatening replication. Sorcery performed now is the same as that performed formerly, because it is taught by father to son, inherited as surely as the father's appearance or temperament. And because of its social repercussions over time, sorcery connotes an incremental aggregation; its consequences may be felt and exacerbated years or even decades after the original insult to a sorcerer. Death by sorcery provides an opportunity for people to interpret the effects of their actions and those of others in terms of the history of their relationships with one another.

The history at issue here is of a type described by Munn (1990) as a process by which people on the Milne Bay island of Gawa "connect given events with other events in and through culturally meaningful practices, so that what one might tentatively call an 'event history' (a specific nexus of events) develops" (1990: 4). In the sequence of sorcery cases described in Munn's account, decisions made by actors in the past were cited as having a direct bearing on events in the present. As she points out, all positive decisions are also negative ones, for example a man deciding to give a Kula valuable to one partner instead of another, and it will be the latter decision *not* to give that may be alluded to later as the reason for illness by sorcery. The illness itself is a visible (physical) manifestation of invisible processes: decisions made, anger felt and concealed, and the magical operations of the sorcerer upon the victim's body. When these processes become visible, a cause is extracted from the past that articulates with present circumstances to create a more or less coherent sequence of events. But because this interpretation of past events is predicated on an understanding of the *potential* for malevolent acts by sorcerers in response to other acts, it draws meaning from possible future as well as past events. Munn sums up her case thus:

> The relations between events are developed in the practices of everyday life through infusing the experience of a given event with pasts (or possible pasts) and futures. Thus the unit of the event history is not simply a "happening" but a happening infused (or becoming infused) with more time and space (more events or potential events) than itself. (1990: 13)

In other words, each node or moment in an event history contains reverberations of past actions and future potentials that affect the interpretation of the present. From death, then, Suau communities move toward a rendering of the causes of death out of historical events. Often these are previous deaths with their source, in turn, lying in an affront of some kind to a sorcerer capable of killing. Such sorcerers are understood to continue killing until they have been compensated for the original insult or are themselves killed. Even the severe death compensations levied during village court hearings are not usually sufficient to deter them from further murderous activities. Death by sorcery could be said to reproduce itself over time, a negative counterpart shadowing the activities of marriage and procreation, which reproduce people in a positively valued relationship to the generation before them.

Sorcery was cited as the cause of death in every case I witnessed or talked about with people throughout the Suau region. In fact, the only ambiguous instance of death I knew of was one in Leileiyafa, where the body had been shipped home from Port Moresby; the stories concerning how the man had died were conflicting and unverifiable. While I am not able to state unequivocally that sorcery is blamed for all deaths in Suau, it is clearly held accountable in most cases and will be prominent in people's minds in connection with an illness or accident. Death is a frequent and expected product of sorcery, which is in turn a product of relations gone bad, those inverted by jealousy, perceived insult, and other sources of anger.

I would like now to present two cases in which sorcery was attributed as the cause of death in the hope of demonstrating this trajectory of negative relationships over the course of years and, consequently, a kind of "event history," such as Munn describes for Gawa. While details of her account, such as Kula partnership, are not applicable to the Suau context, the essence of the idea remains: that the past can be retroactively constituted in terms of negative relationships and their manifestation as sorcery. It could be said that in this environment, deaths do not have causes so much as they have histories.

Two Sorcery Cases: Noenoe's Death Again

Some fifteen or so years before, the same sorcerer held responsible for Noenoe's death killed the wife of Hiuwo, her mother's brother (*bada*), another reputed sorcerer living near Leileiyafa. Hiuwo threatened to take magical revenge for the death of his wife but was apparently unable to do so because the sorcerer deemed responsible was the more powerful of the two of them. In reaction to the threat, however, the other sorcerer was understood to plan the murder of other members of Hiuwo's *ulutubu*—the choice of his sister's daughter is significant because she represents the continuation of Hiuwo's matrilineage, whereas his own children do not.

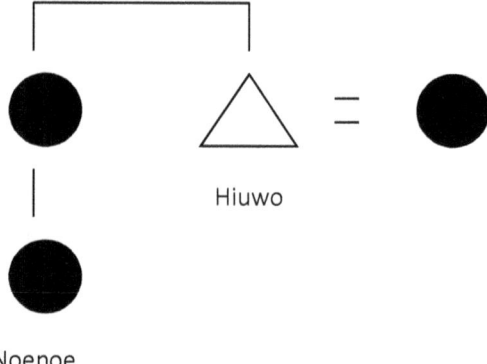

Noenoe

Figure 2.3. Noenoe and Hiuwo. Created by the author

The accused sorcerer was brought to trial at the Leileiyafa village court roughly a month after Noenoe's death. As is usual for sorcery cases, the trial went on for nearly twenty-four hours as he strenuously denied the charge brought against him while the magistrates wore him down. Eventually he confessed, and both he and Hiuwo were ordered to end their feud by contributing 150 kina (about $72 in 1996) and a large pig each toward a reconciliation feast.

Polo's Death

Polo, an unmarried man in his early twenties from Leileiyafa, died after an accident in the mangroves that line Mullins Harbour. He had gone crabbing by himself, and he was discovered by the middle daughter of my hosts lying on his back in the mud, calling for help but unable to move. A party of men from the village carried him back to his hamlet of Ho'owatefana; he was somewhat delirious with pain and shock but said that he had fallen from a log. He told his rescuers not to worry, that he would be fine in the morning. He died that night.

This account, which I present secondhand (I was on Samarai at the time that it happened), suggested to me that he had slipped and broken his neck or sustained a severe concussion; the mangroves are hazardous terrain, an expanse of sucking mud, aerial roots, and fallen trees. I was assured, however, that he had been killed by sorcery due to the fact that when he was being dressed for burial, black marks appeared on his ribs, armpit, neck, and eyebrow: signs of some magic substance having been placed inside him. A sorcerer does not kill in one "blow," I was told, but two. He first "kills" his victim and then resurrects him or her, then at some later date kills again, this time for good. Polo's isolation in the mangroves would have been an ideal moment for the second "blow"—the activities of sorcerers are usually spoken of using idioms of spearing or striking, sometimes elaborated to refer to a magical weapon that can travel and strike by itself.

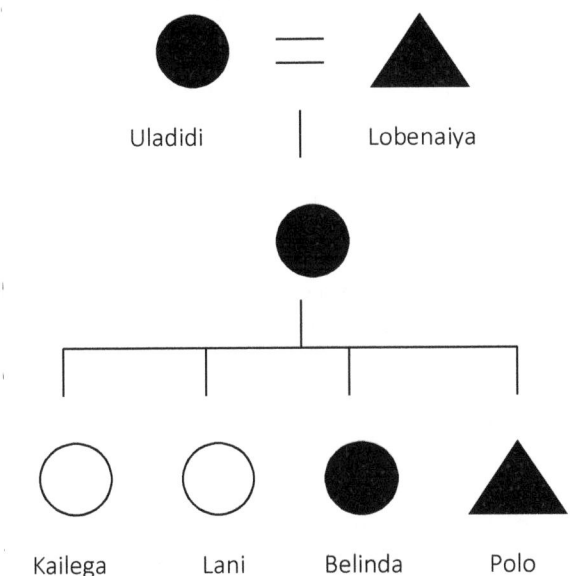

Figure 2.4. Polo's family. Photo by the author.

When the *fafabou* was performed, the stick swung at the name of a sorcerer from Gelemalaiya, a Buhutu village inland from Leileiyafa. The history of this accusation was as follows. Sometime in the 1960s or 1970s, Polo's maternal grandfather Lobenaiya hired the Gelemalaiya sorcerer to kill an enemy of his. As it was considered proper to give a sorcerer a wife in exchange for a commissioned homicide, Lobenaiya promised to give the sorcerer his granddaughter Belinda, Polo's sister. This was an inappropriate pledge since Belinda did not belong to Lobenaiya's lineage but to his wife Uladidi's. If she had hired the sorcerer, she would be entirely within her rights to promise him her grand-daughter, but Lobenaiya was out of line in doing so. Nonetheless, the sorcerer found this acceptable, to the point where he was said to have killed his own wife in anticipation of the new bride. He then dispatched Lobenaiya's enemy, but by that time, Belinda was already married. So, in a fit of vindictiveness, the sorcerer killed both Lobenaiya and Belinda in 1987. Since that time, the family had tried to pacify the sorcerer with gifts of pigs and money, but his killing of Polo was a clear signal that these were not acceptable alternatives to the original agreement. He wanted a wife. When I discussed all this with Elia, he said that his next task after having presided over the *fafabou* was to convince the members of Lobenaiya's lineage to come up with a wife for the sorcerer, since it would have been their responsibility in the first place had Lobenaiya not made his improper pledge. Besides, Elia pointed out, Lobenaiya's lineage had prospered while Uladidi's was dwindling due to the depredations of this sorcerer. The only alternative would be to offer him another of Lobenaiya's grandchildren, but then the members of Lobenaiya's lineage would have to compensate those of Uladidi's with money. Since this could conceivably run to the thousands of kina, it did not seem likely to happen. But the bottom line for Elia was that he would not drag the sorcerer into a court case without al-ready having a designated bride-to-be, as this was the only way to ensure there would be no more killings.

What I wish to emphasize about both of these cases is that in neither of them was the sorcerer held solely responsible for a death. While a *fafabou* divination singles out a specific individual as the "cause" of death, this information is me-diated by the understanding that sorcerers are reactors far more than they are actors. They do not kill arbitrarily but do so in response to some slight or, as in the second case, because they have been hired by someone else. So the history of a death moves "backward" as it were through the person of the sorcerer and into his relationship with the family of his victim, their allies, and their ene-mies. It is they who have elicited from him the response of an act of sorcery, either deliberately or not, and so in many cases they may be held equally liable for a resulting death. Unlike on Gawa, the names of Buhutu and Suau sorcerers (Buhutu ones are held to be more vindictive and powerful) are items of public knowledge, with the result that a *fafabou* can only produce a culprit from a list of "usual suspects" recited during the divination. It therefore is not a foolproof technique—one *fafabou* conducted during my residency in Leileiyafa pro-duced no result at all. Apparently this was because the woman who had died was from a distant coastal village, and so no one from her lineage was available to interrogate her *yaluwa*. It would be attempted again, I was told, if some of her family could be persuaded to travel to Leileiyafa for this purpose. Presum-ably, a closer relative of the dead woman would be more knowledgeable about the possible vendettas held against their family by particular sorcerers and so would say a name to which the divination could respond.

That sorcerers are categorically murderers, or at least potential murderers, is never questioned. They are not, however, shunned or otherwise kept apart from the normal round of social life, because what they are *not* is "antisocial" in the way that, say, rascals[10] are held to be. The relationships they maintain with others may at any point become inflamed with anger or jealousy such that they are inspired to kill, but all that has happened to their sociality is that it has become inverted. Sorcerers have the unique ability to "see" or perceive both positive and negative forms of relationships, or to employ a more Suau-flavored idiom, both good and bad roads connecting them with other people. It is as though every relationship has an ever-present negative potential that sorcerers are able to exploit in physiological terms, and so those who anger sorcerers are often held at least partly to blame for any deaths that ensue. The sorcerer is neither a misfit nor an outcast, but because of the magic knowledge he possesses, he is able to release the latent destruction lying dormant in all relationships.

Funeral Work as the Work of the Future

> To the degree that mortuary feasting becomes the central point of collective social ritual, its entailed expansion of the individual into a generalized social significance becomes the point of origin of society. The dead are truly ancestors, each "renewing" society in his or her turn, because society is all made of them. In this regard the social significance of death is that it is the focal point, and its rites the epito-mizing forms, of the social assimilation of the individual person.
> —Roy Wagner, "Conclusion: The Exchange Context of the Kula," 1989

As mentioned in chapter 1, I wondered frequently during the initial stages of my fieldwork whether the region I was working in could be assigned to the "Massim" rubric, as this appellation was usually reserved for the island region of Milne Bay Province. It was not until the death of Noenoe that I felt unequiv-ocally that what I had witnessed belonged to the complex of funeral practices in the region. That these have a recognizable and more or less consistent format is demonstrated in Damon and Wagner (1989) and summed up in Wagner's concluding chapter of that volume. In his distillation of the preceding accounts from various sites in Milne Bay he outlines some significant characteristics of mortuary practices in the region: a series of feasts that release first the grieving community from restrictions on work and movement and then the significant mourners from the dietary and other taboos they keep, finally culminating in a large-scale distribution of food usually commemorating more than one death. He also notes the uniform appearance of paired categories of "funeral workers" and "funeral consumers," often, though not always, elaborated in terms of affinity and consanguinity.

Of this aspect of funerals in Milne Bay, Wagner writes, "However ad hoc the mourning categorizations, they inevitably present significant kin and social structural oppositions in a ritual transformation, so that the respective ritual and secular involvements of a given relationship stand in a motivating relationship to one another" (1989: 259). Here he identified one of the most salient points in understanding what is being *produced* by funeral workers, assuming that the purpose of work is production. In Leileiyafa, the fact that *tau'anban* are identified by the gifts that they receive in compensation for their efforts is only a partial representation of what happens at a *buga* and, presumably, at *toleha* and subsequent feasts as well. These are all distributive, nonexpansive feasts in which the only disequilibrium that appears is the creation of new debts between *tau'anban* and the lineage for which they are working, but as many debts may be "closed" as "opened." Williams (1933) remarked with some bemusement upon the enormous amount of labor required of participants to bring a pig to a mortuary feast in exchange for which they brought home a different pig of equal size. While people in this region would doubtless agree that funeral work is very heavy (*polohe*, a moral as well as a physical value) indeed, the product of the work is not the pigs and food exchanged but the relationships contained by these gifts that reconstitute and reaffirm the social world inverted by death. That a *tau'anban* arrangement between families can be "spoiled" by intermarriage suggests that the "motivating" power described by Wagner is inherent in the replication of the *same kinds of relationships*, those performed in funerary pig exchanges, over time, in the face of mortality that threatens to dissolve them. Lineages whose members marry their own *tau'anban* disrupt the aesthetic of these exchanges by rendering too similar, or too close, partners in a relationship defined by its dissimilarity or distance. It is as though they are maintaining an interdependent orientation as fugitive as that between the ritual and the quotidian, between form and grief.

What is forgotten when all this work is finished? It may be nothing more and nothing less than grief, or more specifically the pain of encountering an empty space where a person should be. The emotional impact of Polo's death was for me elided with news from home that arrived at the same time, in which I learned that a professor who had meant a great deal to me as an undergraduate had died suddenly a month before. I missed both deaths in that I was not present when they happened, and I struggled with the fact of losing these two very different people: Polo, whom I did not know well but had seen nearly every day for ten months, and my former professor, whom I had not seen for three years but who had had a tremendous influence on my life and career. I could not distinguish between the emptiness left by the one and that left by the other; I was plagued by nightmares (attributed by my friends to Polo's itinerant *yaluwa*) and became ill.[11] After some discussion of these difficulties with my friend and field assistant Kiukiuna, she opined that I was "thinking too much" about the deaths because I had not seen the burial of either person. "If you had been here when Polo died, you would just cry, finish, and then go on," she said, "but since you missed the burial, you think maybe he's still alive." I read a number of things into her observation, aside from the fact that she was probably right. One was that witnessing the vigil and crying immediately following a death has an immediate benefit for the participants: they are enabled to absorb the reality of their loss and carry the burden together, initiating the collective work of forgetting. The other was that what is forgotten is not the person who has died, or at least not their countenance, as Lani asked me several weeks after Polo's death for a photograph I had taken of her brother. It is the relationships with the person that are vital to the business of living, but they are dangerous when still binding one to the dead.

Over time I felt that I grasped a fuller understanding of why Noenoe's family were so reluctant to take her to the hospital. In addition to the great distance and prohibitive cost of hospitalization, there was the fact that the crisis represented by death had *already begun* as her condition worsened. The funeral time that bridged the gap between the originary time of *kastom* and the present day had been activated by sorcery, a destructive—but still morally inflected—manifestation of *kastom*. It was clear to the family that Noenoe was under attack by a sorcerer, which meant that they or some more distant relative had not conducted themselves and their relationships with others properly. An aberrant state of affairs had, in other words, obtained even before her actual death, and of which the death was only one manifestation. This event was construed as a constituent of a larger misfortune, which they must have felt they had very little control over, as it had begun years before Noenoe's illness and could potentially continue to happen if relations between their lineage and the angered sorcerer were not normalized. Seen in this way, death presents a moment of crisis in which people look in the directions of both past and future, as the terrible unknown of mortality is confronted through an imperative to ensure that the appropriate relationships of which Suau society is composed are reproduced for future generations to inhabit.

In the next chapter I consider what happens when these relationships are *not* reproduced—that is, if they are truncated entirely or replaced by different relationships. If an event history is composed of happenings infused with more time and space than themselves, what of events that seem explicitly to create a break with history? These events continue to reverberate on the Suau Coast and still inform a sense of how current life on the coast came to be the way it is now. Death as the moment of social reproduction prompts the work of clearing away relationships that threaten to trouble the living or cause them to be trapped in time; this is critical for an understanding of other world-altering events, such as those described in the next chapter. It is also critical for an understanding of how a people may claim to have lost their *kastom* on purpose, neither because they were deprived of it in some way nor because they were deceived or misled into doing something against their own interests. Both of these models for the loss of "the traditional" deprive those who have discarded practices belonging to that category of any agency, and they also presume a certain conservatism on the part of entire societies where no such presumption is warranted by the evidence.

As I noted in the introduction, these may be difficult propositions for some contemporary readers to stomach, particularly at a moment in anthropology's own reckoning with its colonial history. I do not wish to deny that the events of the late nineteenth century on the Suau Coast, which saw the arrival of LMS missionaries and the introduction of an entirely new horizon for recognizing relationships, changed the shape of life on the coast in a way that seems in hindsight to have been beyond the control of any of the actors involved. But if death itself can be brought under control, in the sense that the rupture of loss is made into the very thing that propels human agency over time, then the transformations ushered in by the mission era represented another mode of letting go of old relationships in order to reconfigure the world.

Notes

1. While I am not entirely certain why Noenoe's daughter put this in her mother's coffin, I am willing to guess she had in mind the prevention of insects from disturbing or consuming the body. The presentation of the body as still whole and beautiful seemed to be of some importance, in accordance with the ideal of creating a lasting "image" of the dead person. Indeed my Leileiyafa friends were appalled when I mentioned that some people in my place were cremated after they died.

2. The name of this period contains the term *tautau*, used for any disembodied image or shape of a person such as a shadow, reflection, or photograph. Battaglia (1992: 8) notes that in Sabarl mortuary practices, the preparation of a body for burial also involves the conversion of the body into an image of itself that will ultimately be detached from the decaying body and exist in uncorrupted form in the afterlife.

3. The same-sex sibling set mirrored by marriage is significant in a society that uses "Iroquois" kinship terminology—in other words, the distinction is between same-sex (*egu doga* in the Daui dialect, *hidagu* in Leileiyafa) and opposite-sex (*lougu* Daui, *egu yofu* Leileiyafa) siblings, rather than distinguishing between what English-speakers might call in absolute terms a "brother" or "sister."

4. These terms are conventionally translated as "the time before" in accordance with a comparable construction in Tok Pisin (*taim bipo*). They nonetheless lack a definite temporal positioning that would equate with a lineal "past-present-future" trajectory

and connote something more like a density or concentration of emplaced time. As such, it is reasonable to say that they refer to something far more open to temporal potential, along the lines of "timey wimey." With thanks to Craig Lind (pers. comm. 2015) for helping me to elucidate this point.

5. Interlocutors who described for me the changes in funeral practices they had observed, or had themselves been told about, were middle-aged in the 1990s.

6. These feasts were recorded by Armstrong (1921: 41) as commemorative feasts (*toleha* and *aiwabosa*) followed by a feast for the disinterment of the deceased's bones (*tumioia*). The latter name, which I have rendered in contemporary Suau as *tumioya*, literally means "garden seeds" or "garden sowing" and may be a metaphoric link between the bones of the dead and the seeds of the garden—this is speculation only, however. Armstrong then placed *hamogululu* (as *laumogululu*; the difference is between a causative and a performative affix) after the completion of these feasts, and cited it as the point at which the skull and other bones of the deceased were reinterred in limestone ossuaries.

7. However, he equates *soi* with *toleha* and identifies them as regional variations of one another, with *soi* belonging to the Suau Coast and *toleha* belonging to the inland and Milne Bay areas. This may in fact have been the case, but Cooper (1970) recorded discussions of both *soi* and *toleha* on the Suau Coast. *Soi* was not identified as a type of funeral feast but as a form for distribution.

8. Certain bereavement observances—cutting of hair or seclusion and warming during deep mourning—are nonnegotiable, and the widow or widower who flouts them runs the risk of suffering several minor but embarrassing afflictions, such as baldness or sores.

9. In accordance with the practice of avoiding utterance of the names of the recently deceased, we were using the name of the dead woman's village of origin instead of her real name. As few people in Leileiyafa belonged to the woman's lineage, her toponym was the most frequent form of address or reference to her even during her life. In fact, before her death she bemoaned the fact that she was dying far from home and among "strangers," which caused those gathered around her to weep, for these were people who had lived with her for decades.

10. "Rascal" (or Tok Pisin *raskol*) is the term used throughout Papua New Guinea to connote criminals and criminality on a spectrum ranging from petty theft to rape and murder. Its oddly jaunty cast in English is lost when one becomes accustomed to hearing its use in an atmosphere of deadly serious anxiety.

11. As it turned out, it was just malaria, and neither Polo's ghost nor grief for my professor that was causing me to feel feverish and weak-limbed.

🏵 3
Times Past, or, the Golden Age

On Eastward in Port Erskine is Suau, well known as South Cape where for years the steady work of a prosperous mission has been carried on. The teachers have been greatly blessed in their work here. There is now a strong church, good helpers, catechumen classes, schools, cannibalism unknown and a quiet people, where formerly they were wild cannibal savages. I need not recount the past but we may rejoice in the present and take hope for the future.

—James Chalmers, in an 1884 report to
the London Missionary Society headquarters

If death entails an apprehension of time that has been brought under the control of the living, what of history itself? Who controls that? One challenge for Suau history is that its written record begins with the colonial moment; ancestral history preceding the arrival of Europeans on the Suau Coast has a different and far more fraught quality (Demian 2013). Some sense of the strangeness of this moment is captured in a translation decision made by either Russell Abel or Benoma Dagoela in their collaborative 1960s Suau translation of the New Testament, which is still in use in churches throughout the region. The final phrase in 1 Corinthians 15:51, rendered in most English Bibles as "we will be changed," has been translated as *ada ao si ori*: "our faces/appearances will change." It did not take the Last Trump for Suau people to experience a sense of complete transformation not only of their social world but also of their very nature as beings in that world. This occurred through missionization itself, but here I want to reiterate a point made in the introduction: Suau people do not regard the missionary era as one in which their "culture" was taken away from them. The story is far more complex than that; historical missionaries have been raised to the status of culture heroes in their own right, and the moment of transformation is one that is celebrated and commemorated.

Nostalgia for a colonial regime expressed by those who were formerly colonized does not sit easily with the political sensibilities of most anthropologists. Its uneasy nature may be a contributing factor to the response of disavowal that produces anthropology's modernity fetish, as I discussed in the introduction. Instead, I encourage the consideration of colonial nostalgia as something far more complex than a kind of false consciousness, which forecloses on the possibility of its role as a form of social analysis. There have been other attempts to take seriously the insistence of decolonized people that the colonial era was a lost golden age. Bissell's (2005) work in Zanzibar offers an example of the way heritage conservation and tourism initiatives led to the proliferation of narratives about Zanzibari history generated both by Zanzibaris themselves and by foreign investors. These "counternostalgias," as he calls them (2005: 228), are among other things a way of laying claim to a historical narrative that may be at odds with those of international development agencies. Such organizations frequently insist, as a component of their own political and historical consciousness, on the preservation of a "lost" or "vanishing" localism when what local people want and miss are international connections. Alongside these counternostalgias we might set the "exonostalgia" proposed by Berliner (2020) to describe "nostalgia for a past not experienced personally. Unlike episodic memory, which connects individuals viscerally to their past, allowing them to return in their minds to events that they have lived, this vicarious nostalgia encompasses a variety of affects and discourses related to loss, but detached from direct experience" (2020: 9). Exonostalgia is a chronic condition among anthropologists, as Berliner observes—but it is also a phenomenon of people who memorialize and celebrate parts of their own history that they have not themselves experienced.

This chapter considers the effects of missionary history on the Suau Coast and its nostalgic (counter-, exo-, or otherwise) evaluation by present generations of Suau people. This evaluation is critical to the project of asking what was both lost and gained through historical relationships that literally appeared on the horizon without warning. If the Protestant missionary narrative is one of introducing not just a new religion but also a new society that was to be engineered from the ground up, the Suau narrative is one of incorporating the stranger through radical acts of hospitality. I hope to show that while these appear to be stories that do not speak to each other in any way—and they certainly are very different, in both the details they emphasize and the agency they attribute—that appearance can be too easily read as the meeting of unintelligible worlds. But both British missionaries and their Suau hosts were engaged in a project of assuming intelligibility, albeit by different means. The nostalgia now expressed by Suau people for a time when foreigners wanted to stay with them, and to introduce entirely new ways of doing things, is an outgrowth of the insistence on intelligibility. If the focus of life on the Suau Coast is overwhelmingly oriented toward the maintenance of particular Christian commitments, then this is as much a commitment to a reading of their own history as having chosen to live in this way, with its ever-present potential to make an equally transformative set of decisions in the future.

A Church Opening at Isudau

Christmas 1999 was to be the date for an auspicious event: the opening of a new church in the coastal village of Isudau. Building a new church takes years as well as a degree of resource gathering that is probably only comparable in scale to the competitive *mata'asi* feasting of the past. So the opening of a new church represents the culmination of years of fundraising and labor and in-debts an entire Local (the smallest organizational unit of the United Church) to its neighbors and kin, from villages just along the coast to far-flung relatives in Port Moresby and other towns. The church opening represents not just the completion of a building but also the completion of a phase of indebtedness and the performance of the efficacy of a Local to an assessing audience the size of which will be seen in the village on no other occasion. It is simultaneously the commencement of the repaying of debts as they are embodied in the struc-ture of a building.

In this way, it replicates and expands the old procedure for bringing a newly built house into use. *Numaso'e*—literally "house opening"—is similarly a revelatory performance in which the relationships that brought the house into being are made manifest in gifts to those who contributed to the house's construction. I was given normative accounts of formal house openings that ran something like this: at the completion of the house, the owner decorates it with flowers and greenery, new clothes, and cash, hung all along the walls. If you have them, you can also display older wealth items such as pearl shells or greenstone axe blades. Then the person designated to open the house, typically a prominent relative, makes a formal speech and opens the door, goes inside, and takes the money and other gifts from the walls. This is followed by mu-sic and feasting, as well as an exchange of pigs between the house owner and house opener. The house owner can then expect to serve as house opener at some future date for the person who opened his house. All accounts of house openings were given to me by senior men, and the building of houses is almost exclusively men's work.

As with houses, so with churches; the opening of the new church at Isudau followed a strikingly similar pattern but on an enlarged scale. The day began early, with attendees from Isuisu (including myself) arriving in the morning via dinghy. Guests milled around, gossiped, and chewed betel nut, while I fee-bly tried to resurrect my inland dialect for old acquaintances from Leileiyafa to the great hilarity of those listening. Long tables had been set up for the serving of tea and food, and it seemed every woman under the age of forty in Isudau and its satellite hamlets had been marshaled to perform these tasks for the entire day. More guests arrived steadily throughout the morning, some bringing contributions to the opening of the church. One party from Isuisu brought a contribution of pigs in a fashion not dissimilar to the presentation

Figure 3.1. Opening the church at Isudau. Photo by the author.

of pigs at a funeral: the group, bedecked in hastily assembled coconut frond skirts, shouted and danced, making as much a spectacle of themselves as they could muster before presenting their pigs to the church opening committee.

The raucous arrival of pigs in the morning stood in sharp contrast to the gravity of the opening itself. A group of men sang the rousing old-fashioned Motu hymns known as *peroveta* ("prophet"), followed by the entire congregation singing relatively newer Suau hymns—although all date to the late nineteenth and early twentieth century. Young people played guitar and shook tambourines to the newest type of charismatic-style songs in English and Tok Pisin, introduced in the recent decades by the evangelical churches that have swept across Papua New Guinea since the 1980s (Lattas 1996; Robbins 2004b; Jorgensen 2005). These were followed by lengthy sermons on the nature of service and the Christmas spirit. But it was evident that more or less the entire congregation was anticipating what followed the formal first use of the church.

When the service had ended, all filed outside, and Isudau Local began to repay its debts. A line of pigs brought by Local members and their kinfolk in other villages had been staked out before the church, with each pig accompanied by a pile of garden food, again identical in its aesthetic to the presentation of pigs at a funeral feast. A "master of ceremonies" read out the contributions of various supporters of the new church—a wealthy resident of Port Moresby who had contributed several hundred kina, the man who had carved the interior beams of the church, and so on—and invited them to come receive their pigs. Some pledged further support when they did so, thereby signaling that the relationships brought to the forefront at the church opening would extend into the future.

The formal pig presentation was followed by the inevitable feasting and a party-like atmosphere. Young men brought out their electric guitars and battery-powered amplifiers. No doubt beer was being drunk somewhere; to my perpetual annoyance, as a woman I would never have been told about it, let alone offered any.[1] My Isuisu companions and I returned home that night, exhausted and filled to bursting with pork, rice, garden food, and homemade buns. And in Isudau, the Local had demonstrated its efficacy in resourcing and constructing a new church, asserting the strength both of its relationships throughout the region, and of the United Church itself in the face of encroachments on its territory being made by the newer churches.

The United Church in Papua New Guinea is the result of a 1968 merger between the Papua Ekalesia, as churches founded by the mostly Congregationalist London Missionary Society (LMS) and some independent Presbyterian missions had come to be called, and the Methodist missions. United Church services now adhere to a generic Nonconformist Protestant doctrine, and in the 1990s they followed the structure of a Methodist "hymn sandwich": a hymn, an introduction with announcements for the week, another hymn, the main body of the service including the sermon, a concluding hymn. These days the services have become far more charismatic in character, doubtless reflecting the preferences of a younger generation of both pastors and their congregations as well as a pragmatic need to see off the threat posed to these congregations by the newer churches. Services are now longer, preceded by numerous popular Christian songs in English, Tok Pisin, and Suau, and the line between the formal sermon given by the pastor and the informal and highly emotive "witnessing" by individual congregation members has become blurred, especially on weeks when the pastor is absent. It could be claimed both that the church has changed in step with changing times in PNG, and also that it has come full circle to the revivalist inclinations of the nineteenth-century missionaries who first brought it there.

The structure of the United Church is composed of regional divisions called Circuits, which are then further partitioned into Locals, roughly corresponding to any village boasting a church and full-time pastor, along with its satellite hamlets. Pastors, who typically serve a tenure of three years in a given Local, are drawn from a pool of both Motu- and Suau-speaking clergy trained at one of the small United Church seminaries that dot the Papuan coast or the larger one at Rabaul in East New Britain Province. The Papuan seminaries are some of the oldest in the country, many of them dating from foundation as an LMS headstation in the late nineteenth century. The most important one for

Suau people was until a decade ago Lawes Bible College in Fife Bay, a coastal village complex located at the western end of their language area. It was named for William George Lawes, one of the first LMS missionaries to establish stations in what was then British New Guinea. But Lawes's namesake institution gave way in 2011 to the James Chalmers Memorial High School, the first all-Suau secondary school in the province, named after the missionary whose career in the region, however brief, is credited with converting the entire coast. Chalmers will reappear in my narrative presently, as he does perennially in Suau conversion narratives, but the church he established must for the moment be foregrounded as it is in everyday life on the Suau Coast.

In the present day, Locals must raise a tithe to their Circuit each year; for example, the tithe required by the Isuisu Local in 1999 was K1,960. This was a considerable sum, and the Local was at risk of falling short by the end of the year. To make up the shortfall, the church deacons organized a *boso-boso*, or basket-to-basket, a strategy borrowed from the women's fellowship, widely acknowledged to be paragons of fundraising. ("As for us men," my host Mamari said to me with a rueful smile, "we just sit around and spend all our money on tobacco.") For a *boso-boso*, each adult member of the church receives a slip of paper on which is written his or her name and the name of someone in another hamlet. By a certain date, the members of each pair prepare a *boso*—a wallet-shaped type of basket made from coconut fronds—containing small gifts and a predetermined sum of money, two kina in this case. On the designated day, the pairs exchange their baskets with each other, with the recipient keeping the gifts and the money going into the tithe fund.

Church fundraising efforts of this kind occupy a significant proportion of economic activities on the Suau Coast, as they do in most Melanesian locales with relatively long histories of integration into both Christianity and the market economy (see e.g. McDougall 2003 for a nearly identical form of fundraising in the Solomon Islands United Church). In Leileiyafa, a *boubou* was also held in 1999, the same year as the Isudau church opening, to fundraise for the construction of their own new church. *Boubou* is an imported fundraising technique from Motu speakers in Central Province, first described in detail by Gregory (1982) in his consideration of Melanesian gift giving as a form of value accumulation followed by sacrifice. Following the time I first stayed there in 1996–97, Leileiyafa had begun construction of a new "permanent" church, as their old one made of bush materials had fallen derelict beyond repair. By 1999 the frame and roof had been completed, and they were awaiting delivery of cement for the floor; the rest of the church has long since been completed. Their primary means of fundraising for this purpose was the competitive *boubou* system, invented in the Motu village of Hanuabada in Port Moresby and probably imported to the Suau region sometime in the early 1990s, migrating eastward up the Papuan coast with the travels of various United Church fellowship groups and individual pastors. During my first period of fieldwork in Leileiyafa it had only recently been introduced by a village court magistrate who had witnessed one while attending a land dispute in a village to the southwest. Leileiyafa's first two *boubou* in 1997 were not very elaborate and raised a few hundred kina each, but the system caught on steadily, growing in both magnitude and performative complexity. Its competitive aspect was particularly emphasized; the 1997 *boubou* featured a period after each presentation when onlookers were encouraged to turn out their pockets and "support" (the English term was used) each gift with a few toea. One girl told me breathlessly as she ran to put her coin in, "If you keep any money for yourself, that's your sin!" This did not happen in the *boubou* I witnessed in 1999, by which point the presentation of donations had become much more formal in style.

At the 1999 event, three kinds of fundraising entity manifested themselves: deacons' groups, usually composed of one or two contiguous hamlets; "families" or representatives of in-married lineages from other villages; and a Local from a coastal village with strong affinal ties to Leileiyafa. The "families" generally appeared as smaller units and did not make quite the theatrical production of their donations as the deacons' groups did. "Families" and deacons' groups overlapped of course and afterward invited individuals who had contributed to more than one category to come and eat with them. At this *boubou*, a pleasure in the aesthetics of spectacle, especially spectacle in the context of gift giving, had given rise to an informal competition for the most impressive presentation of funds raised to accompany the competition for the size of the funds themselves. Several of the deacons' groups dressed up, made banners, and sang and danced their way up to the table to make their donations. Some were presented in a festive manner, with banknotes of various denominations fluttering from the tree branches to which they had been carefully affixed. By contrast, another group tucked its entire donation inside an empty crab shell, a reference to how most of that group's money had been raised: by collecting mud crabs and selling them at the market in Alotau. A flagpole had been constructed next to the old church for the occasion, and the United Church flag was raised by increments after each donation to indicate progress toward the goal. After the main event, the larger hamlets held feasts and invited church and local government council officials, visiting relatives, and eventually anyone who happened by to partake. At this particular event, the pastor noted to me that it was the first time the Leileiyafa *boubou* had reached—and surpassed—one thousand kina.

As Barker (2013) has observed, competitive forms of exchange for political prestige have in many parts of Papua New Guinea been comprehensively replaced with competitive forms of exchange for the purpose of church fundraising, such as the two modes I have described here. In parallel with this process, long-converted groups such as Suau have seen a decrease in the fortunes

Figure 3.2. *Boubou* at Leileiyafa. Photo by the author.

of older forms of political and economic influence in favor of newer forms of leadership, either through the church itself or through the local level government councils for which early mission stations provided the colonial-era blueprint (2013: 153). So while Suau senior men of note (*ba'isa*) no longer engage in competitive *mata'asi* feasting, and perhaps no longer even exist as identifiable personages on the contemporary Suau political landscape, they have been supplanted by economic activities that Suau people may have accepted as analogous to what they already knew how to do, and also by a new set of heroes and heroic powers to which people might aspire in the present day.

Tamate

Eriksen (2006) has written evocatively of "loud and silent stories" told about the arrival of missionaries in Melanesia, how and whether they were welcomed, and most pertinently, who welcomed them and how their messages were actually spread. In many parts of Melanesia with long histories of contact with Europeans and the religion they brought with them, certain arrival narratives have by now achieved a canonical form, or in Eriksen's terms, a loud story. This canonical form as it is told by the converted population may be at odds with how the missionaries themselves recounted their own experiences of introducing the gospel to a new place and people, and indeed with the forms of social organization by means of which these missions succeeded or failed. Conversion stories in Melanesia, as elsewhere, can be "understood as a joint product of locals and outsiders engaged in overlapping projects of imaginative world-making" (Jorgensen 2005: 445). Jorgensen's formulation of conversion as a "joint product" is crucial in moving the anthropology of Christian conversion in Melanesia away from the old "enemies at the gate" model with which anthropologists once characterized missionization (Douglas 2001), because certainly in their own estimation, converted populations portray their own experience of conversion as one originating as much—if not more—from their own initiative as from the efforts of missionaries. Having said this, a joint product is not necessarily a product of relations between parties who consider themselves to be meeting on equal terms. And while the ancestors of my Suau interlocutors may have regarded the relationship they opened with LMS missionaries as one between equals, it is patently the case that the missionaries themselves did not see it this way, and any analysis of what "really" happened on the Suau Coast in the waning years of the nineteenth century must take these incommensurate perspectives on conversion into consideration. Unlike Eriksen, I do not feel that a "total image" (2006: 240) of the conversion narrative is in any way possible to generate; narratives of these events are too far removed from the events themselves, and even if they were not, all narrators of conversion stories are unreliable in that conversion is by its very nature a process of convincing oneself or others that a particular perspective on the world is the sole correct perspective. I do, however, follow Eriksen's important point that only by combining the loud stories with the silent or muted ones can any kind of triangulation of perspectives even be attempted, and this is what I propose to do here.

There is a popular story told throughout the Suau Coast. It has two parts. In the first, the storyteller will describe the landing at Suau Island in 1877 of the Reverend James Chalmers, often referred to by the "Polynesianized" form of his surname, Tamate. The men of the island wanted to kill him. Then a senior woman called Nibeta stood between Tamate and the Suau men, and said "Loni, loni" (peace). (In retellings of this story, Nibeta's exhortation is always, iconically, uttered twice.) The men put down their spears and agreed to listen to what the missionary had to say. Tamate blessed Nibeta for her intercession and said, "Your line will flourish." Which, the teller assures you, it did; Nibeta's descendants are many and prosperous. And then comes the second part of the story, without which the moral and cosmological import of the tale is incomplete. "After that," the teller will invariably say with great relish, "Tamate went to Daru. In Gulf Province. And those Daru people *ate* him! And they ate his *boots*! They thought the boots were part of his *feet*!"[2] The message is clear:

Figure 3.3. James Chalmers, 1841–1901. Photo by John William Lindt, 1885. Public domain.

whereas Suau people successfully recognized in Chalmers the potential for transformation through relationships with almost unfathomably alien others, those benighted savages in the Papuan Gulf failed utterly to see this opportunity and instead destroyed the agent of transformation. This, in a nutshell, is the "loud story" of Suau conversion and, by extension, the genesis of Suau distinctiveness from people in other parts of Papua New Guinea.

This "loud story" also invites some deliberation on how Suau people may have read certain processes of connection and disconnection in what can be called "the world system," or at least *a* world system. The world system in question was the final expansion of Nonconformist Protestant missionary activity into British New Guinea in the late nineteenth century, and my deliberation begins with a possibly inauspicious allusion to cargo. I say "inauspicious" not only because of the extensive literature that has so thoroughly canvassed the limitations of cargo (and its inevitable referent, cult) as an analytic for Melanesian economies, religions, or political movements. The trouble with cargo (to paraphrase Dalton 2004: 188) is that it connects the world, but in "wrong" ways, at least according to the standard narrative. This standard narrative appears to resist all anthropological attempts to correct it, and indeed our very interlocutors appear to confound these attempts at every turn. They do so, I submit, not least because it entraps our attention. Wagner (1981) was undoubtedly on the right track when he suggested that if cargo is anything, it is the earnest attempt of Melanesians to take Euro-American interests seriously and respond in kind: "You want to talk all day about your fabulous technology? Two can play at that game." And it is precisely the dialogic nature of the cargo trap that I wish to pursue here. If cargo is anything, it is communication; and specifically it is an expression of desire to force the recognition of a connection through the use of terms that the other will perceive as part of themselves, and of their own history.

This is to say that connection by means of the material is neither random nor arbitrary. And neither will any old fabulous technology do as a medium for communication, as Strathern (1992) reminds us of the 1930s "first contact" encounter between Australian gold prospectors and the denizens of Mount Hagen in highland Papua New Guinea. When the Leahy brothers offered trade goods in exchange for pigs to feed their entourage, the Hageners were unimpressed and doubtful of the brothers' humanity. But when they offered gold-lip pearl shells, their human status was revealed and the attention of the Hageners was ineluctably seized. This was possible because the Hageners recognized in the pearl shells their own medium for the reproduction of human and clan bodies. The pearl shell "was the one item that already belonged to Hagen; everything else was a mere curio. The marvelous thing about these creatures, then, was what they had within them. Hageners were confronted with an image of themselves" (1992: 250).

Even so, being confronted with an image of oneself is a necessary but not a sufficient condition for the recognition of a connection. The image must be one with a future, otherwise the reflection is a reflection only of mortality and stasis. This is why the pearl shells, indicia of clan perpetuation, so worked on the minds of the Hageners, and why in my own consideration of the history of a translocal connection both this connection and its later attenuation take a local form. In an earlier piece discussing the idea of the local in rural England, Strathern observed that "the bounded local community suggests also that boundaries can be crossed, persons may be detached, belonging may be transient. The notion of localism does not only refer to the value of being local; it refers also to the value of mobility" (Strathern 1984: 186). Whether the locality in question is English or Papua New Guinean, people know themselves as local through processes of awareness of the translocal—and sometimes this awareness is gained at the cost of having lost the infrastructure that made translocalism possible. These are the capacities that, I argue, have been found and lost on the Suau Coast of southeastern Papua New Guinea over the last 140 years. More particularly, what has been lost was a capacity for mobility, which expanded dramatically during the heyday of missionary activity and began a gradual process of contraction following World War II. It was this mobility that enabled Suau to discern an image of themselves among foreign persons whose actions and intentions were initially unintelligible and eventually unrecoverable.

Lost Cargo, Lost Connections

And so to my cargo tale. When I first traveled to the Suau Coast in 1996, the news item still on everyone's lips was the beaching of two containers jettisoned from a freighter that had run into difficulties the previous year. Suau people had retrieved from these containers bottles of cooking oil, clothing, musical instruments and other sundries that they would ordinarily have to buy in Alotau, the capital of Milne Bay Province, at the inflated prices of a country that imports all of its manufactured goods. What struck me initially about the container story was of course the emphasis on free cargo, a discourse to which my receptivity as a novice fieldworker in the Pacific was somewhat overdetermined. With the passage of time I became more aware of the implications that the container story really held, and why my Suau friends were so keen to draw my attention to it at every available opportunity—"You see those cooking oil bottles? They're from the container. The guitar those boys were playing last night? It was from the container," and so on. These artifacts memorialized an anomalous event that served to highlight its quotidian negation. Day after day one could watch container ships literally crisscrossing the Suau horizon, enormous and remote. They were bound from Australia, Indonesia, and Malaysia for other points in Australia, and for Papua New Guinea's major port cities of Port Moresby, Rabaul, and Lae. For these ships, the Suau Coast was just that: a stretch of distant coastline to be passed en route to somewhere else. What was remarkable about the two containers and their contents was not, in other words, that the cargo was free; it was that the cargo stopped moving, and it stopped at Suau.

This chapter is therefore something in the way of a thought experiment. I am interested in exploring the potential of linking up two analytics. One is "old" in that it stems from the long tradition of ethnography in Milne Bay Province; I refer to the high sociological and aesthetic value placed on the contrast between mobility and stasis, on transaction, and on velocity in societies of this region. The other is "new" in that it draws on theories of alienness and alienation that characterize much work in the anthropologies of time, change, and historical consciousness. This literature might also be called an anthropology of attempts to recover a connection from a perceived disconnection. In order to make this move I will have to effect a bit of time traveling between the end of the nineteenth century and the end of the twentieth. The way that people on the Suau Coast assess their current situation is intimately bound in processes that began over 140 years ago, in particular their sense of how these processes connected them to, and then disconnected them from, extended networks in other parts of Papua New Guinea and the world beyond. This process has been well documented elsewhere, particularly for the African period of decolonization. I suspect that one of the reasons it has not been especially well documented in Papua New Guinea is that the period of colonization was itself relatively brief. But another, more pernicious reason is that only recently have anthropologists begun to acknowledge in any systematic way the effects of this "brief" colonial era on the social relationships and cultural formations of people in this part of the world. The problem is especially acute in Milne Bay. The ghost of Malinowski still seems to haunt the ethnography of this region, in which assessments of the long history of contact between Milne Bay peoples and foreigners are somewhat thin on the ground. So my experiment represents the beginning of an attempt to draw out the historical connections that are still felt by Suau people, also in ghostly form. In so doing I want to create a background against which one could discuss later attempts to connect Papua New Guinea to ready-made networks, such as that of British common law, or more recently, those of international entities from the World Bank to Conservation International. If this seems far-fetched, something to keep in mind is that one of the things a network is supposed to do is generate its own context, its own terms of reference. It does so by extending the range of relationships so that scale becomes the way to understand or talk about them: these relationships are "up close," those are "far away," we are local, you are global, or "glocal," or whatever. It is arguable that the "old" network I will describe, that of London Missionary Society headstations, did not do what new networks do—new networks move us out of relation to place, so that it does not matter where we are; we are still connected. By contrast, the infrastructure put in place by the missionaries appears on the face of it to be entirely tied to place and locality. However, what the LMS attempted to do in then British New Guinea was reproduce *exactly* the set of relationships they had previously produced in Africa, China, and India. They were exporting a context. That context was not just an evangelical Congregationalist-Presbyterian cosmology but all its material trappings and imperial connections.

So I would like briefly to return to my inauspicious cargo reference, which will take us into those aspects of their colonial history that still exercise the Suau imagination. For the record, the Suau Coast did actually produce a small and by all accounts short-lived cargo cult in the 1960s. Its prophet (or, according to the patrol reports, ringleader) was a man called Gaileko in the coastal village of Se'ase'a, and he set up a woman named Daphne as "queen" and himself as her "governor." He said that the missionary Charles Abel would come back from the dead, and instructed people to build a wharf for the ship full of cargo that Abel would send them. The queen and her governor were, in the meantime, entitled to suitably royal treatment. People had started piling up stones for the wharf when Australian patrol officers and councillors from nearby villages came to break up the movement. Queen Daphne went to join her husband, who was working in Port Moresby, saying she would send the cargo from there; she spent the rest of her life in "exile" there. Gaileko died in the village, but his relations were rumored still to believe in his predictions. In provincial reports for years afterward, patrol officers were cautioned to alert their superiors to any kind of "regimental" behavior among the "natives," including suspiciously high levels of productivity on the copra plantations.

I note two things about Gaileko's movement. One was that his followers intended to build a wharf rather than an airstrip or radio tower—not especially unusual in the cargo repertoire, but it bears observation. The other is that the returning hero was not the ancestors or even Jesus but Charles Abel. I will return to Abel presently; for now, I raise the question: What if so-called cargo cults were not about material goods but about *mobility*? Anthropologists in Melanesia have already documented how European settlers and explorers expected the locals to be impressed by their technologies; the canonical image of this expectation for my part is the Leahy brothers dragging a phonograph into the Highlands on one of their gold-prospecting expeditions in the 1930s. The issue also emerges perennially in the work of anthropology undergraduates, who seem primed to imagine a first contact or other colonial encounter in which the key feature is not the people but the technologies. My task is then to bring them around to the idea that it was not the airplanes or ships that impressed Papua New Guineans. It was what those airplanes and ships made possible, and the long-distance connections they implied. If some cargo cults predicted that it would be the ancestors who would return on the ships and airplanes, surely this was an idea grounded in analogy. Europeans appeared without any apparent connection to anyone and moved across the landscape (or seascape, or airscape) with impunity (Lattas 2000; Schieffelin and Crittenden 1991). They paid no respect to the boundaries of people's lands and seemed fearless of attack. The question of where these people came from would have been intimately linked to the question of who their relations were, or whether they had relations at all, given that these new visitors could behave in such a cavalier fashion. Since a person without relations is an ontological absurdity in Melanesia, either Europeans were not persons at all or their relations had to be impossibly far away—in the otherworlds of spirits or ancestors. In this sense Europeans too were time travelers, but again, not because of the artifacts they brought with them. Spirits and ancestors frequently do not inhabit the same temporal domain as living human beings; some are extensions of human efficacy into the past or future, and some are intrusions of nonhuman agency or intentionality into the human experience. To imagine that the *unheimlich* newcomers from elsewhere might be transacted with, then, was to imagine the opening up of an almost limitless range for one's own, homely, human agency.

This is a powerful idea for those who now imagine themselves to be dwelling on the margins, with starkly diminished opportunities for connection. As Knauft (2019) has observed, "In remote and marginalized areas, conditions of being reactively modern are thrown into relief and dramatized by relative self-containment and isolation. This does not imply being beyond the reach of global forces. Indeed, lifestyles may be all the more transformed as their continued local emplacement makes them more invisible to or illegible from an outside perspective" (2019: 98). Although, as I noted in the introduction, I do not share Knauft's commitment to the category of modernity as a way of describing what Papua New Guineans aspire to or what they feel they have lost out on, his observation that marginalized peoples may have a better grasp than most on the illusory nature of modernity is nonetheless important. He also brings in the old worries about cargo cultism to inquire whether Papua New Guineans always had a critique of modernity ready to hand. Similarly, but without resorting to modernity as the sign of transformation, Cox (2018: 66) notes the parallels between cargo cult discourses of being left behind by a world in which others prosper and more recent efforts by Papua New Guineans to prosper through participation in financial pyramid schemes. In these two accounts, the idea of cargo is only partly a narrative of having been marginalized. It is also a critique of what "the margins" even are: not a place or even necessarily a condition of impoverishment but one of having been denied a particular flourishing of connection to others.

I hope this meditation on cargo will form a context of sorts for the discussion to follow. Having just said that cargo cults are about movement and connections rather than material things or wealth, I must necessarily describe the material conditions on the Suau Coast between 1877 and my last visit there in 2015, since Suau people themselves are extremely fond of drawing this contrast. The change in their fortunes is directly related to their loss of certain connections, a change that the dropping of the containers brought acutely back to the forefront of their minds in the mid-1990s. But the description itself requires a context, one in which the intersubjective nature of the missionary as well as other "first contact" encounters might be imagined to be at work, still, in the contemporary Suau lived experience.

Hospitality and Abduction

In August 1849, well before the evangelization of the Suau Coast began in earnest, the British survey ship HMS *Rattlesnake* landed at Bonalua Island off the Suau mainland.[3] The account of their congenial visit to a village on Bonalua by John MacGillivray, the ship's botanist and chronicler of its journeys, is worth quoting at length:

> Some women on the beach retired as we were about to land, but a number of boys and a few men received us, and after a preliminary halt to see that our guns were put to rights after the ducking, we all started together by a narrow path winding up a rugged wall of basaltic rock, fifty feet in height. From the summit a steep declivity of a couple of hundred yards brought us to the village of Tassai, shaded by coconut-trees, and beautifully situated on a level space close to the beach on the windward side of the island, here not more than a quarter of a mile in width. No canoes were seen here, and a heavy surf broke on the outer margin of a fringing reef.
>
> On the outskirts of the village we met the women and remainder of the people, and were received without any signs of apprehension. One of our friends immediately got hold of a drum—a hollow cylinder of palm-wood two feet and a half in length, and four inches in diameter, one end covered over with the skin of a large lizard—and commenced beating upon it very vigorously with the palm of the hand, singing and dancing at the same time, as if in honour of our arrival.
>
> Each of us joined in the merriment as he came up, and in a short time the whole of Tassai was in an uproar. Among the natives everyone seemed pleased, bustling about, watching our motions, examining our dress, and laughing and shouting immoderately as each new

object was presented to his view. Meanwhile I wandered about the village, accompanied by some women and children, picking up at the same time materials for my vocabulary. One old dame brought me a coconut shell full of water which I returned after drinking some, but she pressed me in a very motherly way to put it into my bag, having doubtless imagined from our inquiries after water, that even a little constituted a valuable present. (MacGillivray 1852)

As it would be with the anthropologists to follow in his wake over a century later, the linguistic joke was on MacGillivray: the village was not called "Tassai." *Ta sae* in Suau is an exhortation meaning "Let's go up!" In other words, the Bonalua people were not naming their home but inviting the crew of the *Rattlesnake* up to the village a little way from Bonalua's summit. The *Rattlesnake* would not have been the first European ship to visit the Suau Coast, but even by the well-traveled standards of the nineteenth century it would have been an uncommon phenomenon. The hospitality of the Bonalua islanders was a radical, and radically courageous (note MacGillivray's passing reference to the crew's armaments), act of recognition of the foreigner as a human being.

Contrast MacGillivray's account of the landing at Bonalua with the following account of changes in the Suau ethos of dealing with foreigners made to me by a local government councillor in 1999: "Before, when a stranger came by the house, we would kill him and eat him. Now when a stranger comes by, we invite him inside and feed him" (Demian 2006b: 511). The statement is a potent one, despite—or because of—the fact that it is not historically verifiable. This is exonostalgia at its most compelling, with a soupçon of horror thrown in to demonstrate exactly what the missionary era changed for the better. And although it may seem like a digression, a brief acknowledgment of the canonical Suau assertion that once they were cannibals is worth noting as well. Like the presumed aggression toward strangers, there is no evidence that this was the case from any source not invested in a particular narrative; as Arens (1979) noted long ago in his comprehensive debunking of the majority of claims to cannibalism in the modern historical record, "The list of New Guinea cannibals and the recorders of their unseen deeds is almost endless" (1979: 98). The underlying snarkiness of this statement is, to my mind at least, forgivable. Nearly every missionary reporting back from New Guinea in the nineteenth century averred almost as a matter of protocol that the population to which they had been sent were cannibals, in spite of the fact that not one was able to produce eyewitness evidence of the practice. Human skulls were, for the record, found and photographed in Suau houses (see, e.g., plate 28 in Beran 1996: 206). These were in all likelihood ancestral skulls (*kulukulu*) disinterred after burial and given pride of place in the house to guard over their descendants. No archaeologist has, as yet, investigated nineteenth-century

Suau burials for cut marks or other evidence of consumption. But my own agnosticism on the subject of historical Suau cannibalism is irrelevant to the fact that every single Suau person I have ever spoken to is entirely convinced of it. A cannibal past is now indelibly part of their own story of social and spiritual transformation, and their transformation from an unwelcoming to a hospitable people. They are of course different versions of the same story.

The move to extend hospitality is no less than the decision to confer a commensurate humanity on the foreigner, while at the same time recognizing and maintaining their foreignness. "What is a foreigner? . . . It is not only the man or woman who keeps abroad, on the outside of society, the family, the city. It is not the other, the completely other who is relegated to an absolute outside, savage, barbaric, precultural, and prejuridical, outside and prior to the family, the community, the city, the nation, or the State. The relationship to the foreigner is regulated by law, by the becoming-law of justice" (Derrida 2000: 73). In Derrida's formulation, the category of foreigner to whom hospitality is extended is recognizable as a person within the remit of action that he calls lawful but that I might reframe, in the Papua New Guinean context, as relational: to act in a just manner is to recognize a relation with others (Robbins 2009). The foreigner cannot be so foreign as to be regarded as utterly barbaric; this category of person would not merit a hospitable response, and indeed might not even be recognizable as a person. Accounts such as MacGillivray's indicate that at least some Suau received European foreigners in the nineteenth century as persons, such as the senior woman on Bonalua who gave MacGillivray a coconut shell of water. And the boundary-crossing experience of being given hospitality has never lost its power, to the point that it is still occasionally misconstrued for some other kind of relationship. Or as one Papua New Guinean colleague once remarked to me at a conference where we had heard yet another anthropological account of being "adopted" by the host community, "It's very easy to mistake hospitality for adoption."

It is easy for European foreigners to make this mistake because our narrative tropes of adoption by savage-yet-benign Pacific Islanders date at least to Herman Melville's breathless account in *Typee* of being stranded on Nuku Hiva in the Marquesas Islands (Melville 1847). And it is easy for foreigners of all kinds because of a persistent human need to close the gap between experiences that are underscored by acts of hospitality: "It is as though the laws (plural) of hospitality, in marking limits, powers, rights, and duties, consisted in challenging and transgressing *the* law of hospitality, the one that would command that the 'new arrival' be offered an unconditional welcome" (Derrida 2000: 77). The reason a continental philosopher keeps intruding on my discussion of relationships between Suau people and their nineteenth-century visitors is precisely to emphasize the impossibility, to use a term of which Derrida is fond, of reconciling what the Europeans may have thought they were doing and what Suau people may have thought the Europeans were doing. Another European mode of thought will intrude shortly, again, to illustrate how this entire chapter is an exercise in precarious experimentation with an asymmetrical historical record. Suau oral history on the period is perishingly scant and thoroughly articulated with the European written record. European naturalists and missionaries dutifully recorded their own encounters on the Suau Coast, and they recorded them with very specific audiences in mind: also European of course, of a comparable social class, and requiring persuasion, in the case of the missionaries, that the people encountered in British New Guinea were barely people at all but barbarians in desperate need of redemption from their own degraded condition.

Herein lies the central irony of the relationship between Suau people and the missionaries they hosted on their land. While Suau may have been able to instantiate a relation of hospitality with Europeans, this relation was not recognized reciprocally. Nineteenth-century missionaries, especially those of an evangelical Protestant background, did not see themselves as guests but as radical disruptors of the local milieu. And they were unable to recognize Suau or other Papua New Guineans as persons with whom a hospitable relationship had been established; these host communities were, in Derrida's terms, too "completely other" for Europeans convinced of their own transcendent superiority to countenance as either moral or intellectual peers. In a book written for British children who had donated toward the upkeep of ships serving Suau and other Papuan coastal missions, Charles Abel informed them,

> It would be misleading to estimate a Papuan's sorrow by the noise he makes in advertising it. All his emotions are shallow. His heart is limited in feeling, as his mind is restricted in thought. He can neither hate his enemy, nor love his friend, as civilized people can. He may torture and eat the one, and howl and lacerate his face with sharp stone till his blood mingles with his tears, for the loss of the other, but it is not deep feeling which prompts either action; it is custom that demands it. (C. W. Abel 1902: 41)

Abel's words are frankly disturbing to a contemporary reader, and it would be easy to dismiss them as standard missionary rhetoric of the era. Indeed, he manages to invoke the tropes of cannibalism, absence of genuine sentiment, and incapacity for independent thought all in one paragraph—no mean feat! But Abel was a complex figure, a standout maverick in a vocation saturated with maverick behavior. In the above passage he wrote with a Victorian British audience in mind, and he would have known how well that audience was primed to receive all the tropes of alien savagery, especially if it meant they would continue donating to the mission effort. What Abel actually thought about his Suau and other Milne Bay hosts is ultimately unknowable. It is also an unavoidable fact that Abel established the most successful and unusual mission in the entirety of the colonial territories that would one day become Papua New Guinea. Whatever relationship he thought he had with the people of the south coast of Milne Bay, it was clear that they wanted to receive him as a guest, and more than that, they wanted him to receive their children as guests. The uneasy question of adoption arises again, this time in reverse. Or it might, again, be some other form of boundary crossing.

Abduction as an analytic has been imported several times into the anthropological theoretical inventory.[4] First used by Gell (1998) to account for the agency exerted by a work of art upon the agency of its viewer, and later by Battaglia (2005) to describe the privileging of "hospitable exchange over us-them boundary maintenance" (2005: 172) of a North American UFO religion, it has done similar work for both these and other authors. By work I mean the notion that in certain kinds of encounters between incommensurate subjects—person and thing, human and alien—the subjectivity of one of the two positions is perceived to occupy both positions at once. It is the theoretical version of literal abduction, when the subjectivity of a person is overridden by another who removes them, bodily, from one place to another, in partial or total disregard of the abductee's agency or intentions. But the theoretical versions of Gell and Battaglia indicate another important point about agency: there may or may not be any ascription of intentionality or agency at all to the abductee by the abductor, and a component of abduction itself is that the abductee is captured entirely by the agency of the abductor. Arguably, this is most likely to happen under conditions of maximally perceived difference between the two subject positions. In this respect, the theoretical and literal registers of the term begin to merge.

Further to this point, and again fundamental to the discussions of both Battaglia and Gell, is the understanding that in order for the divide between these incommensurate subjects to be obviated, some latent capacity—I might call it, in the interests of provocation, creativity—in one of the subject-positions is drawn out by the other. Whether the genius of an artwork or of an alien civilization is at issue, the end result is the same. In the moment of abduction, incommensurate differences (Gewertz and Errington 1991) become commensurate, and exchange between subjects so differentiated becomes not only imaginable but also inevitable. This is, I would argue, precisely how Suau cast their own history of interaction with missionaries and other aliens. My argument is perhaps aided by the fact that at least some of these missionaries also conceived their activities on the Suau Coast to be abductive in nature, in some cases figuratively and in others quite literally.

In 1877 the third headstation of the London Missionary Society mission to New Guinea was established by James Chalmers at Suau Island. Chalmers was easily the LMS's most energetic representative in British New Guinea, and a larger-than-life figure by almost any standard. Described as the "Livingstone of New Guinea" by his contemporaries, he even managed to die an appropriate martyr's death by being killed and eaten (there is substantial evidence in this case) on Goaribari Island in the Papuan Gulf in 1901. He is commemorated by his own holiday in the United Church calendar, when stories of his exploits are told and sometimes reenacted. Chalmers is regarded in no uncertain terms as a hero by Suau, not least because the story of his death allows them to compare themselves favorably to other Papua New Guineans who initially "failed" to receive the message of Christianity, whereas of course Suau comprehended immediately what was being offered to them. However large he may loom in the Suau historical record, Chalmers in fact only stayed at Suau Island for two years, replaced first by Frederick Walker, who moved the headstation to Samarai Island at the eastern extremity of the Suau Coast. Walker was in turn replaced by Abel, who moved the station to Kwato Island adjacent to Samarai. By 1920 Abel had severed his ties with the LMS and formed the Kwato Extension Association, a standalone mission incorporated in Britain but funded primarily by the New Guinea Evangelization Society in New York. He continued to run Kwato personally until his death from a car accident in England in 1930, after which control of the mission passed to his sons.

It would not be an exaggeration to say that Abel's enterprise at Kwato reshaped the history of Milne Bay as a province, in light of which it is actually surprising it does not loom even larger in the Suau cultural imaginary than it does. In the estimation of one historian of Kwato,

> From the 1920s, Abel's mission was indeed without an equal. Independent, showing its partly secularized Calvinist faith through its fruits in business enterprise; mingling religious exclusiveness with a sporting camaraderie; British in atmosphere yet fuelled by a syndicate of American Fundamentalists with international connexions; there was nothing like Kwato among the missions of the South Pacific. In particular, Kwato was distinguished from other missions in its concentration upon its converts at a headstation and their relative isolation from their own countrymen. (Wetherell 1996: 156)

Wetherell's final observation is telling, and suggestive of why Abel's influence is not memorialized in the same way that Chalmers's is. Abel was to all intents and purposes engaged in nothing less than an experiment in social engineering, according both to himself and the writings of later generations of Abels: "He planned that Kwato should produce a new Papuan society, Christian and manually educated, in which young converts could take their place as independent and useful members" (R. Abel 1934: 97). The prevailing idea in the early part of the twentieth century was that the suppression of local warfare by the colonial administration had left people with nothing interesting to occupy them, leaving them in a state of malaise and dullness. Abel and his associates feared that recent converts sent out into this presumed social and cultural vacuum would either backslide or attach themselves to the kinds of Europeans Abel did not approve of and who did not approve of him. The solution was to keep Kwato converts at Kwato in order to govern every aspect of their education, employment, and personal lives. A complete break with the past was achieved, but only for those raised at Kwato, in whose converts and their descendants a "self-sufficient élitism" (Young 1983a: 5) was fostered.

Kwato became imagined as a "fence" or "garden," with Abel and his converts employing the Suau term *gana* that neatly signifies both concepts: Suau gardens are enclosed with high fences, and inside these fences, a particular mode of cultivation takes place. Outside of the Kwato "fence," the most consistent contact that Suau people had with foreigners during the early missionization period was with the Samoan and Rarotongan teachers who lived among the local people while being supervised by British missionaries at the headstations. Suau responses to these Polynesian teachers ranged from welcoming them with open arms, or at least open curiosity, to killing them outright. "We poisoned their food!" one old man told me with a decidedly mischievous twinkle. Hospitality was not, in other words, extended universally to all foreigners, and nostalgic reflection on these relationships is not universally fond; it is nonetheless potent even in its recollection of past antagonisms. For their part, the Polynesian teachers had some trouble adjusting to their new surroundings, not least because of the toll taken on them by malaria but also because they were accustomed to deferential treatment in their villages of origin (Latukefu 1978), and because most if not all of them regarded the Melanesians as racially inferior to themselves (Prendergast 1968). Suau primarily recall the Polynesians for the ferocity of their religious zeal and of the emphasis they laid on making a complete break with the practices of the past: it was the Polynesians, I was informed, who burned drums, tore down men's ritual houses, and forbade dancing. They also introduced new species of taro and breadfruit and techniques for weaving pandanus mats, coconut-frond baskets, and black palm house walls. Now their names are memorialized in the lists of former pastors on the walls of Suau churches, and in the persons of Suau themselves who have adopted (or abducted) the names into their own lineages.

The experience of British missionaries was even more problematic, at least at the beginning. It is worth reconsidering, at this point, the two stories of "first contact" between Chalmers and Suau. The first is the "loud story" I have related above, an amalgamation of several accounts given to me by Suau interlocutors, drawn from their own oral history of the moment of contact. The second is drawn from Chalmers's own informal memoir of his early mission activities written for the benefit of his second wife.

To refresh the reader's memory of the Suau version of events: Chalmers lands at Suau Island and is immediately surrounded by frightened, aggressive men with spears. Into this tense scene steps Nibeta, a woman described by at least one of my interlocutors as a "chief." Although chieftainship in the sense of inherited political status does not exist on the Suau Coast, she was presumably at the very least a *tanuwaga* or steward of her lineage and in any event a senior woman of note. Nibeta interposes herself between the men and Chalmers and says, "Peace, peace." The men relent and lower their spears. Impressed by and grateful for her intervention, Chalmers promptly blesses Nibeta and tells her that her descendants will be abundant, which they are to this very day.

Chalmers's own account of his arrival at Suau is more detailed but far less thrilling. Rather than a tale of confrontation, intercession, and benediction, he records in his memoir a far more pedestrian, but no less iconic, narrative of the triumph of materiality over uncanniness:

> We found a fine bay between South Cape and Suau. A canoe with one man was fishing and not being able to get away from us we pulled towards him & when some distance off we called, holding up a piece of red cloth & red beads. He looked in great terror & it took us sometime to get him alongside, but when he came he was comforted with small presents. He was an evil looking man & wore on his arm a man's jaw bone. We left him & he paddled as for dear life to the shore. Getting on board we stood over the reef & into the land & came to an anchor in the bay under the lee of Suau Island. It was still early in the afternoon & we were soon surrounded by a number of canoes. The noise was terrible. My wife sat on deck knitting & one old fellow wearing a necklace of human bones took to her & became her friend. When the sun had set as they were all to leave, we allowing no canoe alongside the vessel after sundown, he gave her to understand by signs that he was going to sleep and in the morning he would return with food. (Chalmers n.d.)

Placed alongside each other, each version of the contact story says almost too much about the perspective of its tellers. Suau, keen to distinguish themselves from those benighted savages in the Papuan Gulf who later ate Chalmers, privilege a moment of metanoia (Burridge 1978) in which the prescribed response to alien invasion is overcome in favor of hospitality and communication with the alien, and the rewards are commensurate with the leap of faith taken. The status of the person who makes this leap may also be significant. Nibeta's is the intervening agency, carrying with it both the capacity to perpetuate her lineage in this matrilineal society and also the authority as *tanuwaga* to persuade her kinsmen to act otherwise than they might be inclined.

Significantly, her intervention also represents an act of individual initiative to complement that of the missionary. As Burridge notes, "Because missionaries are themselves exemplars *par excellence* of individuality (the capacity to move from the position of conformist to that of critic), it is this individuality together with its discrepant moralities that they actually communicate" (1978: 17). A missionary is a prodigy of autonomous individualism, certainly in his own society and almost certainly in societies such as that of Suau Island in 1877.[5] And Nibeta, alone among her terrified kinsmen, matched Tamate's uncanny autonomy with an audacious critical move of her own: "Peace, peace!" If Tamate stepping ashore at Suau was a communication act, Nibeta clearly got the message—with the implicit concomitant that those benighted savages in the Papuan Gulf clearly did not. As soon as Nibeta steps between Tamate and the men who want to kill him, she converts monsters into humans, opens and crosses the gap of hospitality, and instantiates the distinction that Suau have drawn between themselves and other Papua New Guineans ever since.

In Chalmers's account, by contrast, the encounter at Suau Island is one in which the uncanniness of himself and his first wife, Jane, is not resolved by the end of the day but is carried over into future interactions with Suau. Chalmers reports with loving detail every moment of amazement caused by his party to people along the Suau Coast: the size of the mission schooner, the pallor and plumpness of a Rarotongan teacher's baby, the sound of the hymns sung on Sundays, the abundance of hoop iron and axes, and finally the strangeness of Chalmers's own person. "It was at Navabo a few years ago," he writes of an eastern Suau village, "on pulling off my boot they all ran thinking I was unskinning myself. One poor old body who was feeling me over, screamed and ran for dear life" (Chalmers 1884: 42). If the Suau narrative of Chalmers's arrival highlights the audacity with which they transformed him from an uncanny presence to a familiar one, Chalmers is keen instead to maintain his uncanniness throughout his sojourn in Suau and other parts of British New Guinea. The connection established by Nibeta in her moment of metanoia is absent entirely from his account.

It did not escape the notice of Chalmers or later missionaries that Suau people appeared unusually eager to adopt the new regime. But according to his writing, he found most noteworthy the process by which trust is won through the (presumably) universal medium of trade goods. Practically all of his accounts of interaction between his party and the people he meets on his travels begin with the offer of trade goods, or the demand for them, or the admonition that they will not be given under duress of any kind. Chalmers habitually went ashore unarmed, a practice neither he nor his later hagiographers failed to emphasize. What he did always carry with him were trade goods, perhaps under the assumption that alongside whatever convictions of the spirit he offered, these would remove any hostility on the part of the Papuans by overwhelming them with desire. Of course there is no reason that Chalmers's version and the Suau version of their establishing contact with one another cannot both be a more or less accurate account of what happened in 1877. But my concern lies not so much with "what happened" at the encounter and more with what each party made of it afterward. Chalmers later praised Suau for their cooperation and the good care they took of his wife while he was traveling. He also clearly attributes the success of the first station at Suau to his and his wife's work, and that of the Rarotongan teachers, but not particularly to the hospitable intentions of Suau people themselves. Suau, of course, point to the events of 1877 as evidence of their own commitment as Christians and of the transformation they see themselves as having undergone in the period following Tamate's arrival. To put it crudely, if Chalmers thought he had demonstrated his intentions by appearing with trade goods rather than weapons in hand, contemporary Suau understand him to have demonstrated his intentions by appearing at all, and appearing to them *first*. Why else would he have approached them if he did not want to recognize a relationship with them? Their success, in their own estimation, lay in recognizing it back.

By the turn of the century there were LMS headstations at both ends of the Suau Coast: Samarai in the east, and Isuleilei/Fife Bay in the west. They supervised, and for all intents and purposes governed, the coast between them; this district was at the time considered to be the only real success story of the LMS project in British New Guinea. Schools and church services were attended, stations were clean and well maintained, and morale among both British missionaries and Polynesian teachers was generally high. During this time the coast was regularly plied by at least ten mission ships and three motor launches, carrying mail and supplies between mission stations. Copra and rubber planters followed in the wake of the missionaries, and indeed some of them were also missionaries: it was in part Charles Abel's determination to make his headstation self-sufficient through plantation income that precipitated his eventual break with the LMS. Gold prospectors in turn followed the planters, traveling up the coast on their way to the gold fields of Woodlark and Sudest Islands. Fife Bay eventually became home to a seminary for "native" pastors.

Meanwhile, at Kwato, Abel had successfully made his station a lodestar for Suau and neighboring peoples with any sort of translocal aspirations. He had instituted the eastern Suau dialect as the lingua franca of the station and had the gospels translated into this dialect.[6] He also insisted, far more than Chalmers or Walker had, on a fundamental division between the "new Papuans" of Kwato and their unconverted kin in the villages. Suau at Kwato distinguished between those "inside the fence/garden" (*gana'alo*) and those "outside the fence/garden" (*ganamuli*), terms that respectively denoted complete or incomplete adoption of the Kwato ethos (Wetherell 1996: 35). Significantly too, Abel preferred his converts to be as young as possible. Suau children were brought to Kwato, bathed, shorn, and clothed in a station uniform. All converts lived on the station and were not to return to their natal villages without permission, although parents were allowed to visit their children at Kwato. Both boys and girls were taught basic literacy, geography, and numeracy; boys were also taught carpentry and boatbuilding, and girls were taught sewing, baking, and other suitably Victorian domestic skills. There was a choir, and regular cricket and rugby matches were held. The descendants of these children, "the first generation" (*iti baguna*, literally "those leaders/firstcomers"), still constitute the Suau elite in Port Moresby and abroad. For his part, Abel considered his greatest success to lie in the complete transformation of Suau children into as-if British children (C. W. Abel 1902), with the requirement that any real influence by the children's parents and other kin be removed from the picture entirely. He remarked frequently in his reports on the eagerness with which Suau parents sent their children to Kwato: "We find everywhere, the parents are willing to let their children come, the hardest work we have had . . . has been to refuse those who have applied, for want of space and funds" (C. W. Abel 1898: 3). Both Abel and his wife Beatrice, a redoubtable presence in her own right, expressed surprise at the willingness of Suau families to "give up" their children to mission education. While I speculate only, it is possible and even probable that most of these families did not see themselves as "giving up" their children at all but rather adopting them out to the missionaries in order to establish a precedent for transaction between them (cf. Demian 2004, 2006a). In other words, the anthropological dream of adoption by the foreigner had its own, specifically Suau manifestation. But what Suau may have seen as adoption Abel clearly saw as abduction, even going so far as to suggest that children be forcibly removed from their villages if necessary, while acknowledging that such a practice would never be condoned by the LMS authorities in London (C. W. Abel 1898; cf. Young 1989). Here again the theoretical form of abduction—the overcoming of incommensurate difference by overriding or refusing to recognize the agency of an other—was imagined by Abel as impracticable largely because he was answerable to those whose agency he did recognize, that is, his superiors in London. What he could not foresee was that he had in some ways been too successful at the abductive relationship with Suau, even if he could not pursue that relationship to its logical conclusion and remove children from their families. Following his death and the decline of Kwato's regional influence, Suau themselves would look at the loss of Abel and Kwato as the end of an era of translocal successes on their part and the beginning of their own diminution and immobilization.

Abjection

World War II saw the building of roads, airstrips, and pontoon bridges throughout Milne Bay Province, and Suau villages were all but emptied of able-bodied men who went to work as domestic laborers for Australian and American soldiers based on Milne Bay itself. The plantations, mission stations, and administration offices at Samarai were evacuated, and after the war most of the foreigners did not return. This period marked the beginning of what contemporary Suau see as a decline in their fortunes. Both soldiers and missionaries were gone, along with the ships and other infrastructures that had supported them. The prices of rubber and copra were both steadily falling on the world market, eventually compelling all planters except those who had married locally to leave. Samarai, which along with Suau Island had once contended with Port Moresby as the new capital for the entire colonial territory (Oram 1976: 20), began to lose ground as a regional commercial and administrative center. Businesses closed, including the shipbuilding enterprise originally established at Kwato. The final blow was dealt to Samarai in 1969 with the relocation of the district capital to Alotau, more centrally located to other Milne Bay populations and boasting a war-era airstrip at Gurney that would become the main airport for Milne Bay Province. Shortly after Samarai's demise as the regional headquarters, the United Church seminary at Fife Bay closed its doors. By the time I arrived at Suau in the 1990s, fiberglass dinghies had become the main means of transport for Suau people, and securing their services was becoming harder and harder for villagers due to soaring fuel prices. Police could not get around for the same reason, and imprisonment orders handed down by the village courts went unenforced. The war-era roads had all grown over or washed away, and debris from the war lay everywhere.

What is the point of this catalog of infrastructural decline? Simply that the things I list here were constantly brought to my attention by friends in Suau as material evidence of their attenuated connections to the rest of the world, of which the distant container ships were only one, particularly visible and galling, example. Of Suau localities, Fife Bay is the only one that can still claim to be "connected." It has a local level government office complete with satellite dish (nonfunctioning because its solar panels have been stolen), a health center, a primary school, a mobile telephone mast, the conversion of Lawes Bible College into James Chalmers Memorial High School, and most significant of all, the extension of the road from Alotau via Leileiyafa all the way down to the coast. But what really matters is that all these things are in Fife Bay solely due to its original role as an LMS headstation; they are there now because they were there before. The connections originally established by the LMS were appended to and built upon by planters, government patrol officers, and soldiers. Those connections are now all gone, but Fife Bay, and

gently decaying Samarai at the other end of the coast, retain an air of subur-
bia in the southwestern Pacific because that is what they once were. Samarai
even continues to boast diesel-generated electricity, indoor plumbing, and
telephone landlines—not because it is an important center of commerce or
government now but because it once was. Samarai and Fife Bay, with the Suau
Coast suspended between them, each memorialize a time when they were
actual nodes of communication between Suau and the rest of the world. As it
happens, Gaileko and his short-lived cargo movement were also located in a
village at Fife Bay.

I will now return to those aspects of his movement that I found interesting.
To begin with, there is the building of the wharf. It is sometimes easy to forget,
now that we think of communication technologies as telephonic, electromag-
netic, and digital in nature, that communication once meant (and still does
mean, in much of the world) physical connections whereby people could move
around. In the nineteenth century they were the connections of railways and
steamships, the latter of which affected the Suau social landscape so profoundly.
Both of these allowed people to travel at speeds and to distances that were previously unprecedented. I think it not too great a leap of logic to claim that just
as railways enabled the previously isolated villages of Britain to think of themselves as "localities" connected to places that were as a categorical consequence
"not local," a similar imposition of scale happened to Suau by means of the
missionaries and their ships. This is not to say that Suau were isolated; far from
it. Trade with Mailu Island to their west and the Engineer and Louisiade island
groups to their east was a fixture of the regional economic system of which the
Suau Coast was a part. But these translocal connections were, for one thing,
slow, and for another, dependent upon established trade relations with particular partners or with people whom one could claim, through totemic (*sulu*) affiliation, as kin. Like many societies throughout the province, Suau are divided
into seven matrilineal clans, each designated by the name of a totemic "bird."
Trade could safely—that is, without fear of sorcery or violence—be conducted
with members of an identical or analogous clan in the islands. As Doreen, an
elderly woman from the eastern end of the coast, explained,

> Men will become our brothers because we have a single origin. Now
> if your totem is green pigeon and if you go to another person and
> you say, "What's your totem?" "My totem is green pigeon," then they
> belong to you. We belong to each other. Flying fox is also like that,
> sea eagle is also like that, it appears in this way of becoming friends
> through totems, we belong. They're not our [lineal] kin, but on ac-
> count of totems we can be with different people.

I realize that with the invocation of totemic connections I have resurrected another hoary concept. It was some time ago that McDowell (1988)

suggested the concept of "cargo cult" had become as analytically exhausted as Lévi-Strauss (1964) once claimed totemism was. Both concepts belong to another era in anthropology. But I insist on allowing these old ideas into my discussion, because the ghostly nature of both cargo and totem is suggestive of the way Suau people memorialize their own history. Their totemic system now lies dormant in everyday life and only appears in the context of disputed land claims, itself an artifact of contested histories (see chapter 5). As for cargo and the infrastructure through which it once flowed, both means and material are now conspicuous by their very absence. The ghosts of totem and cargo produce a sentiment in Suau narratives of the past that I would not hesitate to call abjection. Even in its original psychoanalytic context, abjection indicated the de-recognition of connections that ought to obtain between familiar subjects: "Essentially different from 'uncanniness,' more violent, too, abjection is elaborated through a failure to recognize its kin; nothing is familiar, not even the shadow of a memory" (Kristeva 1982: 5). If abduction is the revelation of one's own agency at work upon others, abjection is its reversal: the suppression of anyone else's agency at work in oneself. Abjection results from a process of defamiliarization so profound that, unlike the uncanny, it cannot be revealed to be the background or latent potential of "home."

Most compelling in Kristeva's formulation is the idea that memory itself can be abjected, that abjection is a retroactive state. I have addressed in previous work a prevalent claim among Suau that they have "forgotten their culture" (Demian 2006b). This forgetting is of course meant not in the sense of a mnemonic disconnect but in the Milne Bay sense of a deliberate project to clear away or unchoose relations that offer no benefits or even present a potential danger. Usually this occurs in the context of death, as was demonstrated in the previous chapter. The introduction of infrastructural connections during the missionary era entailed an entirely new set of relations to be evaluated and, in the event, discarded. These discarded relations included regional trade with totemic "kin" in the islands, those people for whose sake Suau had formerly exerted their foreignness-converting energies but who were now thrown over in favor of the even more enticingly foreign Europeans. They included the ancestors and all the activities the Polynesian missionaries identified with them, from cannibalism to songs and dances. In other words, being connected to a world beyond the southeasternmost tip of New Guinea provided a new context by means of which Suau might evaluate their relationships.

It is not hard to imagine that what Suau found desirable about Europeans was not just that they traveled quickly but also that their travels were apparently divorced from connections of clan affiliation, marriage, or established trade partnerships. Of course, the connections of the seemingly nomadic and kinless Europeans were eventually discovered. And connections to this impossibly exotic place—I mean Europe and Australia, conflated in the category *dimdim*—extended the Suau social field in ways that required a wholesale re-evaluation of both long-distance *and* local relationships. Abduction by present relationships entailed the abjection of past ones. This abjected state is also a haunted state, however, which despite being putatively absent, retains power over the present and those living in it. Brenner (1998) has termed this condition the "unmodern" to describe a space "haunted by the specter of past modernities and their failure" (1998: 14). This space, as Özyürek (2006) has shown for modernist nostalgia in Turkey, can be very intimate in nature, saturated with feelings of affection and love, even for subjects as unlikely as the secular state and its architect, Kemal Atatürk. Both Brenner and Özyürek demonstrate, in the profoundly different contexts of Indonesia (where Islam is positioned as a component of modernity) and Turkey (where Atatürk ejected religion from his vision of a modern state), that the unmodern can emerge in any number of ways, all of them available to incorporation into the haunted space of nostalgia.

If the category of modernity must be dispensed with in these accounts because it did not work out, what orientation to time occupies that space? Brenner notes that "the conditions under which any particular 'unmodernity' is produced are unique and must be explained according to their own distinct social and historical circumstances" (1998: 128). So while the spectral presence of the past in the Javanese setting for her work is asserted through heirloom objects that "possessed their current owners as much as they were possessed by them" (1998: 128), possession by an abjected history on the Suau Coast occurs instead through the ongoing assertion of an originary Christian commitment.

The past could not have this abduction-abjection effect, however, without Suau people themselves having conducted their interactions with Europeans by means of a set of moral-aesthetic values already prevalent in the Suau cultural repertoire and social organization, and arguably found throughout Milne Bay Province. These are the values of movement, speed, fluidity, and lightness, which are in turn preconditions for perpetuating the fame of individuals and the longevity of lineages. Suau mythic culture heroes travel impossibly fast over land and sea and shed or assume their skins to turn effortlessly from one kind of being into another. Formerly, Suau men practiced *udi* ritual asceticisms in order to make their bodies light and hot so as to "turn" the minds of others in favor of bringing pigs and other valuables to feasts. Most fundamentally of all, Suau kinship itself is characterized by movement from place to place. In this matrilineal but virilocal society, with ancestry traced through women who move to their husbands' villages after marriage, lineages are mobile by definition: each time a woman relocates to her husband's place, her lineage identity goes with her. A lineage that stops moving is by definition extinct. This fact casts the Suau account of the encounter with Tamate in a particular light. For

Tamate to tell Nibeta that her lineage would prosper was tantamount to telling her that they would prosper as a consequence of the mobility of their relations, including, by implication, relations with him and his party. The identification of a stranger as "actually" kin, formerly through totemic affiliation, is after all the beginning of a long-term transaction relationship. Nibeta's innovation was to recognize Tamate as kin-like in the absence of a totemic analogy and to be recognized for her pains as the future ancestress of a prosperous lineage.[7] Later Suau innovators would follow Nibeta's example by sending their children to Abel's mission school on Kwato: again, an undertaking that would not be dreamed of if the receiver of one's children were not already recognized in some capacity as kin. "You *dimdims*," said a Suau woman of my acquaintance who was married to an Australian, "have friends. We people don't have friends. We only have family."

Herein lies, I think, the key to understanding the nature of the Suau response to the waning of their economic fortunes since the end of World War II. As Ferguson (1999) has warned, an "ethnography of decline" cannot be reduced to a taxonomy of developmental stages or adaptation to the conditions of modernity: both of these approaches are traps, for they allow the ethnographer to cast local understandings of translocal economic processes as misconstructions, partial comprehension. If one is to take seriously the way Suau call attention to their own regional decline, or process of unmodernity, one must attend to the fact that they initially valued the missionary encounter for the expansion of capacities they *already had and already valued*: long-distance trade relationships instantiated through hospitality, mobility over sea and land, and the addition of new kin to matrilineages characterized by the always-latent potential for extension and relocation. Christianity, education, vocational training, and all the rest of it are retroactively valued by contemporary Suau, and valued quite highly. But the LMS could not have succeeded in precisely the way that it did if Suau people were not able to discern an image of themselves in the actions of the missionaries. Just as it was not the cargo itself but the arrival of the cargo in their locale that intrigued my hosts of the 1990s, it was not the trade goods but the way in which they traveled that intrigued Suau in the 1870s. This process was perfectly intelligible. What was unintelligible was the way that the missionaries and other interests they brought with them departed—and particularly the fact that they departed after the war, in which Suau had labored so assiduously. World War II has its own epochal designation in Suau time reckoning—*hiyala ana huya*, "the era of war"—after which follows an epochal doldrum punctuated only by Papua New Guinea's independence from Australia in 1975, considered by every Suau person I have ever asked to be an unmitigated calamity.

But it is important to note that Suau are not simply caught up in some nostalgic fugue for the ways of the ancestors, or for a colonial regime misremembered as benign in nature. When they speak longingly of the roads along the coast, the free education provided at the mission stations, the Christmas presents, the generosity of American soldiers, and the mind-blowing novelty of meeting "black *dimdims*" who wore the same uniforms and ate the same food as white men, they are making it quite clear that what they miss is connections—of any kind. Now, with both ancestral roads and missionary roads closed to them, they may well ask how they went from being one of the first nodes of connection between Papua and Europe to being nowhere at all. Suau had become not just a locality among other localities, they had dropped off the map entirely, abjected from the world of translocal relationships.

New Mobilities

Foster (2002) cautions against laying too heavy an emphasis on mobility as a barometer for how globalized or localized a population may be. This is an important corrective, especially given that even rural Papua New Guineans, iconically (and legally) tied to their land, are able by means of the popular music they listen to, the soft drinks they consume, and the secondhand clothes they wear to perceive their continued participation in a world in which these things circulate. He recognizes that Pacific nations may wish to remind themselves of their own seafaring histories in order to counter the inexorable message that "in today's world, immobility is an unwelcome sign of marginality" (2002: 134). Marginality is not the same thing as abjection; marginality merely describes a position in deterritorialized economic space. Margins and peripheries are still defined by their position vis-à-vis metropoles and cores. Suau people do not regard themselves as inhabiting a periphery; they regard themselves as inhabiting a place whose very emplacement is in question because it has lost its relation to other places.

What really differentiated the mobility offered by the LMS schooners and whaleboats from the mobility offered by regional trade was that it did not distinguish between kinds of persons in the way that Suau did. Gender and generation, significantly, no longer mattered in quite the way they had before. For one thing, women could now travel in ways that had never previously been possible; a woman was expected to effect one major relocation during her life, that of marriage. The missions, and especially Abel's mission at Kwato, encouraged not just women but young, unmarried women and men to leave home *permanently* and to be inculcated with an entirely new life in which their marriage partners would be chosen not by their families, but by Abel himself (Wetherell 1996: 164). The point is that the infrastructure brought by the LMS was not, obviously, values free but imbued with an explicit agenda of revolutionizing the world of the peoples they encountered. They were not just providing education, healthcare, and "development" projects, as many missionaries in Papua New Guinea do now. The LMS came to Papua in order to create a context in which people could imagine new relations—ostensibly with God, although as the relentlessly pragmatic Abel observed, his aim in educating Papuans and teaching them manual skills was to turn them into model British citizens. So while the deliverers of the system themselves acknowledged it to be an alien one, they also held it to be perfectly capable of reproducing its own context.

It did not, of course, and for many reasons. A striking one is that evangelical nonconformist Protestantism was taken to British New Guinea at precisely the juncture when it was starting to lose popularity in Britain itself (Prendergast 1968: 213), so that by the first half of the twentieth century there was little public support, financial or political, for the sort of "winning New Guinea for Christ" project envisioned by the Victorian missionaries. But another is that context is a product of relationships, not their instigator. While the missionaries saw themselves as replacing one set of relations with another, Suau and undoubtedly other Papua New Guineans saw the new relations instead as additive, by means of bridging the gap of hospitality. I am acutely aware that I have claimed that Suau profess to have forgotten their culture, not added "more culture" to it; it was furthermore relationships with missionaries from the Polynesian teachers to Charles Abel that provided the impetus for this kind of forgetting, this suppression of old connections in favor of new ones.

Forgetting also entails a removal of relations from one's sense of time and movement through it. Abel was determined to invent something like a Year One for his Suau converts, a project underlined by the notion of the "first generation" and the complete break with village relations and village life. Kelly (1999) notes that "common active occupation of colonies by colonizers led to a civilization shared at a price: cognizance of its temporal hierarchy and your place in it. What happened to *that* time, in theory and reality?" (1999: 265). What happened was that Abel created on Kwato a bubble of British middle-class virtue that burst with the loss of funds from abroad and the advent of a truly global war. The "first generation" and their descendants then learned that their new value system entailed only limited mobility: it could certainly take them to Port Moresby, say, but only with extraordinary difficulty or good luck could it take them to Sydney or New York or London. As Ferguson says of middle-class colonial-era Zambians, "It was they who felt the sting not just of exclusion but of abjection—of being pushed back across a boundary that they had been led to believe they might successfully cross" (Ferguson 1999: 236). Abjection in this sense is most acutely felt by those with the most to lose from being stranded in a place that is no place, and in an epoch that appears to have no future. What distinguishes the Papua New Guinean case is that the abjection of Suau may well have been a response to the abjection of the missionaries themselves. It was after all the LMS and comparable organizations who lost a political and economic system that had made the whole dotty endeavor—of sending unworldly, minimally educated, young British men and their Polynesian assistants to evangelize the Papuans—even conceivable in the first place.

There are new connections and contexts to consider, however. Pentecostal and charismatic Christianity have spread through Papua New Guinea like wildfire since the 1980s. While older Suau are occasionally suspicious of what they call "the new churches," there has been some recognition that these churches may provide the kinds of connections and simultaneity of experience they seek to reestablish. As Piot (2010) has noted for a comparable phenomenon in West Africa, the Pentecostal churches offer a new globalism and a set of "narrative machines" (2010: 56) about the world and one's place in it. Combining older ideas of Protestant self-discipline with a new promise of middle-class cosmopolitan attainment (see also Cox 2018), these narratives drive an interest in replacing the social engineering missionary forms of Christianity with the more atomistic plans of God for each individual person.

The new churches also offer a new kind of world-expanding warfare. Dinghies loaded with young Papua New Guinean men and women, identified as "prayer warriors," now ply the coast, holding revival meetings and laying on hands. Their organization is even less hierarchical than that of the LMS had been; they preach a message of direct access and personal accountability to Jesus. Their methods are simple and relatively inexpensive, yet they are affiliated with some of the largest and most well-funded evangelical churches in Australia and the United States (Jorgensen 2005). As Marshall (2016) observes, a number of these churches have been developing a militant, adversarial doctrine of spiritual engagement and its expression since the 1980s. They are also explicitly transnational in orientation:

> As a redemptive faith, charismatic Christianity entails a concerted local engagement with a fundamentally global, transcendent orientation. The latter is figured theologically through the idea of a return to an apostolic origin, a return whose soteriological thrust is realized through a polemical engagement with local cultural forms, idioms and histories that stages a *break* with them, rather than through a process of translation or acculturation. (2016: 95, emphasis in original)

The idea of a break with history and with culture is hardly novel—it is the very principle on which Protestant missionary activity has always been based. It is absolutely what Charles Abel was trying to bring about among his converts at Kwato. The difference with the Pentecostal churches is their antagonistic stance toward any activities, relationships, commitments, and sentiments deemed inadequate for the spiritual warfare that is now demanded by the new evangelical cosmology. The total repudiation of an inadequately Christian

world debased with sin is then made into a precondition for the global connections promised by the new churches.

As Handman (2014a) notes, the cultural critiques offered by Pentecostal
and other schismatic churches in PNG are an opportunity not only for self-
reflexivity but also, somewhat paradoxically, for the creation of public and political forms of unity that have largely eluded a nation with a tendency toward
the pursuit of increasingly fragmentary regional interests.[8] Through an examination of the way new religious ideas are used to experiment with the possibility of realigning cultural and political affiliations both within and beyond
PNG, she observes that "Christianity—even with its many denominational divisions—is not hindering the formation of a public and a way to organize, as it
is so often depicted as doing in secularist Western discourses, but it is actually
producing a way for people to recognize one another across ethnic, linguistic and denominational boundaries" (2014a: 129). The recognition to which
Handman refers is critical. As I hope to have demonstrated in this chapter, the
entire Suau enterprise of welcoming missionaries in the nineteenth century
was a labor of recognition that could, by their own account, have been so many
other things instead. The Christian critique of one's own practices in order to
extend relationships to unknown others is among the forms of social analysis
that Suau people regard themselves as having deployed almost from the moment of Chalmers's arrival.

It remains to be seen whether the new churches will convince Suau that
they are the appropriate replacements for old relationships found and lost, but
especially for young Suau they hold out the possibility of a new sort of mobility and new ways to turn non-kin into kin. This is precisely what alarms their
elders, because it threatens also to turn kin into non-kin through denominational schism (Jebens 2006). But the appeal to the young of being accountable
to Jesus and Jesus alone is undeniably appealing. An accountability to a spiritual authority rather than, say, their elders or a formal church hierarchy, that
requires an ongoing process of self-critique is precisely how the new churches
present the possibility of connection to other Papua New Guineans that has so
far eluded projects of Papua New Guinean nation making. It certainly holds
out the possibility of connecting Papua New Guineans up to a global ecumene
that obviates any need for Papua New Guinean identification in the first place
(Robbins 2004a). If that happens, then the Pentecostal churches will have
proven to be the most effective communication technology to have reached
the Suau Coast to date.

Further to this, it is worth noting that not all the foreigners abandoned
the coast after World War II. Abel's children in particular returned, some married locally, and his grandchildren and great-grandchildren now run some of
the most successful businesses in the province. One of them, along with a series of both foreign and naturalized *dimdim* business partners, kept the last

large trade store on Samarai afloat long past the point of economic viability before finally cutting his losses, fully aware that he had been providing a public service to the entire coast. But even Gaileko's prediction came true, after a fashion: Charles Abel, the great-grandson and namesake of the pioneering missionary, is at the time of writing a parliamentarian for Milne Bay Province. The road from Alotau to Fife Bay is his project, and one that many Suau people are watching intently to see if it can deliver the prosperity and long-distance connections they once enjoyed. While they can never experience in Alotau the linguistic and regional dominance they enjoyed in the heyday of Samarai and Kwato, Alotau nonetheless represents that beguiling potential, a connection leading to other connections.

Notes

Part of chapter 3 was originally published as "Canoe, Mission Boat, Freighter: The Life History of a Melanesian Relationship," *Paideuma: Mitteilungen zur Kulturkunde* 53 (2007): 89–109.

1. In Suau villages, "good girls" neither drink nor smoke. Only a few older women of my acquaintance smoked, and absolutely none that I knew of drank alcohol. On one occasion I was caught with my carefully hidden and rationed bottle of duty-free Scotch by Baigayo, my host in Isuisu. "Melissa, are you drinking?" she asked me incredulously. I admitted that I was. She laughed and teased me lightly, but by the next day the entire village knew about it, and it became clear that my reputation was in jeopardy. I took the whisky to share with some European friends on Samarai on my next visit there, and I never brought alcohol to the village again.

2. This boots-eating trope in European–Pacific Islander encounter stories predates the demise of Chalmers at Goaribari by at least fifty years. The story may initially have been applied to European whalers and traders and later "migrated" to the deaths of missionaries in Fiji and Vanuatu before making its way to Papua New Guinea. With thanks to the collective knowledge of the ASAONET listserv for bringing the antiquity of the trope to my attention.

3. MacGillivray uses the English term for this island group, Brumer Islands; I am employing the Suau names for individual islands. It is evident from MacGillivray's description that Bonalua is the particular island at which the *Rattlesnake* stopped: "The large Brumer Island is long and narrow, running East-North-East and West-South-West, two miles and two-thirds in greatest width; it is situated in latitude 10 degrees 45 minutes 30 seconds South and longitude 150 degrees 23 minutes East" (MacGillivray 1852).

4. The concept was imported from the philosophy of Charles Sanders Peirce, who proposed abductive reasoning as a process distinct from, but complementary and in some ways preparatory to, deductive and inductive reasoning. Abduction for Peirce was, among other things, the process by which an inference can be made before other modes of reaching the inference come into play. It is sometimes described as "Inference to the Best Explanation" to indicate that it is a means of reaching an inference without necessarily requiring the establishment of a truth-value (McKaughan 2008).

Abduction can be a way of forming the justification for pursuit of a scientific hypothesis, for instance, and also one for reaching an understanding of history by means of the evidence left behind (Niiniluoto 1999). Part of the problem with defining the philosophical usage of abduction was that Peirce worked on the principle over many years, leading to its taking on more than one possible interpretation, all of them "Peircean" in nature (Fann 1970). This is precisely the sort of indeterminate or contested quality that can make a philosophical concept ripe for poaching by anthropologists.

5. Prendergast (1968: 15) observes that the LMS, as a *de facto* Congregationalist organization, emphasized more than most missionary groups the status of its missionaries as individual Christians rather than representatives of a particular doctrine or occupants of particular roles in a church hierarchy.

6. Predictably, this dialect is now touted as "real Suau" by its speakers, and all other dialects are felt to be corrupt offshoots of a proper language. As for the Suau New Testament, it was sometimes compared by my friends to the way they speak English: perfectly intelligible, but it would never be mistaken for a document written by a native speaker. More recently, the PNG Bible Translation Association has stationed translators from Costa Rica in the midcoastal village of Savaia, who are in turn working with local assistants along the entire coast. In time they may produce both Old and New Testaments that not only sound right to Suau ears but also break the Kwato-instigated dominance of the eastern dialect as the only one claiming to be "real" or "pure" Suau.

7. No Suau person of my acquaintance ever remarked on the structural similarities between this story and the promise of God to Abraham in Genesis. Nor would they be likely to; the Old Testament is not yet translated into Suau and is still largely mediated for Suau people through English-language Bibles and the sermons of their pastors.

8. In a shorter period of time than it took to complete this book, two new provinces (Hela and Jiwaka) were carved out of existing ones in 2012, and a province with limited autonomy (Bougainville) voted overwhelmingly for independence from PNG in a referendum held in 2019.

4

Old Roads, New Roads
Temporal Cartography

Our *ulutubu* came from Wari Island. We came from Wari and later went to Suau. At Suau there is a little village called Gadawiwi. There at Gadawiwi we lived. That was our ancestors, our *ulutubu*. At Gadawiwi they lived until they went to Pwa'iu. They went to Pwa'iu and then they went to Saga'afo and lived there. At Saga'afo they lived until they had children. There was a "big death" [*pe'i la'ila'i*, epidemic?] there. Eventually all the people at Saga'afo died, with one left who came up to Buhutu. At Buhutu that person lived, got married, and had one girl child. There was one girl child, and it proceeded until that woman herself had a child. She also had one girl child. After that one girl child she gave birth again: a boy. . . . [Some misadventures with a witch follow, and a war between lineages is averted.] . . . They lived until they had another boy. They had another child. Giuwede. They had Giuwede. Until it was finished, and they had another. Waileya. Until it was finished. They wanted to stay together, and they came down to the foot of Monailo River. . . . They built a house and time passed while they lived there. Then they gave birth to Laukapore. After that they also gave birth to me. They bore Tauyabuna. There we lived and then later we lived at . . . what's-it-called . . . at Puyuwa. Another hamlet called Puyuwa. There we lived until . . . we lived at Daiyela. Later we lived at . . . what's-it-called . . . Boboulo, a place called Boboulo. We lived at Boboulo until Misibibi came and gathered us together. The government. Misibibi came and gathered us together, in the mountains where we were all living at the time. We came here to Bwabwatiti. At Bwabwatiti we stayed together.
—Tauyabuna, around seventy, telling the history of Saga'afo *ulutubu*[1]

My account in the previous chapter of some pivotal moments in Suau history refers repeatedly to the arrival and movement of missionaries on the landscape, as well as the implications of their staying put, as in the case of missionaries like Charles Abel. The significance of their having done so is twofold. Firstly, to recapitulate a point made in the introduction, the Enlightenment—

that is, European—apprehension of space as being fundamentally empty until something is "made" of it was a component of the asymmetry in missionary relationships with Suau. As I will show in this chapter, no space is ever empty but is replete with actions and intentionalities, stemming from the past and the present, inclusive of human, nonhuman, and quasi-human agency. The modern constitution, which seeks to divide a before from an after, fails repeatedly in Suau perceptions of their land and its capacities. This chapter is where my discussion of a Suau historical consciousness will take a sharp turn, as it were, in the direction of deep history and its perduring presence in the landscape. While this presence only sporadically emerges into everyday discourse, its effects are still felt. The themes explored in the previous chapters, of what it means to forget one set of relationships in order to pursue other, more lively ones, may seem to be at odds with this assertion.

I would only remind the reader that claims of a break with history are precisely that: claims, made in aid of rhetorical or other immediate social effects. Consider: what if James Chalmers must be memorialized with a day in his honor and a secondary school named after him because, otherwise, his memory really would disappear? Memory practices of this kind—commemorative holidays that repeat on an annual cycle, institutions with people's names on them—are a colonial introduction to the Suau cultural repertoire, as they are for most if not all Papua New Guineans. My focus here shifts to another kind of memory practice, alluded to in chapter 2 in the ways that Suau people build graves and plant significant trees and shrubs to fix their dead in the landscape. The land itself is at issue here, along with the ways that it continues to offer to the Suau imagination a way of thinking about movements across space and through time that belong both to Suau people and to other kinds of people who have made their presence felt in the reckoning of history.

The Topogeny of the Suau Coast

Tauyabuna was one of Leileiyafa's oldest inhabitants when he provided me with the foregoing history of his *ulutubu*, which I have chosen to gloss somewhat inadequately as "lineage," in 1997.[2] When I returned to the Suau Coast two years later, he had died, and junior members of his *ulutubu* wanted copies of the tape I had made of the account in case they should be called to reproduce it in the course of a land dispute.[3] It is a typical ancestor account provided by Suau speakers: if you ask someone to tell you about their lineage, you will be regaled with a catalog of places and the people who inhabited those places, usually including the order in which they were born. Any *ulutubu* account will start with the earliest ancestress known to the speaker and proceed through the marriages of her descendants, each of which would also constitute a move to a new village in this predominantly virilocal society. *Ulutubu* are described as relocating for other reasons as well: in various *ulutubu* accounts I have heard, women are kidnapped, some people are chased away by hostile affines, others are invited to live somewhere else by friendly ones, and others still, in the early twentieth century, were relocated by the Australian administration to bring them closer to patrol routes. In each case, the matrilineage relocates, and each location forms the history of an *ulutubu* that is also an account of the places that belong to it and to which it belongs.

Fox (1997) calls this type of knowledge practice "topogeny," and as he observes, it is a signature characteristic of societies descended from the Austronesian cultural complex. Elaborating on the idea, he further notes that "in so far as a sequence of names can be attached to specific locations in an inhabited landscape, a topogeny represents a projected externalization of memories that can be lived in as well as thought about" (1997: 8). The idea that topogeny represents a particular form of remembering is one that has received extensive discussion among anthropologists working with Austronesian groups, not least because the argument can also be made that topogeny facilitates a particular form of forgetting.

In her consideration of the starkly different purposes of monuments through history and between cultural groups, Küchler (1999) adopts a distinction drawn by Aleida Assmann between two mnemonic forms. One is a temporal mode, "capable of bridging across a lost present to a desired future" (Küchler 1999: 60); the other is a spatial mode, "which initiates a momentary collapse of past and present by forcing past and present, distance and proximity into a single point" (1999: 60). Küchler asserts that the second, spatial mode is emphasized in Austronesian memorial activities, drawing primarily on her own work on the construction of funerary artifacts in New Ireland. She observes of the experience of this form of memory "the fact that while it can be repeated, it can never be recollected" (1999: 60). The importance of this observation cannot be overemphasized, because by taking seriously the temporal mode suggested by topogeny, it is easier to avoid the assumption that topogeny is simply a means of remembering—in the sense of recollecting and reanimating—the ancestors and the places in which they lived. It is also a means of letting them go, in that a literal or a narrative movement through the places of ancestral dwelling does not necessarily form a bridge from the past to the present. It anchors the past in place, where the power of the past is both safeguarded and quarantined, so that its efficacy can be "collapsed" or even "exploded" (both terms employed by Küchler) into the present when it is invoked under ritual—including, in the present era, legal—conditions (see chapter 5).

An instance of Suau topogeny, Tauyabuna's *ulutubu* account shifts seamlessly between a progression from place to place and from sibling to sibling, each geographical and narrative movement between locations and persons encapsulating the passage of time. His own birth, which he added with a mischievous half smile, is embedded in a sequence of births and deaths of which the flow of time from past to present is constituted. His inclusion of himself in the *ulutubu* account was simultaneously a retrospective and a prospective move because it pointed to his own imminent transformation into an ancestor. He would only be able to "see" the itinerary of his *ulutubu* as far as the hamlet of Bobontiti, after which it might relocate again if his sisters' children moved elsewhere. In the telling of the lineage history, he anticipated his own fixing in the landscape and in time. But precisely because he could envision becoming a named ancestor, he was imagining how future generations of his *ulutubu* would in turn look back on him and on the place in which he lived and would die.

As the oldest living member of his lineage, to whom younger members could come for accounts like the one I have excerpted above, Tauyabuna was uniquely entitled to locate himself as an ancestor-to-be in his telling. The other siblings named in his history were all dead. In Suau topogeny, the names of ancestors and the names of abandoned hamlets form a constellation of reference points from which people can take their spatiotemporal bearings. As Küchler (1993) has written of New Ireland, "In the absence of any emphasis on genealogy, the history of social relations is embedded in the process of mapping. Mapping is the product of place transmission which, together with the transmission of personal names and skills, effects the virtual reconstitution of social relations over time" (1993: 96). Places and deceased people become functionally interchangeable in this conceptualization of movement through space and time, as they serve the same purpose of orienting the present generation in the histories of their lineages. The problem for the ethnographer in the case of Suau topogeny—and occasionally also for Suau people themselves—is, what exactly is a lineage? Which is also a way of asking, what kind of landscape is created through placing the emphasis on different modes of connection between persons and through time?

Reckoning Relationships, Reckoning Time

Early ethnographers who visited the Suau Coast (Seligman 1910; Armstrong 1921; Williams 1933) reported a clanic social structure with between four and six exogamous matriclans (*sulu*), each identified by four associated totems of a bird, a tree, a snake, and a fish. These were translocal affiliations, linked to analogous clans (*susu*) in the Engineer Group (Macintyre 1989) and elsewhere in the Southern Massim (Lepowsky 1983). It is reasonable to assume that these island-mainland connections helped to facilitate partnerships both for grand-scale ceremonial exchanges, such as *mata'asi*, and for trade (*une*) in regional specialties, such as clay cooking pots from Wari Island, carved ebony lime spatulas from the Suau Coast, and shell valuables and stone axe blades from the distant Louisiade Archipelago. *Sulu* exogamy also meant that men would have had to search assiduously beyond their natal villages for wives. *Sulu* relationships simultaneously reflected and fostered economic interdependence between language groups, facilitated by men and women who made journeys to other regions for very specific purposes such as trade, ceremonial feasting, and marriage. Indiscriminate travel would have been not only pointless but also dangerous, due to the risk of death by sorcery or straightforward physical violence.

Significantly, *sulu* are not associated with places and recent history in the way that *ulutubu* are, but are instead associated with a time-distant or even time-detached mythological history. An example is the story of the *bunebune* (glossed locally in English as "green pigeon," a species of *Ptilinopus* fruit dove) *sulu*, as told by one of my hosts in Leileiyafa, May, who is a member of this *sulu*:

> One day a woman and her daughter went to the sea to gather *iwai* [a fat clam-like bivalve]. When they had plenty of *iwai* in their baskets, the daughter opened one to eat it. She saw there was meat in only one-half of the shell and started crying. "What are you crying for?" said the mother. "That's how *iwai* are, when you open them the meat stays in one half of the shell." But her daughter said, "I want meat in both halves!" and she kept on crying. She cried and cried until she turned into a green pigeon and flew away over the trees, still crying [the green pigeon has a mournful call]. Her mother picked up the open *iwai* shell and threw it at the pigeon. The shell struck the bird on her forehead and it started to bleed. This is why the green pigeon has a red mark on its forehead.

While taking the form of an unremarkable just-so story, the green pigeon *sulu* origin includes several key elements: matriliny (the tale concerns a woman and her daughter), transformation (a feature of very many Suau myths), the departure of girls from their natal family, and a nonassociation with either place or time: this story could have happened anywhere, at any point in history. Because it could have happened anywhere, the *sulu* associated with it can potentially be found anywhere.

This aspect of *sulu*—its placelessness and ubiquity—appears to be precisely what has caused its decline as an index of identity and relationship for Suau people. When I first arrived on the Suau Coast in 1996, identification by *sulu* had dwindled in importance to the point where almost nobody knew more than their bird totem (although everyone knew at least that one) and *sulu* endogamy was considered perfectly acceptable. Only land mediators, who were all senior men and who by definition worked with more "classical" categories of social organization than most people, took *sulu* affiliation seriously enough to insist on its contemporary relevance in the course of land disputes (see chapter 5). It appeared that *sulu* had gone from being one of the most salient aspects of Suau identity in the past to an abstraction almost completely divorced from social reality in the present. Its status as group identifier seemed quaint or nostalgic, useful for the naming of village soccer teams but little else.

In the current era, most Suau people place far greater emphasis on their *ulutubu*, a kind of "last known address" for their apical ancestress (*wahabili*). *Ulutubu* names are all place names, some still inhabited, others long since abandoned, from which people's matrilines are known to originate. Terms sometimes used interchangeably with *ulutubu* are *tanohi* (land) and *boga esega* (one womb). The idea is one of rootedness in a place that is semantically equated with the body of the ancestress who lived there. And while *ulutubu* accounts frequently cross the boundaries of dialect groups, as Tauyabuna's did, they are largely located within the Suau language cluster, suggesting that this category of relationship encompasses only the least "foreign" of places.[4] Marriage to members of either one's matrilateral or patrilateral *ulutubu* is inappropriate—which is not to say that it does not happen, and is often pointed to by older Suau people as a sign of the degradation of contemporary society. An emphasis on concrete, geographically and linguistically accessible origins, as well as membership within traceable descent groups, has supplanted the former translocal sensibilities and identification with more amorphously composed "clans."

The most coherent account of *sulu* affiliation offered to me came from Tubufuyo, who in 1999 was probably in his seventies and who discussed the difference between *sulu* and *ulutubu* as follows:

> When you think about it, *sulu* is: when we meet a person, and we talk about *sulu*, they'll say "This is my *sulu*." And I'll say, "My *sulu* is the same," and that's how the friendship begins. That's it, that's the road. Our *ulutubu* is: different origins, because one person has a different *ulutubu* and other people have a different *ulutubu*. For *sulu*, if somebody says "This is my *sulu*," we say, "I have the same *sulu*," there we put them together and he becomes your brother, as though from the same womb, that's *sulu*'s part. The meaning of *sulu* is like I've said, I've explained it. If this person's *sulu* is flying fox, his *sulu* is flying fox, we are all flying fox *sulu*, that's the meaning.

One of my closest interlocutors in Leileiyafa, a senior man named Elia, demonstrated this felicitous potential for co-identification when he explained to me that *sulu* could be determined by examining the lines in someone's palm.

Naturally I then offered my palm for inspection, whereupon he declared, "Malibon—yau doha" (Flying fox, the same as me).[5]

Whereas *ulutubu* indicates fundamental difference based on identification with specific and named ancestors in the more or less recent past, *sulu* indicates the possibility of common origins located in a mythohistorical past, a time-out-of-mind. Some *ulutubu* are the names of extant villages or hamlets; others are places where no one has lived for decades. But the point is that they are all geographically concrete and temporally accessible, since the relevant ancestress may have lived there only a few generations prior to the one claiming her place as *ulutubu*. *Sulu*, by contrast, is a highly abstract relationship, spanning hundreds of miles and located in "time immemorial." A *sulu* is also categorically static by virtue of its encompassing the entirety of the Suau Coast and neighboring peoples, whereas an *ulutubu* is categorically mobile as a consequence of the processes of matriliny and virilocality.

So how did *sulu* come to lose prominence in Suau discourse? Obviously there is no single reason, but a number of possibilities present themselves readily, and they are all to do with shifting patterns of mobility in this region, an altered emphasis on both the range and depth of movement to and from other places. *Sulu* relationships would certainly have been integral to the maintenance of long-distance trading routes that formerly existed between the Suau Coast, the Engineer Group of islands to its east, and Mailu Island to its west, since they may have determined the distinction between trading partners and enemies. They would have served the same purpose closer to home, where exchanges of valuables and of violence between lineages were also common. It is tempting to speculate that the de-emphasizing of *sulu* identity was a dual product of pacification and the diminution of the old "roads" (*dobila* or *eda*) of trade and ceremonial exchange in light of new possibilities for productive relationships opened up by the missionary encounters described in the previous chapter. The older roads are by no means dead, but are maintained primarily by senior men who still possess some shell valuables or by younger island-mainland couples sending gifts of food, pigs, and money along the "road of marriage" (*tawasola dobilana*).

If people ceased to identify themselves translocally, then it is important to ask why this is no longer necessary, or rather, if the nature of translocal identification has changed such that regional sources of value have been supplanted by national or even international ones (cf. Kirsch 2004a). For while Elia may have been able to assert common *sulu* identity with a *dimdim*, his assertion was of course dependent upon the *dimdim* both knowing and caring what *sulu* meant, a set of conditions I established by asking about it in the first place. But apart from the idiosyncratic desires of an anthropologist to learn about old forms of social organization, *sulu* appears on the face of it to have not much of a future in everyday Suau discourse—precisely because its past is too deep and too spatially dispersed. By contrast, *ulutubu* identification is historically grounded, literally; with similar literalness, it tells people what their place in the world is and on which local relationships they can depend. More prosaically, *ulutubu* present Suau people with a more manageable corporate form in which to stake land claims, an issue to which I will return in chapter 5.

If a Suau sense of history has become limited to the past three or four generations, this gives rise to questions of what happened to the indeterminate "ancient history" to which *sulu* relationships belong. I take my cue in approaching these questions from Toren (1995), who has documented similar processes for Gau Islanders in Fiji. On Gau, identification with the remains of ancestral house sites once provided people with access to ancestral efficacy in the form of the legitimation of political forms and exchange relations between kin. Now the power of these same sites is regarded as the source of success in school and business ventures. And with the value of land in some parts of Fiji being converted into lucrative kava farming, the potency of the ancestors is conceived by some people on Gau as that which will bestow upon indigenous Fijians the ability to compete in the world of business with Fijians of Indian descent. In sum, Toren demonstrates the way in which the same principle— the immanent efficacy of ancestral actions upon the landscape—is recognized as animating different forms of action by those people in the present day who can claim a relationship with the ancestors who lent the land its power. In a similar vein, Guo (2003) notes that activities carried out in the past by Langalanga people in the Solomon Islands, notably the building of artificial islands, are still those that form the basis for Langalanga identification with the landscape. Never mind that they do not create islands any longer, or indeed that most Langalanga people now live on the mainland of Malaita rather than on the islands their forebears made. The fact that Langalanga people *used to* create artificial islands is still evident in the enduring presence of many of the islands and is therefore sufficient to endow contemporary generations with the capacity to reflect on their own historical efficacy, reflected back on them in the present era.

Which brings me back to the problem of *sulu* identification for Suau people, and what has happened to it—by which I mean, what has happened to the history to which *sulu* belongs. A moderately obvious remark to start with is that *sulu*, unlike house sites in Fiji or artificial islands in the Solomons, and notably unlike *ulutubu* on the Suau Coast, is not linked to a topogeny. That is, *sulu* lacks the direct connection between the living and their ancestors whose movements across the landscape are recorded in *ulutubu* histories. But more subtly, the kinds of relationships that were activated or recognized through *sulu* co-identification are "roads" that Suau people no longer use.

This is materially observable. There is a notable absence on the Suau Coast of the types of items that were once traded or ceremonially exchanged across the "Southern Massim."[6] Intact shell valuables like the red shell disk *bagi* strings are increasingly rare, as they are cut up to distribute among heirs as memorial items or simply to make into necklaces. Every so often I would be shown a *bagi maʻuluʻuluna* (*bagi* "with its hair," that is, inclusive of shell, seed, and glass or plastic bead ornaments), a pearl shell (*giniuba*), or pig's tusk valuable (*kaipesi*), kept and cherished as an heirloom but no longer in play as a form of wealth. Clay pots have been supplanted by aluminum ones bought in Alotau. The competitive feasting of *mataʻasi* is a moribund institution, and so pig exchange networks are now mostly limited to those maintained for bride-wealth and funerary purposes, which necessarily covers a smaller geographical area. The fact that the material signs of translocal relationships are nowhere in evidence suggests a cessation of trade and ceremonial exchange beginning many decades ago, but only "complete" in the past twenty to thirty years.

At the same time as important trade and exchange items from "before" were being replaced by novel valuables (aluminum cooking pots, store-bought food, cloth, money), warfare between neighboring groups on the Suau Coast ceased under pressure from government and mission pacification efforts. Residence patterns became more nucleated and even isolated in the wake of this newfound security (Williams 1933), and regional identification correspondingly narrower and more particular. Former enemies were now potential exchange partners and even affines, thereby obviating the need to look farther afield. The new economic centers of activity were in turn Fife Bay with its seminary, Samarai with the colonial district headquarters, later the provincial capital of Alotau, and later still the oil palm plantations of the Sagarai Valley, all of which effectively brought the new forms of wealth and prestige progressively closer to "home" for Suau people.

Finally, one event in living memory may have done as much as or more than all the other factors combined to privilege local over translocal identity. World War II and its aftermath have taken on a mythological quality for people in this region, complete with physical relics left behind: downed aircraft, decaying pontoon bridges, anonymous engines gently rusting away beneath the aerial roots of mangroves. One material left over from the war era, the perforated steel Marston Mat designed for the rapid construction of airstrips, is now ubiquitously found integrated into everything from hearths to fences to pit latrines. My assertion of the mythological status of the war must be qualified, not only because of these physical remains but also because it is still vibrant in the memories of the generation that experienced it. But for younger Suau, the war may as well have happened hundreds of years ago—not that there is any great disparity between them and my own generation of Americans in this particular respect.

But it is what happened after the war that is of the most significance to contemporary life on the Suau Coast. As noted in chapter 1, Mr. Vivian/

Misibibi, the assistant resident magistrate of the mid-twentieth century, is credited with having relocated entire lineages to coastal or estuarine locales in order to render them more accessible to government. Exasperated with the land squeeze along the coast, some of the residents of Isuisu—and presumably of other coastal villages as well—have taken to building gardens a day's walk inland, at the sites of their former *ulutubu* land.[7] And some people in Leilei-yafa maintain that Leileiyafa is not a real place at all but rather an invention of Misibibi. Out of eight *ulutubu* that had come to Leileiyafa and its satellite hamlets through in-marriage, senior members from four of these lineages told me they had been relocated from the mountains and given land there by Misibibi himself. Another married in and was given gardening land by one of the Misibibi-sanctioned lineages. I questioned none of these assertions until seeing a reference to Mr. Vivian in Young (1971: 31), wherein he was also credited with relocating entire villages on Goodenough Island, not to mention seducing all their women, in the manner appropriate to trickster figures and morally ambiguous culture heroes everywhere. It is evident that whatever Mr. Vivian actually did, his memorialization as Misibibi in the Suau region and beyond has assured that his decisions and policies had effects that far outstripped the ordinary bureaucratic intentions of a midlevel colonial administrator. And who knows, perhaps he did sleep with half the women on Goodenough Island. This was, after all, a not unheard-of practice among single European men stationed in colonial Papua; the son of the last Australian patrol officer on the Suau Coast was serving as the elementary school teacher in Isuisu the last time I stayed there.

The point is that, whether on the grand scale of relocating villages or the more intimate scale of leaving children behind, colonial officials in Milne Bay throughout the twentieth century left their mark on the landscape of social relations. Which is simply a way of saying that they affected the landscape itself, given that the physical landscape and the social landscape are not differentiated, in this as in many Melanesian societies (cf. Rodman 1992). It seems reasonable to assume that the mass relocation of people away from their *ulutubu* land would have had profound effects on the way that they conceived of their relationships to others, both in the aftermath of the relocations and in the present day. In some respects, what Mr. Vivian did was revolutionary; in others, it was simply another way for *ulutubu* to relocate. What made it revolutionary was the fact that many *ulutubu* relocated all at once, leaving large areas of the Suau hinterland abruptly uninhabited. Could it be a consequence of this element of Suau history that led to a hyperprivileging of *ulutubu*? Certainly the old "rules" of spatial identification seem to have been altered during the war era and afterward, when Suau people were suddenly obliged to readjust their horizons from being a pivotal theater of battle to just another Papua New Guinean backwater. Suau people had grown accustomed to acting—by which I mean marrying, working, transacting, traveling, studying—either in terms of highly localized relations, or highly translocal ones. The value of the medium-range translocality of *sulu* identification could well have diminished in the face of opportunities to transact with (work for, learn from, sleep with) extremely foreign foreigners such as Europeans, Australians, and Americans.

This is not to say, however, that *sulu* is entirely defunct as a means of recognizing the relationships along which value travels. Its belonging to another era is still a source of efficacy for at least one specialized forum in contemporary Suau life, and this is the land dispute. The nonassociation of *sulu* with any place names or features of the landscape is precisely what aids land mediators in their strategies to persuade disputants to come to an agreement, a topic to which I will return in more detail in chapter 5. While the placelessness of *sulu* may seem a paradoxical form of persuasion to draw upon in debates concerning the ownership of land, it is arguable that this is precisely why land mediators find it effective. Land mediators in Papua New Guinea hold a peculiar position in the legal system of the country. They have no power to adjudicate and their decisions cannot be enforced, but they are empowered by the state to hear and mediate disputes that cannot be heard in the village courts. The point of land mediations, in other words, is to prevent disputes over land from ever reaching the formal court system. While this does not always work in practice, most Suau people are committed to using the land mediation system as a means of "straightening" (*hadudulai*) relations within and between families in order to prevent disputes over land from causing wider problems still, ranging from sorcery attacks to village court hearings over grievances that are subsidiary to land disputes.

With the obsolescence of former exchange routes and the shifting of travel to very distant places rather than neighboring language groups, perhaps the old system of translocal totemic identity has, in a very real sense, disappeared from the map. What matters now are the extreme ends of the social continuum: groups defined by the consolidation and contraction of their spatial and temporal identities (*ulutubu*), and travel among peoples so different from themselves that relationships with them must be conceived in wholly different forms from those of clan affiliation. If Leileiyafa was indeed altered radically by the influx of new lineages in the early 1950s, its residents can hardly be blamed for feeling that the old roads between themselves and distant clanfolk are now defunct. They have had to reinvent themselves to suit the new political-economic dispensation. Or, as I was told time and again by numerous people, as though apologizing for their lack of the sorts of "cultural knowledge" they thought I wanted, "We used to know these things [magic, dances, *sulu* totems], but now we've forgotten everything." This was nothing less than an assertion of their engagement with the new roads available to them. The landscape had changed, thus requiring them to alter their bearings within it.

These different ways of reckoning identity have their corresponding implications for economic life on the coast. *Sulu* is now mainly of concern to those engaged in situations calling for a high level of rhetoric and repositioning of identity, and sometimes to Suau who find themselves elsewhere in the province for school or employment and in need of a way to establish positive relations with people in their new home. (Significantly, educated Suau speak of their old school friends in language that closely resembles the way in which they might also speak of friendships grounded in a shared *sulu*, e.g., "We're just like brothers." Schooling to secondary or tertiary level is becoming an increasingly important means of establishing long-distance relationships.) For people who do not have these very specific negotiations in mind, *ulutubu* is the primary means of identification. This localization of identity accompanies—not accidentally, I think—changes in the ways in which Suau have engaged with each new economic dispensation, as suggested earlier. Individual mobility has increased, for women especially; whereas before a Suau woman might relocate only once in her life, at marriage, now she could conceivably go to school in one place, find a job in another, get married in a third, and travel to church functions in many others. More recent origins may hold more relevance than those located in a past to which the contemporary imagination appears to have less and less access. In the village, political lines are typically drawn between *ulutubu*, and often deacon's groups within the church are also demarcated according to the *ulutubu* of the deacon. Identity has become somewhat contracted; the immediate evidence of this are the ways in which people envision the material manifestations of their relationships with one another.

A land mediation that will appear in more detail in the next chapter is a case in point. In that instance, the disputants presented themselves as differentiated because they belonged to different *ulutubu*. But the mediators insisted they were *not* differentiated because they belonged to the same *sulu* and therefore had no cause to quarrel because the land belonged to both parties. The view of the mediator eventually prevailed, though not, it appeared, without some misgivings on the part of the disputants. But land is unusual, because it has a quality unique among the forms of wealth now transacted among Suau: it is perdurable, unconsumable. The *products* of land, such as garden food, cash crops, and timber, are most certainly consumed, but the land itself, and its generativity, remains. This quality was also attributed to "old time" valuables made from shell, tusk, and stone, which are hardly in circulation in the Suau region any more. Significantly, the forms of wealth still in use—pigs, garden or trade store food, and money—are all "used up" at some point in their lifetime. As transient objects, they appear to have accompanied the more itinerant and immediate form of identity, *ulutubu*, into contemporary preference.

When Suau people say they have "forgotten" the practices of the past, they are of course making claims about their relationship to the present. In each of the epochs of their experience over the past hundred years, they have deliberately adapted to novel forms of wealth, novel systems for attributing value, and novel ways of maintaining positive relations with one another and with the arbiters of each new economic dispensation. Among the most important changes they have seen has been the integration of money into the gift exchange repertoire and the effect this has produced in the way value is reckoned both qualitatively and temporally. Suau people like to contrast themselves with people from Central Province with their bridewealth payments in the thousands of kina, but their own transactions have in fact undergone a different kind of "inflation." Instead of being expected to produce *more* and *better quality* wealth, as in the past when pigs and food given at *mata'asi* dazzled the guests of knowledgeable and efficacious big men (*ba'isa*), Suau are now expected to produce wealth *faster* for *more kinds of transactions*. This altered emphasis on value from both quantity and quality to speed and multiplicity, taken together with the abstracted-value principle of money, has meant that one form of wealth is now exchangeable for almost any other form of wealth. These transformations have gone hand in hand with transformations in other areas of social life, notably the depriveging of a type of identity, *sulu*, that did not emphasize places of origin but rather mythological events of origin and belonged to an era of long-distance travel for the express purpose of formal exchange. The emphasis now is placed almost exclusively on an alternative mode of identification, *ulutubu*, which is grounded in the local and the recent, because these are the arenas in which exchanges are now conducted. Just as the most popular contemporary forms of wealth are those that are consumed and replaced in short succession, so identifying with one's *ulutubu* reflects a similarly brief "cycle," as each generation moves from one site to the next, to be replaced by others following them.

Precedence, Movement, and Rootedness

Stationary and mobile states mark particular phases in the lives of Suau people, and the relocation of entire groups may ultimately be affected by one of these lived phases. The elaboration of an ideology of mobility on an individual level may be seen as reflective of movement through and ownership of land by whole lineages. Three elements of varying strictness—matriliny (nonnegotiable, despite the best efforts of young men at land disputes), exogamy (often violated at *sulu* level but less frequently at that of *ulutubu*), and virilocality (ideal but flexible)—combine to produce highly mobile lineage populations that nonetheless place a heavy emphasis on identification with specific places. This is not as paradoxical as it might seem, as I shall discuss later, although it does necessitate an ideological acknowledgment of principles of both rootedness and travel.

These typically Austronesian concerns with origins and precedence are also elaborated at the level of birth order. Firstborn children (*taubaguna*, "leader"), whether male or female, are understood to be the "bosses" or stewards (*tanuwaga*) of their junior siblings (*taumulita*, "follower"), requiring particular respect from them and their spouses.[8] Married couples address each other by the names of their respective hamlets or lineages until the birth of their first child, after which they may also practice teknonymy using the name of this child.[9] Firstborn children are often the holders of lineage origin stories and are the nominal stewards (*tanuwaga* again) of lineage land, although the authoritative knowledge of *tanuwaga* may be supplemented by more abbreviated, "genealogical" versions of lineage histories are written down for use by any lineage member in case they are needed for land disputes. In the event of the death of a firstborn sibling, authority transfers to the second eldest, and so on down the line of birth order. Sibling groups are thus metaphorically conceived as traveling single file, which is the preferred spatial arrangement for people journeying from one place to another; walking two or more abreast is sometimes referred to jokingly as "*dimdim* style." Single-file spatial sequences appear elsewhere as well, from the line of pigs staked out for all formal prestations to now-defunct dance forms in which dancers proceeded in a single-file circle around their drummers or else in parallel ranks.[10]

The special status of firstborn children is also condensed in the unique relationship they have with their fathers, to whom they are said to "belong" (*taubaguna tamana enana*, the firstborn is the father's). That is, they may inherit land from their father's matrilineage, although many people say also that this arrangement holds only for one generation, and the land reverts back to its original matrilineage upon the death of the firstborn who inherited it. This relationship contains as much potential for the mobility of a lineage as does virilocality, for in both cases the land available for inheritance or use is shifted from one location to another. In this respect, a firstborn child can truly be said to "lead" his or her siblings to a new home, should the option of inheritance from the father's matrilineage be invoked. It also creates additional tensions in a system of land tenure that is already fraught with ambiguities, as I shall demonstrate. The burden of firstborn children is to embody both principles of rootedness, in that they hold the knowledge of their lineage origins and authority over the disposal of their land, and rootlessness, in that they may or may not ultimately occupy and work this land. In the case of a firstborn woman, the issue is compounded by the fact that she may potentially claim identification with—and therefore rights of inheritance to—land belonging to her own lineage, to her father's lineage, to her husband's lineage, or all of these at different junctures in her life. Firstborns are *par excellence* the creators of new paths for their lineage to traverse, but they can only do so at appropriate points in the life cycle. Mobility is only considered suitable for certain people at certain times.

The moral valence of motion and stasis is primarily affected by two variables, which are age and gender. Their alternating emphasis at different stages in a person's life is perhaps the only reliable distinguishing trait of progress through the life cycle, for since the cessation of full-body tattooing of prepubescent girls in the 1930s, Suau people do not observe any rites of passage other than the funeral sequence. However, periods of enforced stillness have in the past accompanied certain transitions in an adult's social life, and these will be discussed shortly.

Until marriage, the ideal social image is one of stationary girls and mobile boys. Female children and unmarried young women (*hasala*) rarely leave their hamlets unaccompanied, and at night they are expected to stay in their houses: boys seeking romantic assignations must come to them, never the other way around. Girls only make journeys to other villages or the market at Alotau in groups and for specific purposes, never alone and never "going around for nothing" (*laulau gaibu*). Male children and unmarried young men (*hewali*), by contrast, are notoriously itinerant. Their whereabouts are sometimes unknown even to their parents; they move about freely at night socializing with young women and each other; they may hare off to Alotau or even Port Moresby on little more than a whim and an invitation from distant *wantoks*.[11] I was astonished to learn that my Leileiyafa host Saunia had, as a young bachelor, gone all the way to the Ok Tedi gold mine in Western Province for work. In spite of the fact that there was wage labor to be had closer to home, he said, he had wanted to travel, and agemates going to Ok Tedi had presented him with the opportunity. This wanderlust evidently ran in his family, for when I returned to Leileiyafa in 2008 I learned that his third daughter had also gone to Western Province to work for a timber company. The departure for other parts of the country in search of income and adventure had been established as a familiar pattern among Suau people before they marry and settle down; what made the case of Saunia's daughter novel was that a young woman had done it.

The fact that girls are expected to contribute toward "women's work" at a much younger age than boys will perform "men's work" is undeniably a factor in this scenario; it is also a fairly standard feature of subsistence economies. An adolescent girl who is looking after younger siblings, washing her family's clothes, and cooking the evening meal while her parents are in the garden simply does not have the time or opportunity to *laulau gaibu* that her male agemates do. However, it is not just the work but also the ideology surrounding the work that keeps girls near their homes, because with marriage this same domestic imperative means that they will in all likelihood relocate to their husbands' villages. While virilocality is not strictly observed by Suau people, it is the preferred arrangement cited by everyone I asked. And in the past when entire lineages co-resided and rules of exogamy were more assiduously observed, it meant that a young woman could expect to leave her natal hamlet more or less permanently upon marriage, when she would relocate to the hamlet of her husband's lineage. This practice is still reflected in the nicknaming of "foreign" women with the names of their villages of origin, as most people in their marital village will not belong to their lineages, and consequently they cannot be addressed by their given names but are subject to the practice of *geba*, respectful name avoidance.[12] In-married women from other places are therefore constantly reminded of both where they have come from and where they are now residing, as it is their status as outsiders that necessitates the nickname.

For young men, however, marriage represents a shift toward domesticity and a more serious expectation to participate in men's work, most notably for their parents-in-law.[13] This is not to say that they no longer travel, as this certainly happens up until they have had several children. By this time there is considerable garden work for them to do in order to support their family, they may have become involved in village politics or the church leadership, and they may also be growing cash crops such as coconut, cocoa, or oil palm or helping relatives to process their cash crops. Adulthood and marriage "root" men in their villages in an almost literal sense, as their attention is drawn toward activities that are linked with growing things: gardens, pigs, and houses, which continually decay and are rebuilt or altered according to the requirements of the family. Perhaps the most significant growing (in the transitive sense) done by men is the growing of their children, who consume the fruit of all the other labors cited, and whose health and well-being is read off as an index of the work and broader moral state of their fathers (Demian 2000).

Men's work, although it starts at a later age than that for women, is extremely specific in its parameters and moral weight. The most telling example of this was a man I met in Siasiada, a village about ten kilometers inland from Leileiyafa. He had formerly worked for the National Broadcasting Corporation in Port Moresby as a programming manager for their radio station, but he resigned when—according to him—an inexperienced *wantok* of the station director was promoted two levels above him. When I asked what he planned to do in the wake of his resignation, he smiled and said, "Plant my oil palm and my sweet potatoes; stay in the village. Some people go to the cities and don't come back until they're too old to work, they have no strength left, and I didn't want to do that." What I heard in this remark was the implication that urban employment, particularly the sort of white-collar job he had had, did not count as work: gardening and perhaps cash cropping were the only work that merited consideration. Both of these are of course related to the use of one's own land. I remarked that his had been the sort of lifestyle that many young villagers dream about having. He acknowledged that this was true, that villagers always think about moving to the city and earning money, while during his time in the city all he could think about was returning to his village. Although he worked at a job with high prestige in Port Moresby, the fact that this took place far from home and that his work bore no relationship to his own land severely diminished its "village" status as work and, consequently, his own status as a responsible adult. Neither of these value systems is unambivalent, of course—otherwise, he might never have left the village in the first place. As Rachel E. Smith (2018) has also observed for returned seasonal workers in Vanuatu, the channeling of wages earned elsewhere into village housebuilding and similar "retirement" plans has multiple layers of significance with different and sometimes conflicting moral implications. Returning to the village to build a house and engage in cash cropping can be read as a morally laudable commitment to one's family and to the local economy. It can also be seen as an audacious and even aggressive assertion of a land claim.

While the return of the programming director to Siasiada was dramatic in its scope, it was not at all unusual in its content; this man was one of several I knew who had left his village for waged employment in a town, a mine, or a plantation and returned eventually to build a house and garden in the village. The rootedness of adult men in their villages is a compelling ideological imperative, although, as with women, what can be identified as "their" villages is debatable. They may claim belonging to their natal village, the village of their lineage if this is different, or occasionally even their wife's village, as was the case of one oil palm plantation supervisor who entered into a land dispute at Leileiyafa on behalf of his wife and children. They won, because their claim could be traced directly to a matrilineal ancestress, whereas the incumbent occupant of the land in question had claimed it via the rule of patrilateral primogeniture. It was, arguably, a case of one type of "rank" or precedence against another: birth order versus the immutability of matrilineal inheritance.

I should note that it is not only men whose ideal work resides in the village and garden, although my research suggests this ideal may serve to anchor men more than it does women. The sentiments of the former programming manager had been prefigured some months earlier by a discussion among older women disparaging the kinds of "work" taught to girls at school. "They learn A-B-C, come home and cut a little grass, and they think that's work!" one woman had exclaimed with equal parts hilarity and disgust. The caricature of the young person who has neither enough education to seek employment in Alotau or further afield nor the knowledge and fortitude to do proper garden work haunts the imaginations of Suau parents struggling to balance the cost of sending children to school against the risk that they will acquire nothing of use to their families. By contrast, a child who stays out of school, remains in the village, and becomes skilled at gardening can at least be counted on as a future provider. "He's really industrious!" my hosts' daughter Marie exclaimed as a young man, the son of a neighbor, returned from his garden one afternoon in 2008. "That's good," her aunt remarked. "He'll get married and all the things in his garden will be ready." The word Marie used that I have glossed as "industrious," *taubiga*, also carries connotations of nurturance and husbandry in the agricultural sense—but her aunt clearly saw it as a sign of his future potential as true "husband material," as a man who excels in caring for his garden is a man understood to take all his familial responsibilities seriously. It is also the sign of a maturing young man who has stopped roving around and is in the process of anchoring himself to a place, and to a future wife and children.

Such elaborations of stillness and motion at the individual level are the most visible or accessible manifestations of the movement of lineages. It is as though they are a part of submerged processes that protrude into everyday life in the form of moral constraints upon men and women, deference to senior siblings and affines, and occasional, radical cessation of activity as is still the case during the sequence of mortuary events described in chapter 2. But these processes are by and large invisible (or camouflaged) to an ignorant observer, because they are literally embedded in the landscape as "natural" features. It is important to note here that "land" and "landscape" are not necessarily discrete concepts when talking about their use by Suau people, since both the meaning and value of land are derived or interpreted from its physical features. These include living people and the alterations they make to the landscape: houses, paths, gardens, graves, and plantations. For example, on a long walk to the hamlet of Filawan from Leileiyafa in 1999, I was guided by Tawa, the then twelve-year-old nephew of my hosts. Tawa gave a running commentary as we traversed significant features of the landscape by means of a bush track:

> This is a garden road. Bubu's [a generic term for grandparent] garden. You hear those people's voices? They're in their new garden up there. That's Cecily's new road. This old road is bad. That's the way we came before. We'll take the upper road; the lower road is muddy. That's the road to the flying fox cave [followed by an extended account of his adventures there]. These are our betel nut palms. Polo planted them . . .

And so on. The reference to Polo had precisely the effect it was meant to: I was saddened as I regarded the trees in question. To our even younger walking companion, the pastor's son, Tawa pointed out other features relevant to a seven-year-old: a bird's nest, wild foods to snack on, betel pepper with no ownership sign (*katilipu*) on it, that is, fair game for anyone who wanted to pick some.[14] In his commentary on the route from Leileiyafa to Filawan, Tawa was demonstrating explicitly for his foreign guest the knowledge that most Suau people carry implicitly: that the landscape is saturated with human actions and human intentionality.

Furthermore, all these human actions and intentions—not to mention the actions and intentions of nonhumans—remain features of the landscape long after the people who shaped it have gone. And the further back in time one goes, the more dramatic the alterations wrought upon the land are reckoned to be: ancestral actions are marked not by paths, gardens, and fruiting trees but by springs, rivers, caves, and islands. Because the activities of ancestors were understood to modify permanently the geography they traveled through, there is no reason not to assume that contemporary people are included in this conceptual sequence of land changers. Both the moving-through and the staying-in-place of people has effects upon the land, and many of these effects remain visible long after the people have gone.

Suau people also deliberately inscribe their presence on the landscape (see Tilley 1994) so that they will be remembered for having been there. Usually this takes the form of planting desirable trees such as coconut, betel nut (areca), and mango, but it might also involve cutting a new track between hamlets (as Tawa's cousin Cecily had done), widening the clearing of an existing hamlet, and the periodic clearing and burning off of new gardens characteristic of swidden horticulture. These are all logical extensions of the ideologies discussed in this chapter, because there is nothing so effective as a mark left on the landscape to "fix," albeit only temporarily, the uncertainty of one's ultimate destination as a husband or wife.[15] Visual signs of human presence such as fruit trees, old house posts, and gardens reverted to bush are a record of people's residence in and passage through an area, often in the absence of any other kind of "recorded" history—which is to say, these signs on the landscape are the historical record. The marking of human movement across the land is thus also an assertion of human temporality. The names of lineages are sometimes all that remains to commemorate sites no longer occupied by people.

The ephemeral nature of the human lifespan and its relationship to historical events points to particular ways of regarding the effect of lived time on the landscape and its intrusion into later epochs, even in the absence of a physical memorial. Take, for example, the case of ancestral origin houses in East Timor, many of which were obliterated during the period of Indonesian occupation (Bovensiepen 2014). In some parts of the country, these origin houses are asserted to be still present in the landscape in spite of the physical absence of the houses themselves: "The houses never stopped being there; the houses were there but one could not see them. Thus, a house does not cease to exist when the edifice is destroyed" (2014: 295). However, the Idaté speakers with whom Bovensiepen worked also felt it imperative to rebuild the destroyed origin houses, "mediating the tension between the radical historical transformations that had taken place in the country and the need to maintain the view that these houses endure in an unchanging way through time" (2014: 295). East Timor is an extreme example of the quintessentially (not to say stereotypically) Austronesian preoccupation with rooting or anchoring lineages in the landscape and of the duties incumbent on the living to take care of the dead. There are few other recent examples of disruption to lived time in the Austronesian ecumene on such a cataclysmic scale, except perhaps for the ten-year civil war on the island of Bougainville. But the very extremity of the Timorese context indicates the capacity for the potency of land and its ancestral inhabitants to continue to animate the relationship between living generations and their land, even after they have been forcibly removed from it. What differs is how people engage with these ancestral capacities, and what powers they are felt to hold over the living.

Many Suau lineages were also, of course, moved off their land during the colonial era, albeit without the violence of the more recent Timorese experience. Perhaps far more significant was the Protestant cosmology of a complete break with history that Suau people embraced, in contrast with Timorese people's conversion to Catholicism, which for them was an additive rather than epoch-defining spiritual process (Bovensiepen 2009). But even though the ancestral and nonhuman potency of land has become somewhat quarantined to particular sites, as I will show later, Suau nonetheless retain conceptions of emplaced ancestors and other nonhuman agents, who in stories are rooted to the sites of their activities by powers both human and nonhuman in origin.[16] These ancestral figures appear as "natural" features in the landscape rather than "artificial" structures such as houses, although as Bovensiepen's Timorese material suggests, the line between what constitutes a natural and an artificial feature of the landscape is ambiguous at best and at worst an entirely inappropriate set of categories to impose upon the Austronesian milieu. Ancestral alterations to the land in Suau are sometimes portrayed as unintentional and at other times deliberate, but their own eventual merging with it means their emplaced names are remembered now as a record of ancient itineraries and era-changing discoveries.

Marking Time

> Once there was a woman named Hinaumasali, and her village was called Anauli. She was the chief cook in her village, and when everybody else went to the garden, she would peel their taro, sweet potato, and other foods and simply dry them in the sun. But her own food she cooked: she would make the fire with magical substance from her armpits and put it under her cooking pot.
>
> This went on for some time until one day, a piece of Hinaumasali's food got mixed in with the other people's food by accident. A man tasted it and said, "This is really nice!" He shared it around to show the others how good it was. So they had a meeting and decided one man, Tauleletauhoina, should hide and see what Hinaumasali was doing to make her food taste different. He hid in her net, and he saw her take the magic from her armpit and put it under the cooking pot.

So he reported to the others when they returned; they decided that Tauleletauhoina and a second man, Taukulukalakala, should hide in her net the next day and try to steal some of the fire. They did this. When everyone else went pig-netting or to the garden, these two men hid and they stole the fire. Hinaumasali saw them running away and she ran after them, calling, "Bring that back, it's mine!" But they kept going. She called out, "If you bring it back, I'll teach you how to make the fire!" They kept going. She called out, "If you bring it back I'll teach you how to find springs in the ground for your water!" They still kept running, and by this time the fire was burning their hands so they had to pass it back and forth between them. But finally they dropped it, setting some kunai grass ablaze. People from far away saw the smoke and wondered what it was, as they had never seen smoke before. The two men called out to Hinaumasali, "Go down to that stream there and you'll be safe from the fire!" She did, and in the middle of the stream, she turned into a stone. She called up to the men, "Go to the top of that hill and you'll be safe!" They did, and they also turned into stones. All those stones remain there still.

—Told by Elia Seromai, 1997

Sometimes I think this place has no history.

—Author's field journal entry, March 1996

The cliché that the easiest way to hide something is to place it in plain view is nowhere more evident than during first-time fieldwork. I was, at the time of writing the above words, in despair over the apparent shortness of memory evident in Leilieyafa. The rigid—to me—categories of "before" (*beabeana*) or "the olden times" (*huyahuya yai*) and "now" or "today" (*aho te*) seemed to preclude any discussion of past events as having a relationship to contemporary concerns. Whole areas of knowledge and even objects were consigned to "before": competitive feasting, ancestor accounts, cannibalism, songs and dances, residence patterns, gardening magic, architecture, tattooing, shell and stone valuables. If I wanted to know about any of these, I was sent to the most senior residents of the village even if some of the institutions in question had only ceased to be viable a decade previously.[17] Legends occurred at an indeterminate point in the past, as one would expect them to, but then so did translocal events such as World War II and Papua New Guinea's independence in 1975. The latter was at least celebrated every year on 16 September so that it could be "remembered" in a formalized way. The anniversary of the arrival of James Chalmers in 1877 was also commemorated. But the main point emphasized by my interlocutors about most things that occurred "before" the present era was that they had been *forgotten*. I initially took this to mean that when a period of time and the events it framed had ended, they simply vanished over some kind of temporal-cognitive horizon, hence my disorienting initial sense of there being "no history" in Leileiyafa or its environs.

This was of course not the case, but it was some time before I could discern a Suau sense of history because it was located not in oral accounts of the past but in the landscape itself. Oral history provides a certain amount of interpretation, as in the story related above, but one suspects it is as much "about" the appearance of the landscape near Anauli as it is about the original theft of fire-making knowledge. Not only did the principal players in the story end up as specific geographical features but one of them, Taukulukalakala ("Scabby-head"), also lends his name to a type of very knobbly eroded limestone found throughout the region. The introduction of new knowledge in this story (using fire to cook food) is accompanied by a minor disaster (a bushfire) that announces, by means of the smoke it produces, that what was previously a secret is no longer one. The "marks" left on the landscape by the petrified protagonists document the sequence of events and fix them in memory. The relationship between the past and the present is evidenced by the fact that while the events themselves happened "time out of mind," the actors in these events are *still there*. The transformation of people into stones concretizes, as it were, the transformation of historical events into current knowledge. A landscape is a map of the past.

McDowell (1985) also suggests a trope of metamorphosis in the temporal scheme of Bun in the East Sepik Province of Papua New Guinea. She uses Gellner's concept of episodic time to provide an exegesis of the radical distinction made between past and present dispensations by Bun people, such that the transformation of one kind of time into another also entails the transformation of one kind of person into another. There can therefore be no possible relationship between them. What is interesting about this account is that McDowell also embraces Gellner's image of episodic time as "a train crossing a featureless landscape" (Gellner 1964: 1, cited in McDowell 1985: 29), temporal movement that is nonetheless dissociated from incremental change. Gellner's choice of metaphors, and McDowell's use of it, are significant. Such a formulation for episodic time may indeed resonate in Bun and other Yuat River societies, but it does not in Milne Bay Province, where the most salient point of the passage of time (and the passage of people through time) is that the landscape changes. What appears at first to be all-consuming, all-transforming episodic time is revealed, with the accumulation of stories about a given place, to be something rather subtler.

Rather than "episodes," Suau time may be perceived or rendered as "epochs." While both exhibit what Greenhouse (1996) has called "the dense concentration of agency" (1996: 88) characteristic of so-called "timeless" societies, the difference lies in the effect produced by this agency. Greenhouse is concerned with how "agency is thought, shown, or claimed to animate the social universe" (1996: 105), and how its effects are registered as different temporal perceptions. Taking her cue from Lévi-Strauss, she argues that the relationship between "before" and "after" contains the effect produced by these temporal categories. I would extrapolate from this to suggest that in episodic time, the effect may be located in the obliteration of all that passed "before," whereas epochal time accords an equally "real" status to both "before" and "after" but imputes a different perceptual quality to each. On the Suau Coast, "before" is anchored to the landscape, immobilized and "finished"; "now" is life-in-process, mobile, actively and avidly affecting the land upon which it is lived. Each of these epochs contains the seed of the other, for the immobile evidence of what happened "before" bespeaks the potential to create such lasting monuments in the activities of daily life "now."

Stories such as the one I have cited above, in which protagonists end up as stones or even more significant features of the landscape, are extremely common throughout Melanesia. Kahn (1990) provides ample documentation of this phenomenon, as well as what was at the time a long-overdue plea for more attention to the historicity embedded in this anthropomorphic geography. Her own exploration of people-into-stones myths on the north coast of mainland Milne Bay Province leads her to perceive stories encoded in the landscape as evidence of the movement of time:

> The past is often anchored to recognized, tangible, and named forms in the landscape. In rendering geography sacred, people are able to reap the harvest of the historical landscape in their contemporary lives. Geographical features are instrumental as sources of living tradition that inform, modify, and are modified by ongoing relations. Moreover, such physical markers of the past may serve as mnemonic devices for individuals and groups, thus helping to establish their identity. These landmarks then have two functions; they mark the ancestral itinerary, and they serve as a physical memorial. (1990: 52)

This is the case not only for mythological stories, she argues, but also for everyday accounts whose grounding in a particular and familiar site lends them a veracity they might otherwise lack (1990: 60). Because the listeners have presumably seen the surroundings to which the speaker refers, the visual cue of the story's location provides a certain amount of proof against suspicion of trickery. Places and the events that transpire in them are inextricably associated by virtue of the privileging of visual knowledge. The "ongoing relations" Kahn mentions are not only those between people but those between people and the landscape they inhabit—which is, in turn, associated with people of the past.

As far as establishing a spatially located identity is concerned, Kahn notes the tendency of people in Milne Bay to greet each other with questions along the lines of, "Where are you going?" (1990: 62). To this I would add the Suau practice of using shibboleths to ask this question, which immediately identify the speaker as belonging to a particular dialect group, a practice identified elsewhere in PNG as one of lexical play with concepts of ancestral origin and relationship-extending exchange (Slotta 2012). For Suau and its hinterland, to ask "Ai somo?" indicates a Buhutu or Leileiyafa speaker; "U lau saha?" indicates a Daui speaker; variations on this "Where to?" greeting continue to shift accordingly as one proceeds eastward along the coast. For speakers of Suau and its constituent dialects, as for many other Papua New Guineans, language itself is rooted in particular locales and their accompanying ancestral histories. Within any given place on the Suau Coast—but especially dialect-boundary-straddling ones like Leileiyafa—residents of different hamlets may use different interrogative idioms, which identifies their lineage origins. This is sometimes complicated by the fact that place names can become divorced from their dialects, however. When a woman relocates during marriage, her children and grandchildren will probably speak the dialect of their new home rather than that of her lineage, but they will nonetheless be identified with the original place, even if they have never been there. Potentially, with the passage of time only the names and stories of lineage origins will remain to mark the place where the ancestors of an *ulutubu* once dwelled.

Tauhou and the Ancestral Landscape

About an hour's walk inland from the coastal village of Isuʻae is a limestone cave. The cave is the one-time home of Tauhou, a preeminent culture hero in the Suau mythic repertoire. Formations in the cave are identified as Tauhou's pig-net, drum, and chair, and the rooms of his two wives. An old-fashioned clay cooking pot is wedged into a corner of one of the chambers, the limestone grown around it. The cave is also filled with graffiti; every provincial high school student and Peace Corps volunteer to visit has left their name behind them. During my own visit to the cave, I asked a woman of the lineage on whose land it is located whether any respectful procedures had to be observed before entering. She said in the past this would certainly have been necessary, but since missionaries prayed over it decades before, its potency or "heat" (*gigiboli*) has dissipated. Nevertheless, her daughter told me, the cave remains immaculately clean, as though someone were still sweeping it every day.

Tauhou is, like other Milne Bay culture heroes of ambiguous moral status (Young 1983b, 1984), also ambiguously human, born of a pig or a witch. He is white skinned, white haired, and possessed of extraordinary magical pow-

Figure 4.1. Cousins Margaret Sunday and Ken Ah Chee in Tauhou's cave, Isuʻae, 1999. Behind them is an old-fashioned clay pot wedged into the wall with the limestone grown around it. Photo by the author.

ers and charisma. His exploits are characterized by mutual deception between Tauhou and the communities he visits, a tendency to assume different skins or change into various animals, and a voracious sexual appetite. Like all good tricksters, he is credited not only with wreaking mayhem but also with introducing discoveries such as betel pepper, sago, certain freshwater springs, and in some stories, the substitution of pigs for people at feasts. In the course of his travels he is said to have created many of the islands along the southern coast of Milne Bay Province, when the speed of his magically propelled canoe severed them from the main land mass. After his death at the hands of sorcerers in the Sagarai Valley, he turned to stone and sank to the bottom of a river, where he remains to this day.

Tauhou's strange appearance and physical mutability render him both fascinating and frightening to each of the places he visits; what makes him monstrous also makes him heroic and enduringly compelling to the contemporary Milne Bay imagination. Milne Bay elites in Port Moresby wrote about him during the era of PNG's independence; one posited him as an indigenous answer to Jesus (Anere 1979), while another compiled—and, in the grand tradition of nationalist folklore everywhere, made additions to—a collection of Tauhou stories from various localities around the south coast of the province in a publication called *The Epic of Tauhau* (Kaniku 1975).[18] This epic reproduces the space of "home" using writing to recall the landscape, complete with a map illustrating Tauhou's journey from one end of southern Milne Bay Province to the other. The intended effect of the epic appears to be not unlike that described by an urban Trobriand Islander remarking on the "importation" of the yam harvest festival to Port Moresby: "You've lifted the land and brought it here" (Battaglia 1995: 80). In a part of the world where land in general and gardens in particular act as a reflection (that is, an externalization) of the gardener's internal (that is, moral) state, "lifting the land" implies far more than re-emplacement of displaced persons. Lifting land or recalling the landscape serves to extend a rhetorically displaced perspective back to its putative source in order to facilitate self-reflection (1995: 93). It allows the activation of an aesthetic assessment of relationships that would not be possible, or would not be possible in the idioms of "home," without the reflexive agency of the land from which both contemporary human and past heroic efforts can be read.

Younger Suau people sometimes say that they did not believe the Tauhou stories until they visited some feature of the landscape with which he is associated—a spring, a cave, a rock formation on a riverbed. Their accounts of conversion from unbelief to belief follows a common distinction in Suau assessments of news and stories: did the teller see the events described?[19] If not, belief is suspended until the hearers can at least witness the effects of these events for themselves. The mark of Tauhou's presence is not "evidence" in the sense of an effect that may be associated with other, visible effects in a chain of causality, but rather it has to do with the weight added to a story by witnessing the story's remains, its impact on the physical world. Just as lineage history accounts take the form of a topogeny that can be indexed to existing geographical locations, the history of Tauhou's exploits can in one sense be read off the landscape. The past is anchored in place, literally, by the physical manifestations of its effects. If it were not, it would become dangerous: people would have to keep it constantly in mind, dragging at their imaginations and feelings. This psychic weight, in turn, would obstruct the possibility of future-oriented practice because of the absurdity of attention focused on relationships (with the dead, with the mythic past) that literally have no future.

Battaglia (1993) has employed the Freudian concept of screen memories to describe the process by which Melanesians and others use ritual protocols to forget—that is, to suppress or unselect *deliberately*—those relationships whose foregrounding in memory would be disruptive to the potential for future action. People seek control over memory and forgetting, she argues, as a mode of future-oriented action, of leaving behind relationships that might impose an emotional and psychological burden on the present:

> They gain this control within an ever-changing field of historical contingencies, political realities, and the like. And it occurs to the extent they are able to recognize and participate in influencing the cultural process of things—or social histories of relationship—falling apart. They also gain an experience of control only to the extent that they are able to fill the vacuum created in eliminating not merely the cognition, but the active force of the unreleased energy of the memory confronted. Within these terms, *control inheres in acts of relinquishing it as an admitted purpose.* (1993: 433, emphasis in original)

It is important to note that the control sought in this case refers not to the domination of a subject over other subjects but to the deliberate backgrounding of particular relationships. A successful "screen" is not one that obliterates referents to the past but one that contains them, and it is in the process of containment that temporality is phenomenally encountered. For Suau, lineage histories, ancestors, and heroes from "the old times" (*huyahuya yai*) are all fixed in place so that they will not be lost. They are also fixed in place in order to be got out of the way. If living people had to constantly walk around with the memory of all the events and people that had gone before them encumbering their thoughts and feelings,[20] they would be obstructed from generating new relations with each other and with the world around them. They would, in other words, be lost in time.

Toren (1995) suggests one of the modes in which people prevent them-selves from becoming "lost" in this way. Drawing on the grounding of ances-tral efficacy in the Fijian landscape, she observes that

> the transformational potential inherent in the awareness of "time em-placed" renders the ancestral past not as a frozen, timeless, mythical domain, but as historical and dynamic. And even as this dynamic past continues to inform the dynamic present, the changes wrought in the present are made integral to the land, and the present comes to over-lap, becomes as it were continuous with, that ancestral past. (1995: 164)

While Toren's notion of the dynamism of the past and Battaglia's notion of its containment may appear at first glance to be mutually contradictory, it is worth stating again that both anthropologists worked in Austronesian socio-cultural contexts. With this in mind, it becomes possible to see how these two concepts—the landscape as that which anchors time and also as that which continually revitalizes it—are *complementary aspects of the same complex of values emplaced in the land.* The mobility of people, and their capacity to seek out new forms of spiritual and economic action, is a direct outcome of the containment of the past by the land.

The actions of ancestors and their effects on the land and its resources also express this concurrent capacity for emplacement and forgetting. The actions of ancestral figures, and the people and places upon whom they exerted their efficacy, are a direct result of their emplacement in the landscape and con-sequent "bringing under the control" (in Battaglia's formulation) of current and future generations. Such ancestor figures also derive their efficacy from their uncertain humanity, itself a problem resolved through solidification into a feature of the land. Tauhou belongs to no place, travels through many places, and in the end is only compelled to remain in one place by age, illness, death, and petrification. He manages to belong to no people and yet leave his name behind with nearly all people in the region. There is even evidence that he was at one time appealed to as a spiritual agency that could be induced to take an interest in human affairs (Cooper 1970: 108). In Kaniku's version of the myth, Tauhou becomes increasingly disoriented as he visits places that remind him of his origins in the Tawala-speaking part of Milne Bay due to his recogni-tion of taro cultivation styles, women's tattoos, and houses. In Tauhou's eyes, distance becomes collapsed by the appearance of signs of home, and the dif-ferences between the peoples he has visited are elided. He ultimately belongs everywhere.

It is a compelling thought, and one that arises peculiarly from the na-ture of Kaniku's text. Kaniku's title for his collection of stories is apt; indeed, when all the different regional accounts about Tauhou are laid end to end, so to speak, his life takes on Ulyssean proportions.[21] The key issue is that his text is a collection of stories from different parts of the southern mainland of Milne Bay Province and not the reproduction of a unified story that was ever recited or otherwise recounted in epic form. It is entirely probable that no one village or language group in this region ever knew "all" the Tauhou stories or produced them with the Western-style narrative continuity that Kaniku did. Kaniku created an epic of heroism, occasionally shading into soft pornography—it was the 1970s after all—based on a selection of the Tauhou legends. But is it an account *of* Tauhou?

I would argue that in one important respect, it is. Kaniku constructs a linguistic and geographical map of the Suau region and beyond by means of a sequence of stories grounded in actual, physical locations. While Tauhou's lifespan does not exactly follow the normal stages of development (he is born fully grown), Kaniku plots out sequentially a youth in the Tawala-speaking region, middle age along the Suau Coast, and dotage in the Sagarai Valley: because by traveling through space, he must also have been traveling through time. An epic narrative structure is made possible precisely because the various Tauhou stories come from different places, and in the act of compiling and synthesizing them, Kaniku generates a spatial image of these places. This in turn drives the narrative's temporal movement. The flow of time is made manifest by the physical journey, which in turn is rendered "true" by the appearance of different people, different languages, different landmarks. Toward the end of this epic, Kaniku's Tauhou questions the reality of his travels because his surroundings *look like* home: the physical and social landscapes have not changed sufficiently for him to believe he has traveled the distance that he has. Tauhou, not unlike a disoriented anthropologist, is deceived by the attractiveness of his own story.

If it seems as though the problem of people's actions upon the landscape belongs solely to a mythic past, it may be useful to place a more contemporary conundrum alongside the life and times of Tauhou. The story with which I will conclude this chapter continues to unfold at the time of writing, and it illustrates both the dynamism and the emplacement of landscape in Suau people's reckoning of the consequences of their ancestors' actions, as well as their own actions in the present day. It also serves, alongside the continued if attenuated presence of Tauhou's actions in the mythic past, as a reminder that topogeny is informed by nonhuman as well as human agencies.

Like a number of Suau coastal villages, Isuisu has water problems. Among the many considerations that did not enter into Mr. Vivian's decision to relocate inland settlements to Mullins Harbour and to the coast was the fact that water supplies are far more reliable in the hinterland mountains, abundant with rivers and streams. In Isuisu, rainwater is collected in concrete or fiberglass tanks during the wet season (May to August) and available as the rains taper off in the intervening months, until about halfway through the dry season (November to May). Then the tanks run out, and villagers must wash their clothes, dishes, and bodies in the brackish water drawn from shallow wells, and walk several hours inland to collect good river water for cooking and drinking.

A solution to this problem is available, and my host Mamari along with other village leaders have long sought provincial funding for a pipeline to be built from the inland Bomtoha River down to Isuisu, Saga'aho, and several smaller coastal communities. During fieldwork in Isuisu in 2008 I asked to see the river, and so Mamari arranged a day's expedition. I went with Mamari, his then-teenaged daughter Marie, and two members of the river's stewarding lineage, Kingsley and Leisi. The walk was long and tiring, over uneven ground and sometimes no ground at all, with the five of us clambering over and balancing our way along the trunks and branches of trees that had been felled to make a new garden. As we approached the river, hearing it long before we saw it in the dense bush, Kingsley and Leisi at times asked us to speak in low voices, or not to talk at all, and absolutely not to laugh.

Finally we arrived at the river, a splendid cataract down a steep series of terraced limestone pools. Before we emerged from the bush to view the river, Kingsley asked us to wait. He went ahead, and appeared to speak to the air for a few minutes. Then he returned and said it was all right for us to approach the river and drink its water. "Who was he talking to?" I asked Marie. "*Kokome*," she replied—the little people. Marie went on to tell me that Kingsley had spent the latter part of the walk pointing out these people's miniature resources to her: dwarf areca palms for their betel nut, tree boughs for their houses. And we had been asked to keep our voices low in order not to offend them. Marie said it was unusual to encounter a place where *kokome* still lived, as I was already aware from what other people had told me on previous visits. Formerly, of course, *kokome* had lived cheek by jowl with human beings, and interactions with them were frequent. "That was before when we were in darkness, when we didn't know about Jesus," Marie said. "Since the light came, they don't live here anymore."

But they still live at Bomtoha River. We spent an hour or two resting, eating the lunch we had brought, and drinking the ice-cold and beautifully pure, if somewhat chalky, water. Marie went with the river's owners to see a higher and deeper pool that might someday be used as a reservoir for the proposed pipeline. She came back awed, saying she had never seen so much good fresh water in one place. Before we left, Marie placed an uneaten bun from our lunch on a rock by the pool where we had sat, saying it was a gift for the *ko-kome*. "They'll be very happy about that," Kingsley told her with a twinkle. He also said they had bid us farewell when we left the river.

Bomtoha River is a place of ramifying temporal potential. Beautiful and valuable, it is also in a sufficiently remote location to serve as a refuge for spirit people who have for the most part withdrawn from relations with human people. This withdrawal was attributed by my young friend to the turning of human attention away from them, and toward relations with Jesus and the Christian God instead, and her attribution was one shared by a number of Suau friends. As such, the river belongs to a past in which humans and *kokome* coexisted and interacted. Elsewhere in this past are the exploits of Tauhou and the other elements of deep mythic history that gave rise to the identification of people with each other by means of a *sulu* totem. Although none of these elements of Suau history have literally disappeared, given that they persist as features of the landscape itself, their power continues to recede from the pre-occupations of contemporary people who have more pressing needs, such as a source of fresh water for a burgeoning population.

As the site of the potential water pipeline, the river's value extends into a possible future in which the western end of the Suau Coast would be supplied with potable water year round, and the *ulutubu* on whose land it lies might ask for royalties if the pipeline is built. But in the meantime, its human owners must continue to show respect to its spirit owners or else risk illness and misfortune visited upon their lineage. Should the remoteness of the river be breached by the pipeline, with the river physically connected up to *ko-kome*-free human villages miles away, will the *kokome* remain? Or will people say that they have moved further into the bush, as the isolation of their dwelling places increasingly parallels their isolation from relations with thoroughly Christian humans who rarely if ever have them in mind anymore?

These are an anthropologist's questions, of course, and unlikely to be foremost in the considerations of people who really do need a reliable, year-round source of safe drinking water. And because most Suau regard themselves as having broken utterly with the past, the problem of where the *kokome* might relocate will not be of utmost concern to them in the happy event of the pipeline's future construction. But I will offer the speculation that it might be of some concern to the *ulutubu* on whose land the pipeline would be built, if it is built: for it is their descendants who will look back on the actions of the ancestors and on the changes these actions have wrought upon the landscape and lives of people on the coast. The ramifications of potential alteration to the river extend not only into the future but also into the past, as any permanent alteration to the landscape is an alteration to memory and to the history that accounts for that memory.

Notes

1. This is the name of the coastal village of Saga'aho, rendered in the pronunciation of the Buhutu dialect now spoken by members of its *ulutubu* who have relocated inland. The F-H shift is probably the most common marker used by Suau-speakers to distinguish inland from coastal dialects. Tauyabuna's labialized consonants ("Bwabwatiti" instead of the Mullins Harbour pronunciation "Bobontiti") also mark him out as a Buhutu speaker.

2. More accurate glosses for *ulutubu* might be something like "origin" or "initiation point." The most literal gloss would verge on the overly abstract: "ancestral head." It is a collocation of two highly flexible and important lexemes, *ulu* (head) and *tubu* (ancestor, grandparent, fatness and vitality of a living body). Used with a causative prefix (*hatubu*), the latter term also means to begin or commence an activity. Taken together they connote the bodies of the living whose "head" or origin is coterminous with the bodies of the ancestors.

3. That they should want the tape is worthy of note. The normative version of the passing down of *ulutubu* accounts is that a senior member teaches it orally to one or more reliable successors. Young Suau people do not necessarily rely upon this method, either because they have not been taught the lineage history or because they recognize a potential value in additional methods of record keeping. Once I came across an adolescent girl, Dore, carefully recording an anthropological-type genealogy in her school notebook. I asked what it was, and she said, "My family. In case we have a problem [*pilipili*] with land." The Suau term for a problem or complication, *pilipili*, again literally means "entanglement," and the word is frequently employed as a euphemism for land and other major disputes, such as those over long-term debts or sorcery accusations.

4. The most distant *ulutubu* I identified in Leileiyafa, Dubunamwasiu, was said to have originated on Logea Island. Several *ulutubu* in coastal villages such as Isuisu originated on Wari Island or on Kolaiwe (pronounced 'Olaiwe in Suau) in the Engineer Group of islands.

5. Flying foxes (*malibon* or *maliboi*) are classified as birds in Suau taxonomy. The other *sulu* totems that people have identified for me at various times are green pigeon/fruit dove (*bunebune*), hornbill (*bina*), white cockatoo (*wadaheya*), sea eagle (*magesubu* or *madunali*), and wagtail (*kulokulo*).

6. There may still be exchange and trade networks in the Engineer Group or the Louisiade Archipelago, but to the best of my knowledge the mainland is no longer included in these networks.

7. It is perhaps worth mentioning here the linguistic identification of gardens with bush or inland locations. Suau speakers use two words interchangeably for their gardens: *gana*, which also means fence, and *oya*, which also means hill or mountain. The first term indexes the high log fences built around gardens to exclude pigs and the prying eyes of other people; the second term indexes the upland locations of many gardens—and in former times, many *ulutubu*.

8. See Young (1994: 265) for similar birth-order classification on Goodenough. Young labels this particular manifestation of hierarchy "normative rank," as it is constant and undisputable, unlike other Milne Bay hierarchies that obtain from strategic gift giving.

9. Suau teknonymy appends the name of the firstborn child—usually—to the appropriate parental kinship term. For example, my host in Leileiyafa, May, was addressed in the

local dialect as Buwowo Tinana, "Ginger's Mother," using a nickname (Buwowo) for their red-haired daughter Agula. This practice is somewhat negotiable in cases where the firstborn moves away or falls out with his or her parents. In these cases the parents will switch to using the name of a later child, often based on which name sounds the best with the parental terms. What remains constant is the teknonymy itself, the reflection of the child's name back onto the parent, obscuring the issue of whether identity emanates from the past or the future.

10. There is ample evidence of this spatial aesthetic throughout Milne Bay Province, particularly for presenting wealth, such as "paths" of stone axe blades in Sabarl mortuary prestations (Battaglia 1990) and of yams at festival exchanges on Goodenough (Young 1971: 235).

11. Tok Pisin "one talk," indicating a member of the same language or ethnic group and often the same village.

12. The requirements of *geba* can sometimes result in creative or comical efforts to avoid speaking words that even sound like the names of those to whom one is unrelated, and especially one's affines. My Isuisu host Baigayo had an in-law named Peggy, whose name was unfortunately homonymous with the Suauized English loanword for laundry pegs, *pegi*. So Baigayo resorted to calling laundry pegs *he'ahe'apudidi*, literally "hanger-uppers." Another acquaintance called an affine named Michael, as well as any other Michael he happened to encounter, "Somare" after Papua New Guinea's first prime minister, Michael Somare.

13. Some people told me that in former times there was a formal expectation of bride-service for young men following marriage, and although this is no longer observed to my knowledge, I did note that recently married men tended to spend an unusually high proportion of time looking after their wives' parents, repairing their houses, and working in their gardens.

14. A *katilipu* is most often simply a palm frond tied to the tree or forest crop that is claimed by someone: the trunk of an areca palm, for instance, or the thickest vine of a betel pepper. The absence of a *katilipu* means either that no one owns the resource in question or that if someone does, they do not mind if other people take fruit/nuts/leaves from it.

15. See, e.g., Battaglia (1993: 431), Küchler (1993: 99) for notions of "marks" or "traces" left behind by the deceased in other Austronesian Papua New Guinea societies. In New Ireland, where Küchler worked, eradicating the "marks" of a dead person's life (such as trees planted) constitutes part of the management of memory in mortuary practice. By contrast, Suau people are more likely to leave these "marks" intact in order to moor memory in one place.

16. This is not true throughout Milne Bay Province, however. Elsewhere on the Milne Bay mainland, some petrified ancestors elsewhere do still have an interest in, or at least an effect upon, the well-being of their descendants (Kahn 1996).

17. There is a striking example of this practice. I was told to ask the oldest man in Leileiyafa about *mata'asi* feasts, when later it transpired that anyone over the age of twenty during my 1990s fieldwork periods should have had some recollection of them, as *mata'asi* were still being held in the early 1980s (Young 1981: 35). As far as people in Isuisu were concerned, the last significant *mata'asi* in their vicinity was held sometime in the 1970s or 1980s.

18. The name of this hero varies with the dialect of the people referring to him. Kaniku, a Logea Islander, calls him Tauhau, as do speakers of Eastern Suau. In the Buhutu-speaking hinterland he is Taufwau, while among speakers of the Daui dialect on the western half of the coast he is Tauhou (see Cooper 1970). I employ the Daui pronunciation because my primary exposure to this mythic complex occurred during fieldwork in Daui-speaking villages.

19. A storyteller who suspects that people doubt the veracity of her news will insist, "Matagu yai!" (in my own eye!). That is, the teller saw things with their own eyes and is not repeating someone else's tale.

20. One Suau term, *nuwa-*, is used for both concepts. It takes an "inalienable" possessive affix, implying on one register that it is constitutive of persons, and can as easily refer to someone's state of health as it can their state of mind. See Mallett (2003: 124–26) for a discussion of this root, common among Milne Bay languages.

21. Probably a more appropriate comparison might be made with other "compiled" epics like the *Kalevala* and the *Mabinogion*, both of which were "discovered" in order to demonstrate that the nations from which they originated (Finland and Wales, respectively) produced epic poetry on a par with the Homeric tradition. Kaniku's aim in his collection appears to be similar.

Times Present, or,
"No Government Here"

Law has two parts: the church side and the government side.
—Eliot Sunday, village court peace officer,
at a village meeting in Isuisu, 1999

What do we need more laws for? We already have too many laws!
Don't do this, don't do that!   —A man at the same meeting

Five thousand years ago, the government was rocks, trees, mountains.
—Morris Towasae, land mediator at a dispute
in Duhumodawa, 1999

There is no government here. Only us: we are the government.
—Elika Mumu, village court magistrate, at the same dispute

In this chapter I take up the subject of law as one of the primary social orders that Suau people must negotiate in the postwar and postindependence world, and in particular as a social order by means of which some Suau feel their own forms of social organization must be understood. This is directly related to the subjects of the previous chapter, although it may not be immediately apparent. But how people on the Suau Coast think about land, how they think about the way their own relationships are organized in a formal sense, and how they think about "the law" are all implicated in each other. In turn, the law as a primary organizing principle of contemporary life—even, or especially, under the conditions of withdrawal by the Papua New Guinean state—continues to vex the Suau social imagination.

In its performative mode at village court and land mediation hearings as well as at village meetings and informal dispute-settling processes, law provides the arena in which Suau can communicate to each other their ongoing commitment to state forms of action and those sanctioned by the church as constituting part of the Christian life appropriately lived. In both cases, however, I argue that relationships with church and state constitute a part of the Suau social imaginary, as these institutions are brought into being by means of the performative mode rather than through any efficacious communication between the Suau Coast and the "real" institutional entities that might be imagined to encompass it. The infrastructural decline experienced by Suau since World War II has meant that neither church nor state can "see" the attention paid to them by Suau people and their institutional pursuits. In chapter 3 I addressed the role of the church in Suau history and contemporary life; in this chapter, I propose to ask whether Suau participation in the mechanisms of the law can be read as anything similar. Relations with the state are far more ambivalent for most Suau and do not carry the overwhelmingly positive set of associations that attend participation in church activities.

The Suau Coast is not remote, in a strictly geographical sense. But as in most rural Papua New Guinean locales, the state is functionally all but absent for Suau people. Schools and medical aid posts exist, but all are undersupplied with staff and materials and are frequently broken into. Depending on their village of residence, most children who attend school must either walk for a minimum of an hour to classes or board with relatives who live closer to the school. School costs are prohibitively high for rural families who do not have the support of *wantoks* working in the towns. And there is no guarantee that teachers who have gone home for the Christmas holidays will return to a job for which they are paid only sporadically, have insufficient teaching materials, and may have no linguistic or cultural connection to the communities in which they teach.

There was for many years a small police station at Fife Bay, but this was so chronically underresourced that most of my acquaintances disparaged the officers stationed there for using up what little dinghy fuel they had on obligations to kin and other *wantoks*, so that the local village courts no longer bothered to issue imprisonment orders that would never be enforced by police with no transportation. Finally, there is the Western Suau Local Level Government Council, also headquartered in Fife Bay. The council meets to discuss the maintenance of villages, aid posts, and public water tanks if there are any; to bring up "law and order" issues; to try to formulate infrastructural plans for their region; and nominally to liaise with other representatives of government interests. The councillors representing each ward (roughly encompassing a village and its satellite hamlets) frequently express frustration at the indifference or "wrongness" of the relationship between themselves and provincial and national government. Dan David, who in the late 1990s was councillor for Suau Island and the council president, once expressed this frustration in the following terms, when he and I were discussing the chronic problem of low stocks of medical supplies in village aid posts. According to Dan's model of aid post impoverishment, what happened was that medicines and other supplies started their journey in Port Moresby whence they were sent out to the provinces, then too much was used in Alotau before it was distributed to local health centers, and finally the scant remaining supplies would end up at the

Fife Bay medical center, which is why there was never any medicine in Fife Bay for distribution to village aid posts. What ought to happen, he told me, is that each of these levels of government should "top up" (his term, in English) the medicine stocks instead of depleting them further.

Dan David's account of the incorrect flow of resources from center to periphery is a classic example of Suau frustration with their relatively recent status as a periphery. It also illustrates Suau moral concerns with discovering what lies behind the failure of state resources to travel, grow, or otherwise proliferate in the way that wealth circulating through positive relationships is supposed to do. A relationship through which resources continually diminish is in a parlous condition indeed, one marked by animosity, greed, and perhaps even witchcraft, the archetype of human beings acting as though they were not human. In other words, empty aid posts and locked-up schools are sometimes read not just as indifference or incompetence on the part of the state but as active state contempt for relationships with rural people that, in the view of many such people, ought instead to be nurtured. In light of this perceived hostility, the question arises as to what Suau people think they are doing when they invoke the name of law and engage with the mechanisms by means of which the law most explicitly appears, such as village courts and land mediations.

The Origins of Law

One could claim that the presence—or more accurately, the visibility—of law stems from Suau experiences of the colonial era, with the surveillance of Australian patrol officers, the relocation of people from the mountains to the coast to expedite this surveillance, the jailing of murderers, sorcerers, and cargo prophets, and significantly the performative disavowal of old practices demanded by European and Polynesian missionaries. The influence of these experiences is undeniable, yet I also submit that they would not have taken hold of the Suau imagination in the way that they did if there was not a complementary set of knowledge practices to do with visibility and rectification on the part of Suau people themselves. Law could only be apprehended as a capacity of the state in the first place because it was apprehended as something Suau people already had, and in this important sense the state is superfluous when it comes to the operations of law.

In fact, the state and its popularly perceived insistence on a *code of conduct* may not even be welcome in Suau understandings of law and its purpose. The most common gloss for "law" in Suau is *laugagayo*. But *laugagayo* connotes moral instruction largely in the form of proscription: don't do this, don't do that. Which is why, at the meeting in Isuisu in which Eliot Sunday said that the law had both a church component and a state component, he then went on to suggest that Isuisu ought to have some laws of its own, and was angrily confronted with a portrayal of contemporary life as sufficiently constrained by "don'ts" and not in need of any more, thank you very much. The idea of law as proscription is expressed by Eliot's doubling of law's sources: the Church brought Nonconformist Protestant and Victorian prohibitions as well as the radical social and cultural interventions promulgated by LMS missionaries and the later Kwato experiment; the Australian administration brought patrols, the relocation of villages, policing, taxation, corvée labor, incarceration, and perhaps most significantly an end to local warfare. All of these factors served to make the law of the state appear primarily in a constraining or coercive form, expressed so succinctly in the objection to Eliot's proposal. The paternalistic view of law and government expressed by some missionaries and patrol officers, particularly in the early part of the twentieth century, has not much of a place in contemporary Suau imaginings of what purpose the law serves. And while the law administered these days by village courts carries some of the weight of proscription, it is far more oriented toward the reconfiguration of relationships than it is toward the punishment of transgression. Having said this, there is also some interest among Suau people in what kinds of transgressions really do merit punishment and what moral or spiritual basis there might be for doing so. In 2015 I spoke to a man in Isudau who was assisting with a new translation of the Bible into Suau, which would include, for the first time, the Old Testament. He was hard at work on a section of Leviticus when he said to me, "The law of Moses is a good law. We should have some of this law for ourselves." When I asked why, he noted how clear and uncompromising it was, and also that it appeared to come directly from God. The external sources of law lend it weight and attractiveness for many Suau, but they also sometimes generate tensions in relation to their own social forms, as I will demonstrate later in this chapter.

To appreciate how these tensions are produced, it is important to consider how "the law" in the sense of exogenous interests was reintroduced to rural people, including those on the Suau Coast, following the end of Australian territorial administration and the emergence of Papua New Guinean statehood. Prior to independence, patrol officers were almost the sole representatives of government interests to rural people: although they had delegated local authorities in the villages, on their patrols they embodied administrator, police, judge, and occasionally executioner all rolled into one (Gordon 1983; Sinclair 1984; Dinnen and Braithwaite 2009). With the dismantling of the patrol officer system, the eyes and ears of the state disappeared from the rural Papua New Guinean experience, replaced somewhat unpredictably and certainly unsatisfactorily by the visits of police, health workers, agricultural extension officers, and, during elections, campaigning politicians and polling officials. But none of these representatives of the government could really "stand for" the government in the way that the patrol officers had done, because they did not embody the law of the government. This was the void that village courts and land mediations were supposed to fill.

The intended purpose of the Village Courts Act 1973 was twofold: to provide legal access to rural people without the interference of lawyers, and to attempt to integrate the categories of "custom" and "law" (Scaglion 1990: 19) by creating a forum for the application of custom by local magistrates invested with state authority. Village courts were taken up very gradually throughout PNG in the period following the act, with the Suau region adopting them by 1990. This period also saw intense interest in village courts on the part of anthropologists and legal scholars, who had before them the opportunity to watch the unfolding in real time of an experiment in introducing local-level magistrates' courts to societies that had never had such institutions. As Lawrence (1969) observed of the perils of fashioning a legal system for PNG on the eve of the country's independence,

> This has proved to be the Achilles heel of decolonization . . . the attempt by the metropolitan power, as part of its programme to establish stable national autonomy, to leave behind its own legal system in a society which traditionally is in no way structured to assimilate it. This is a crucial issue because its outcome is usually an index of success or failure in the whole experiment of nation-building. (1969: 15)

The village courts were an attempt to rectify several problems. They were meant in part to replace the various paternalistic and race-based Native Ordinances of the Australian era, as well as the Local Courts Ordinance 1963–66, which was the beginning of the integration of the legal system to cover both European settlers and indigenous Papua New Guineans. They aimed, as stated earlier, to harmonize "imposed law" with "customary law." And they contributed to the project of nation-building, precisely because they would provide the mechanisms of a unitary legal system to rural people, with the actual content of these mechanisms to be determined by "customary" usage.

It was the latter provision that provoked some debate on the part of early observers of the emergent legal system in PNG, including the introduction of village courts. Several of these (Fitzpatrick 1980; Paliwala 1982; Scaglion 1990; Westermark 1986) observed a tendency on the part of village courts to adopt the physical trappings, hierarchical style, and legalism of higher or European-style courts. Before the Village Courts Act came into force, Strathern (1972) had noted that residents of Mount Hagen in Western Highlands Province were reluctant to draw much of a distinction between the then local courts and their own informal disputing processes, and that any introduced system of mediation (such as the village courts) was likely to be valued by

Figure 5.1. A village court hearing in Isuisu, 2015. *From left to right:* magistrates David Novau, David Kaisa, and Tau Mimino. Photo by the author.

Papua New Guineans for precisely the opposite reason it was valued by its European authors: "Mediation may be successful to a European because it is removed from a court context; to a Hagener it may be successful precisely because of its approximation to a court process" (1972: 137). In other words, and contrary to some predictions of the 1960s, many rural Papua New Guineans were quite prepared to appropriate the authority of the state, and to discover for themselves state forms in places that the state itself may not have intended.

There is nonetheless the unavoidable fact that magistrates are often called to "stand for" the state even, or especially, when the state is presumed to have absented itself from the local arena. A prime example is land disputes. Elika Mumu, the magistrate quoted at the opening of this chapter, attended the 1999 land dispute at the inland village of Duhumodawa largely as an interested observer and additional representative of state authority, but under the provisions of the Village Courts Act, village court magistrates cannot hear land disputes. These are instead the remit of land mediators, who do not have the power to adjudicate at all but only to act as repositories of the histories of landholding lineages and to reveal these histories when asked to do so in the context of a formal dispute. At the dispute in question, two village court magistrates were present and requested to make note of the proceedings (and, I suspected, to represent the interests of "law and order" in case the dispute got out of hand). Elika spoke before the hearing properly began to remind the disputants of the different functions of a village court case and a land mediation. His remark about the absence of the government was both an observation and an exhortation. On the one hand, he was reminding those present of the popularly perceived indifference of the state to rural Papua New Guineans, and of its functional invisibility. On the other, he was also asking his listeners to contemplate the necessity of settling their disputes themselves, without recourse either to the authority or to the more material resources of the state.

I propose to take Elika's remark seriously and ask what it means to operate a system of law in the perception that the state is ineffectual, indifferent, invisible, or otherwise understood to have removed itself from people's everyday lives. The underlying question is one of what we mean when we refer to law or legal mechanisms under the conditions of a "weak state." However, I want to attempt this discussion without recourse to the rhetoric of the failing state that has dogged popular discourse on politics in Papua New Guinea since the 1990s. An invisible state is not quite the same thing as a failing state, and the concerns of rural Papua New Guineans are not always convergent with those of Department of Foreign Affairs and Trade staff in Canberra. Elika's assertion was not novel, but it was part of an ongoing debate in Suau and indeed throughout much of rural Papua New Guinea about how to maintain institutions that are seen nominally to emanate from the state but enjoy no support from it. These institutions, from schools to police to hospitals, are valued by Suau people as indices of connection to the metropole, participation in some of its processes, and sharing in some portion of its wealth, however inadequate. But their reasons for valuing such institutions are not self-evident, and to ask what is the value of, say, village courts and land mediations is to ask how people create value for a nominally state-sanctioned institution when that putative source of value is so unreliable. To do so, the state must be preempted or obviated: we are the government here.

Another way to describe the problem is to say that it is about the limitations of the law as perceived by Suau people. But again I would stress that these limitations are not simply the result of international influences such as the structural adjustment programs imposed by donor agencies in the 1990s, national conundrums such as the ongoing issue of corruption among politicians, or whatever: they are imposed by Suau people themselves. Suau village courts are used to prosecute very specific types of cases, and among these, sorcery stands out as the only one easily recognizable as "customary" in that it is presumed to involve an attempt on the life of another person by magical means.[1]

The most serious of these cases are prosecuted following divinatory or other forensic procedures to discover the identity of a sorcerer responsible for a death or series of deaths in a given lineage, such as the *fafabou* process described in chapter 2. They are in this respect comparable to murder cases, although magistrates may also serve as mediators between the family of a sick individual and the sorcerer they believe to be causing the sickness, in which case the village court may be said to intervene before a "murder" has actually taken place.[2] Sorcery hearings are widely acknowledged by magistrates to be the thorniest and most exhausting kind to convene, but they are relatively infrequent. More often, a village court will be convened to hear such quotidian cases as unpaid bridewealth or other debts, destruction of property (a garden ravaged by someone's errant pig; a house damaged during a fight), adultery, domestic violence, "defamation of character," and other inflammatory language.

What all these cases have in common is that they are a public exhibit of relationships in a negative state. The village court is usually a last resort for such problems, coming after interventions by family members, the magistrate in his capacity as mediator, or the church pastor acting in a similar capacity. The task of the magistrate is to convert a negative or "skewed" relationship into a positive or "straight" one. Straightness (*dudulai*) is both an aesthetic and moral value in Suau ethics that can refer to a person's interior state, her relations with others, the material manifestations of such relations, or any combination of these. It may be contrasted with various undesirable states described as crooked (*gewagewa*), complicated (*pili*), or difficult/problematic (*pilipili*— really complicated). A crooked house, for example, may be read as evidence of discord between kin; I was once even told a story of a portable sawmill that would not cut straight boards because its owners had failed to reassure their ancestors that trees cut down on their land would only be used to saw timber for members of the landholding lineage. But perhaps the most elegant demonstration of the principle of straightness is a hand gesture sometimes used at, or in reference to, court hearings and other disputes. People in relations of concord can be represented with the hands placed palm to palm; in relations of discord, they are represented with the hands back to back. Straightness, then, refers not to the presence or absence of a relationship but to its moral and communicative state. A relationship that is not straight should be converted into a state of communication rather than stoppage. "Straightening" (*hadudulai*) can be informally achieved between people who have been angry with one another, typically by airing their grievances in the presence of a respected third party such as a village court magistrate, local level government councillor, or pastor, then saying a brief prayer together and shaking hands. These informal *hadudulai* meetings happen frequently and may not even require a third party to mediate them: a statement of contrition and a handshake may suffice.

The realization of straightness through the village court, however, is usually only achieved by the levying of compensation, which is a measurement of the gravity of the situation. So on one occasion when I had lost my temper with the eldest daughter of my Leileiyafa host family in the mid-1990s, her father told me with barely controlled exasperation, "If you don't *hadudulai* with her, then I have to take both of you to court. The magistrate will make you kill a pig for each other, and where are you going to get a pig?" His point was that I had no local relations to lend me a pig, no body of support on which I could rely, and therefore no grounds on which to continue my quarrel with his daughter. If one does not have the wherewithal to straighten a relationship gone awry, one had better tread carefully. This incident also impressed upon me that the threat of the village court is not necessarily used as a means of punishing bad behavior but one of bringing a skewed relationship back into alignment. Like their district court counterparts in the cities and towns of PNG, the village courts constitute a public forum to which grievances are brought in the hope of their rectification. But unlike the district courts, the village court operates without support or even much in the way of acknowledgment by the organs of the state (Goddard 2009; Demian 2014). The easy thing to say at this juncture would be that village courts reproduce the form of law but not the content. How can law be present when the state is looking the other way, so to speak? Instead, I would like to suggest that the social form constituted in the village court *is* the content, in the sense that as far as Suau are concerned this form is law, and that it is law because it does what law does. That is to say, it brings people and their complex relationships into a state of visibility and clarity (*ma-salaha*, "out in the open"), such that the complexity may be straightened, even if only temporarily.

Some of the village court magistrates I have spoken to have made reference to the notion that the desired outcome of a court sitting is not grounded in the law of proscription, so much as it is in the law of value in relationships. That is, the point is to find straightness not through the application of an abstract code of conduct emanating either from the church or the state but through the most expedient way to convert relations in a conflict into a state of concord rather than one of further strife. For example, after a village court hearing in 2015 for a young man accused of wrecking the water pipeline to the village of Siloa Pota and neighboring hamlets at the eastern end of the coast, the presiding magistrate told me his aim had been to keep the youth out of the district court in Alotau—where he "ought" to have been sent for destroying government property. But the destruction was part of a larger pattern of the young man's behavior, which was the real issue that had to be dealt with by the community. Also, the magistrate said, this lad spoke almost no English, had minimal experience of town life, and would not stand a chance in a formal court setting. He should not go to jail: he should stay at home and have his actions corrected by his family and the village as a whole.

So to describe straightness solely in terms of rules or even morals is to miss the point. Straightness as a component of the aesthetics of social relationships describes these relationships in their desired state and indexes other positively valued attributes of relationships such as their openness, visibility, and the unimpeded flow of their movement between persons, places, and lineages over time. Few if any Suau people would necessarily associate straightness with *laugagayo*, whose connotations of prohibition, stoppage, and in general the foreclosing of possible courses of action are not suggestive of any form of "law" that could be generative of positive relations.

Putting the Law in "Law and Order"

> Take the real savage, keen on evading his duties, swaggering and boastful when he has fulfilled them, and compare him with the anthropologist's dummy who slavishly follows custom and automatically obeys every regulation. There is not the remotest resemblance between the teachings of anthropology on this subject and the realities of native life. We begin to see how the dogma of mechanical obedience to law would prevent the field-worker from seeing the really relevant facts of primitive legal organization. We understand now that the rules of law, the rules with a definite binding obligation, stand out from the mere rules of custom. We can see also that civil law, consisting of positive ordinances, is much more developed than the body of mere prohibitions, and that a study of purely criminal law among savages misses the most important phenomena of their legal life.
> —Bronisław Malinowski, *Crime and Custom in Savage Society*, 1972

The "don't do this, don't do that" of law manifested as *laugagayo* recalls precisely the custom-driven automaton in Malinowski's caricature. Malinowski's project was to dismantle the notion, held over from nineteenth-century cultural theory, that "savages" were subject only to an innate knowledge of custom and its edicts, which they followed involuntarily and without question. In order to refute this caricature, Malinowski had to demonstrate that his interlocutors in the Trobriand Islands did in fact distinguish a field of positive behavioral prescriptions based on economic necessity rather than some pre-logical terror of violating custom. In other words, the disparaging language he employed to describe Trobriand Islanders in the 1920s was a sort of backhanded compliment: the so-called "savages" of his acquaintance had liberated themselves from the dusty presumptions of Victorian ethnology precisely by means of their blithe disregard for custom.[3]

When Malinowski was writing on Trobriand law, however, his basis for comparison was not other Milne Bay societies but what he referred to as the "anthropologist's dummy," the figure unable to question the tenets of custom or act out of any sort of free will; this was also of course the missionary's dummy, who appears in Charles Abel's assessment of Suau emotional capacities in chapter 3. Malinowski, who met Abel and likened him to a character in a Joseph Conrad novel (Malinowski 1967: 43), offered as an alternative a complex of social "forces" that, by means of both prescription and interdiction, ensured the mechanisms (as he perceived them) of Trobriand society could proceed smoothly: "I venture to foretell that reciprocity, systematic incidence, publicity and ambition will be found to be the main factors in the binding machinery of primitive law" (Malinowski 1972 [1926]: 68). His insistence that anthropologists look beyond "custom," understood then as a complex of implicit and explicit prohibitions, was clearly a much-needed one at the time that he made it. And while Malinowski could not have foreseen that the category of custom would eventually find its way into the Constitution of Papua New Guinea in 1975, he did establish what would become one of the central problematics in both the anthropology of Melanesia and the anthropology of legal systems the world over: when people talk about their custom, are they talking about something identifiable as a form of law?

It is worth considering an expansion of Malinowski's own terms of negativity and positivity to describe what might be called a Suau legal consciousness (cf. Merry 1990: 5). At issue in the village court is the reestablishment of positive social value, which has for one reason or another been inverted or gone awry. Reciprocity, ambition, and the rest have not disappeared, they simply become adapted to the court environment. And they are appearing not only in village courts but at almost every level of Papua New Guinean political life. The intriguing thing is the way in which they are consistently glossed in terms of "law and order," one of the most abiding rhetorical terms employed by politicians from parliament all the way down to the local level government councils in rural areas such as the Suau Coast.

It is difficult to resist a gesture toward Malinowski's classic observation about the inappropriateness of casting Papuan legal sensibilities solely in terms of negative proscriptions or "criminal law." On the face of it, this is what "law and order" sounds like, at least when journalists in PNG's national newspapers invoke it. "Law and order" in their accounts actually refers to the *absence* of both terms, manifested in the form of the endemic thieving, violence, and corruption currently held to plague Papua New Guinean civil society. But for "law and order" to be a popular item of rhetoric in relatively peaceful Milne Bay Province presents a particularly interesting problem. To get at why Suau are as fond of talking about "law and order" as politicians in Port Moresby are, it is important to ask what else this utterance carries with it along with the frightening figure of the gang member. One possibility is that it is a way of demonstrating that local interests are in alignment with those of the state; it is a discursive method of knocking down the distinction between the center and the periphery.

Elia Seromai was the first village court magistrate I ever met, during my period of residence in Leileyafa, and was at that time renowned throughout the region as a specialist in the *fafabou* sorcerer-identifying divination technique. In an early interview he made the somewhat cryptic remark "laugagayo esana laugagayo," which I have chosen to translate as "the name of law is law." Elia seemed to be suggesting that law is a package containing its own reputation, connections, and capacity to rise or fall in the estimation of those it affects; like the Victorian missionization project, it is supposed to be transmissible from one context to another relatively intact. It is also possible that Elia could define law recursively in this way because he was steeped in the history of the village court as an institution of the Papua New Guinean postcolony. Its identity has become self-evident to the extent that he may not have felt it necessary (never mind desirable) to explain what he meant. But I suspect he was referring to more than this; that, rather like Malinowski, Elia knew that custom honored in the breach rather than the observance provided a means of demonstrating appropriate relationships by means of their inappropriate expression, the effects of which were registered in the social environment. Law is named, that is, visible, only when it has been set into motion as a form of action. And like the name of a person, its moral cachet rises and falls with the actions it is perceived to effect.

Malinowski's was one of the earlier empirical efforts to show that non-Western peoples "had" law, or something analogous to it. Part of the functionalist project was to demonstrate that all societies place a premium value on "order," no matter how this order might be expressed, so that, in Strathern's words, "even where we cannot find counterparts in other societies to our formal judicial structures we nevertheless like to discover regulatory mechanisms, in however a diffuse or generalised form. They may be uncovered as 'customary law'" (Strathern 1985: 113). Strathern's observation casts doubt on the general assumption that customary law is an inevitable product of the colonial encounter, that is, a translation between exogenous and indigenous visions of order. The irony here is that while the architects of PNG's village court system in the late 1960s saw themselves as creating an institution that would harmonize state law with local customary law, Suau people refer hardly at all to custom in their village court hearings (Demian 2003). There are many reasons for this, not least because they rarely speak of custom as if it were a charter for social order (but see chapter 6 for some recent refinements on this practice).

Having said this, order, as in "law and . . . ," is in fact a matter of abiding concern to many contemporary Papua New Guineans, as their political leaders and the international press alike bemoan the "chaotic" or "anarchic" condition of the country. Criminality is endemic; police are underresourced, demoralized, and frequently abusive; Papua New Guinea is chronically represented as a place of "lawlessness," a place without law. Nothing could be further from the truth, of course: the problem isn't whether there is or is not law in Papua New Guinea but how the law is locally inflected and whether the law of locality is in any way associated with the perceived interests of the state. Hirsch (2004) has provided a telling example from elsewhere on the Papuan side of the country, where the younger generation among Fuyuge people in Central Province debate over whether "disco is law"—that is, to what extent the efficacy of innovative forms of music and dance are to be associated with Europeans or with Fuyuge. In particular moments of ritual exhortation, disco, money, and law become coterminous, all versions of the same concern with timely action and its display for the critical assessment of others. Meanwhile in Eastern Highlands Province, West (2006) has documented the experimentation of Gimi and neighboring peoples with the adoption of conservation NGOs as the new representatives of government and governmentality, in the face of the national government's record of inefficacy. I set these two brief examples beside my own account from Suau to try to demonstrate that the Suau experience is not particularly idiosyncratic in the wider Papua New Guinea context but rather an indication that Suau are only one of many peoples throughout the country who have quite happily disaggregated law from any association with state interests or mechanisms—if indeed they ever regarded these entities as associated with each other in the first place (Demian 2015). "Law and order" can be read as an expression of alignment in the face of disconnection: you may not support what we are up to here, but we want the same things you do.

"Law and order" also provides some of the few instances of actual engagement between representatives of the state and village life in Suau. One of the relationships that Papua New Guinean politicians are fondest of emphasizing is that between the state and the person *qua* citizen-subject. The passion among Papua New Guinean officeholders, from MPs on down to village court magistrates, for holding up "law and order" as the ultimate object of their actions in their capacity as officeholders suggests a model of law that is predicated on a particular, positively valued relationship between persons and the state. The "law" in law and order, then, may be readable as a product of an emergent political imaginary in PNG, in which the value of the relationship between the state and its citizens is assessed according to both "exogenous" and "indigenous" models of political agency. These models may be combined or separated according to the agenda of those who employ them, depending on the source of authority deemed to be most persuasive at the time they are employed. The aim here is not to describe the cynicism of politicians but rather to flag the appearance of a theory of political action in PNG whose source is not readily reducible to discourses of the center versus the periphery, or the indigenous versus the exogenous.

It is easiest to show these processes in action by means of the type of case that most Suau say is on a perpetual upward trajectory in frequency: a land dispute. The relocation of entire villages described in previous chapters, the mobility of lineages inherent in matriliny combined with virilocality, and a contemporary boom in the population of the coast all add up to a recipe for land disputes becoming the preeminent form in which Suau people attempt to work out their relationships gone awry. Furthermore, matriliny itself is precisely the kind of "custom" that grassroots Papua New Guineans are presumed to be using in village courts, but it is far more common for Suau people to invoke this category of action in land mediations. It is also in land mediations that Suau people become most explicit about when they are, or are not, doing something called law.

Law, Land, and the "Problem" of Matriliny

In November 1969, A\$50,000 was paid by the Australian colonial administration to a number of "landowners" in the Suau census division of what was then Milne Bay District (now Province) in exchange for timber extraction rights. The patrol officer at the time, one John Balderson, noted in his annual report that there was some dissatisfaction among "people belonging to one of the Clans holding full rights over the timber in question, but residing in another village at the time of purchase, thereby receiving no monetary compensation" (Balderson 1970: 9). He also remarked that one plantation owner at the village of Maliawate expressed concern that he would not be able to log because the "real" owners of the land in question had not been paid (1970: 10). However, Balderson wrote that "overall satisfaction with the sale was expressed nonetheless, and the impression gained was that the payees are now waiting patiently for the Government's second move to see if it is as silly as its first" (1970: 10).

Twelve years later, in a report written as a result of a social feasibility study for the introduction of oil palm to the province, Michael Young noted that land tenure among the peoples of the southern mainland was remarkably "insecure" in comparison with the island peoples with whom he had the most experience (Young 1981a). By "insecurity" he meant the flexibility with which land could be transmitted. Although the default is inheritance through the matriline, several mechanisms exist for obtaining use-rights and even "permanent" transferral of land ownership through the father, or more precisely, from the mother's matrilineage to the father's. As one of his informants told him, "We have *too many* ways of getting land" (1981a: 15, emphasis in original). Young noted that the issue was not simply one of matrilineal versus patrilineal inheritance but also one of the mythohistorical relationships to the land discussed in the previous chapter. The Goodenough Islanders with whom Young had worked before could be claimed to have a more "secure" or "stable" system of land tenure not only because patriliny and virilocality meant that the same lineage remained on the same land for generation after generation but also because each patrilineage could claim its origin in a cave opening on that land. Origin accounts among mainland peoples such as Suau are far more indeterminate.

As mentioned in chapter 1, my original sponsor to live in Leileiyafa, Matilda Pilacapio, told me on several occasions that my job would be to record "the matrilineal kinship." Her use of this phrase was clearly a shorthand reference to something more complex, and in characteristic fashion she left it to me to work out what it was. My eventual conclusion was that she perceived Suau matriliny to be under threat, particularly as it pertained to the transmission of land rights. The threat in this case was the possibility of land being claimed through patrilateral ties and perhaps even legally registered as such, although the cost of hiring a surveyor and filing a legal claim would be prohibitive to most people on the Suau Coast. Her concerns, as I ultimately learned, were inflated but not baseless. Because of the mission and plantation history of the region, Suau speakers and their hinterland neighbors were exposed early and intensively not only to the property regimes of Europeans but also to those of people from nonmatrilineal societies. While it could be argued that the former was more vigorously imposed on Suau, the impact of the latter could not be discounted, if only for the way in which it enabled them to imagine how outsiders might perceive them and in what terms they might or might not continue to differentiate themselves from those outsiders.

As a matrilineal society, Suau constitute a minority within the panoply of systems by which Papua New Guinean societies reckon descent and inheritance. Matriliny in PNG tends to be found among coastal and island peoples speaking Austronesian languages, while the majority of non-Austronesian language speakers on the mainland (and on some islands) reckon inheritance along patrilineal or cognatic lines.[4] But the region to which Suau belong, with a scant handful of exceptions, is almost entirely matrilineal. A recurring theme in ethnographies about this corner of PNG is the notion that matriliny provides a blueprint or charter for a particular configuration of relations between men and women and the forms those relations are likely to take. In the latter half of the twentieth century, anthropologists were concerned to elaborate the ways in which matriliny contributed to the political and economic influence of women in "Massim" societies (Weiner 1976; Kahn 1986; Lepowsky 1993). Not unreasonably, all of these studies took as their object of analysis women's control over particular material forms, from food to ceremonial valuables to land. While it had to a certain extent been recognized all along that women in these societies enjoyed a more active role in the "public sphere" than did women in many other parts of PNG, it was not until the dual emergence of feminist and Marxist thought in anthropology that matriliny was construed as playing a significant role in women's lives outside of their obligation to reproduce the lineage and their status as future ancestresses through whom property and identity would flow.

In fact, until the 1970s, the focus had for the most part been on the implications of matriliny for men. Matriliny appeared to present a peculiarly difficult situation for fathers, who were assumed to be torn between the interests of their children and those of their sisters' children, that is, their heirs (Richards 1950: 246). Later studies, notably those from Melanesia, suggested that fathers in matrilineal societies are not as conflicted about their obligations as previously accepted (Clay 1977; Battaglia 1985; Bolyanatz 1996; Sykes 2001). The imperatives of reciprocity through which fathers are compensated for their fathering work, provisions for particular property forms that fathers can transmit to their own children, and new obligations to the state all contribute to a model of matriliny in which fathers can quite comfortably distribute resources of various kinds among their children and their sisters' children. The assumption that fathers invariably prefer to devolve property to their own children, and are only prevented from doing so by the demands of matriliny, has also been called into question by studies of polyandrous societies (Levine 1987), and this notion has even come full circle to meet its mirror image. Matriliny has now been conceived as promoting solidarity between lineages, rather than fission within them, by means of the "dual role played by men: on the one hand, father and husband, on the other hand, mother's brother and brother" (Petersen 1982: 138). Far from the splitting or diluting of men's kin identity imagined in the 1950s, their identity is now thought to be doubled or otherwise amplified by the provisions of matriliny. Key to both images, of course, is the notion that kinship can be added or subtracted by the "rules" of unilineal descent. With the addition or subtraction of kin relations is implied the addition or subtraction of property relations.

In the 1960s, an apparently new problem emerged: matriliny appeared to be on the verge of dissolution in the face of capitalism's inexorable advent (Gough 1961). If, as the theory went, matriliny was associated with "abundance and unrestricted access to resources" while capitalism was associated with "scarcity and restricted access to resources" (Poewe 1980: 342), then matriliny stood no chance of survival. Later assessments of the death-of-matriliny announcements noted that they were based on the modernization theory prevalent at the time (Colson 1980: 359), which proceeded from the assumption on the one hand that capitalism would sweep all before it, and on the other hand that it would reproduce the social forms that had produced it, namely, private property and patrilineal inheritance. Underpinning the second assumption was in turn the evolutionist sensibilities of Victorian anthropology, to which the rather peculiar association between matriliny and the absence of private property can be traced. For Lewis Henry Morgan and those influenced by him, most notably Engels, both kinship and resources were imagined to undergo incremental "enclosures" progressing from a state of "primitive promiscuity" to polygamous matriliny and finally to monogamous patriliny, with the final stage accompanied by full-blown private property regimes (McKinnon 2001). The final two social and economic forms brought each other about because, in contrast to the maternal relation, which was thought to generate a natural form of social relation in the matrilineal gens (but one whose maternal communalism was inherently antithetical to ideas of individual property), the paternal relation was seen as incapable of generating any social form *until property was added to it*. (McKinnon 2001: 284, emphasis in original)

A century after Morgan, social theorists still assumed that private property and matriliny were fundamentally incompatible. Although that notion has been tempered by abundant evidence to the contrary, it still lurks behind the concerns of those who would "preserve" matriliny from the depredations of capitalism. Property and matriliny, as institutional social forms, are not antagonists. This is an unsustainable position, both philosophically and ethnographically; it is tied to the Victorian idea that matriliny constituted an older, more "primitive" form of kinship speculatively shared by all human societies at some point in their history. However, what I hope to show in the remainder of this chapter is how the ambiguity of property in the matrilineal Suau context—"too many ways of getting land"—leads back to the question of what law is on the Suau Coast, where its provisions begin and end, and how this presents an increasingly pressing set of questions to a Suau conception of life in the present.

My own ethnographic perplexity with matriliny is twofold. The first issue is whether, when we refer to matriliny, we are really talking about a *system of inheritance* as it was conceived by twentieth-century anthropologists. The second follows directly from this. If Suau land disputes arising from them are in fact becoming the free-for-all many of my interlocuters say they are, due to a ballooning population and a diminishing understanding on the part of young people about how land inheritance is supposed to work, is matriliny actually under threat, as the twentieth-century anthropologists predicted it would be? With time and further experience on both the Suau Coast and in the district courts in Alotau, I became more confident that the "preservation" of matriliny was not the issue, or at least not the most pressing one (Demian 2011). While land claims and the disputes that arise from them are indeed a space in which matriliny is debated, they are also a space for debate about the history of the Suau Coast and the current relationship of its people to the country in which they now find themselves.

What Kind of Landowner?

An attentive reader will notice that this book has been filled with terms like who does the land "belong to," or who is its "steward"—there has been very little in the way of ownership so far. The European model of landownership, the fee simple estate, has little to do with how Suau people conceive of their relationship with land, as chapter 4 illustrated. PNG is a country in which, famously—and to the chagrin of economists—some 85 percent of land continues to be held under customary tenure, including most of the Suau Coast. In common with much of PNG, identifying a "landowner" in Suau, in the sense of a single individual or even a single family with unambiguous and uncontested rights of use over a piece of land and disposal of its resources, is an almost nonsensical proposition. As in the case of the money paid to "landowners" for timber extraction rights in the 1960s, such a transaction will always leave out other landowners whose ire may fester for generations. This problem will reappear in chapter 6: for now, I wish to focus on who may be recognized at a given moment in time as having a certain authority over the land and what happens to it.

As I briefly noted in chapter 4, the Suau term *tanuwaga* is often glossed as "boss" by Suau people who also speak English. It is also, significantly, the term applied to schoolteachers. The role is a flexible one; normatively, it falls to an older member of the matrilineage (*ulutubu*)[5] residing on the land belonging to that *ulutubu* and holding detailed knowledge of the *ulutubu* history and topogeny.[6] Despite being a nominal "boss," a *tanuwaga* cannot decide unilaterally what happens on their *ulutubu* land but must instead muster agreement from a majority of lineage members to make decisions. There may be more than one person occupying this role in a given lineage, and the role may also be contested if there are multiple senior people with the relevant knowledge and diverging ideas about how their land should be used. It is hopefully clear that for all the attributes of a *tanuwaga*, exclusive authority over land and exclusive benefits arising from that authority are not among them. The actual role of a *tanuwaga*, to organize something approaching consensus about land use within a lineage that has moved across the landscape throughout its history, bears little resemblance to the kind of "landowner" that companies and NGOs from outside of PNG might imagine themselves to be negotiating with. For every "landowner" signing a contract or otherwise entering into negotiations with bodies wishing to do business, there is a potentially limitless number of other landowners who can claim that they have been left out of the consultation.

Suau people recognize that this is a problem and have every so often sought their own solutions. Toward the end of 1999 I was able to witness one such attempt, at a meeting in the village of Saga'aho. A group of educated men wished to start a timber extraction company with the proposed name "Saeleu," after Duiduisae and Duiduileu, the traditional designations of the eastern and western halves of the coast, respectively. This inclusive company would explicitly operate as an alternative to the Malaysian timber companies that some

Suau and neighboring villages had already experienced to their detriment. These companies were known to pay below-market value for logs, clear-cut the forest despite having made a selective extraction agreement, and leave nothing but scorching grassland and crumbling infrastructure in their wake. This new company, Saeleu, would be different, run by Suau people themselves.

I discussed with one of the men who called the meeting the question of who would make decisions about bringing their lineage members on board to partner with the company; he used the term landowner and *tanuwaga* interchangeably at times, and at other times maintained the distinction between them. There was also some question of whom the meeting convenors had actually sought to involve, since there were three women present and thirty or forty men, notwithstanding that the role of *tanuwaga* is not a gendered one, nor is it fixed in any other respect to a category of person apart from the contingent categories of seniority, residence, and knowledge. When I asked the meeting convenor about the small number of women present, he appeared to misunderstand the nature of the question and said that he wanted women to come so that no witches would become jealous of the project and sabotage it. At the same time, all of the convenors seemed keen to imagine the community-wide benefits that would eventuate—the schools, roads, and aid posts that the company would make possible—but only if everyone agreed to participate, suggesting that they really did want any *tanuwaga* who came to the meeting to persuade, cajole, and otherwise coerce a consensus from their lineages that this was a good idea. In anticipation of the inevitable discord that might arise if some "landowners" felt left out of the proceedings, they invoked a critical value and end goal in Suau intralineage meetings: *nuwa esega*, the "single mind" that an *ulutubu* should reach when making a significant decision about their land. In this sense, it did not matter who was actually present as long as decisions could be reached within each *ulutubu* to make the company happen.

To my knowledge, the Saeleu company never eventuated. But the meeting to discuss it was a manifestation of an enduring desire to relocalize translocal processes, such as resource extraction, and to claim ownership—with its broader suite of meanings including not only control but also responsibility and even sovereignty—over these processes that, as Suau people are painfully aware, are not only happening elsewhere but also orchestrated elsewhere. So to speak of ownership of an economic decision, such as cutting down trees or deliberately retaining them, will never only be a debate over classical anthropological issues of descent and inheritance, although these cannot entirely be removed from the picture without doing an injustice to how seriously these issues are still taken. Social organization, especially as it affects the course of land disputes both actual and anticipated, throws into relief people's interest not only in what makes them different from other Papua New Guineans and from, say, biblical patriarchs, but also in who ultimately will decide the future of the land from which people continue to derive their livelihoods. Will it be the disinterested PNG state? The rapacious Malaysian timber companies? Or some combination of more local instigators and authorities, using that category so beloved of the decolonizing moment, "customary law"?

Matriliny Tested: The Land Dispute

I noted earlier in this chapter that land disputes cannot be heard by village court magistrates, although the latter are often present at land mediations and many of the cases they do hear in the village court are, at their core, actually about land or have land use as a component. The exclusion of conflicts over land from the jurisdiction of the village courts stems from a colonial-era concern that these cases were too complex for the kinds of "petty" village issues imagined to be the proper remit of the courts, and that exclusion was retained once the courts were formalized after independence (Goddard 2009). Land disputes are indeed very complex in nature and, again, contain the potential for almost perpetual ramification into the future; I have attended land disputes at the district court in Alotau that had been ongoing for years. Such disputes only make it to the district court if they have proven too intractable for land mediators to handle, or if the younger members of a lineage or clan are actually interested in pursuing the kind of all-or-nothing end result the district courts can give them (2009: 177).

In the normal run of events, however, a land dispute must first be heard by land mediators, who become appointed to this role because they are older community members who are knowledgeable about the "correct" systems of land inheritance for their ethnic group and also about the histories of most of the families in the area they serve. In common with village court magistrates, they also must be skilled at guiding their disputants to reach an agreement—even if that agreement does not entirely satisfy everyone involved. Unlike magistrates, they are not regarded as representatives of the law of the state: their remit is customary law in its broadest and most indeterminate sense of indicating a shared set of values about how land ought to be used and devolved from one generation to the next.

If a land issue brought to them proves beyond their powers to resolve, they can then send it to "the law" in its manifestation through the district courts; there is one such court in every provincial capital in PNG that serves as the entry point to the country's formal legal system. This is considered a highly undesirable option by many land mediators, as well as disputants who wish to avoid the zero-sum result of a district court hearing in which one family is granted all the rights to a piece of land and another goes away with none (Demian 2011: 52). Land mediations are socially and temporally very different in texture from village court cases as well. They can be months and even years in the planning, can take a day or more to bring to completion, and during that time can take on an almost celebratory atmosphere, due to the enormous effort involved in bringing them together. Given how different land disputes are from other kinds of conflicts, the question then becomes, what is a land dispute about?

In his work with Arosi people in the Solomon Islands, Scott (2007) draws attention to an axis along which cosmologies of unilineal descent (such as matriliny) can be construed as both negotiable and immutable. This has to do with their temporal as well as their spatial placement. Scott posits two temporal modes in Arosi matrilineage making. One, based on Arosi narratives of originary nonhuman ancestral progenitors existing independently of either land- or human-based relations, he calls "utopic primordialism" (2007: 347). The other mode, based on the kind of topogenic narrative of human agents moving and acting upon the landscape I have described in chapter 4, and present among Arosi as in most Austronesian-speaking societies, he calls "topogonic primordialism" (2007: 348). Arosi people may appeal to either primordial mode of claiming lineage origins in deep time, or both, again depending on how and against whom the claim is being made: whether in a public land dispute or in a private, secretive discussion with the ethnographer. This is to say, matrilineal land claims may be made in a sense that is entirely extralegal or even extrarelational if reliant on Scott's utopic mode of primordialism. One could even ask whether, in this sense, they are claims or some other kind of speech act, insofar as a "claim" is an act made against the potential or actual claims of others, so that even a nonrelational temporal mode is marshaled in the interests of a particular relationship. The point here is that the kind of hypermobile unilineal descent suggested by matriliny is complicated by distinctive originary times as well as distinctive originary places. Even the relatively less deep time of topogonic primordialism offers such complications, as it "envisions conditions in which it is possible, even likely, that the history of more than one matrilineage will impinge on and come to reference the same geographical terrain" (2007: 349).

These kinds of primordialist-yet-overlapping histories are observable in the wrangling that Suau people engage in over land claimed by means of *ulutubu* and *sulu* distinctions, and also in attempts to claim land through their fathers. The latter is actually possible, but only within a certain set of conditions; otherwise, the matrilineal default reasserts itself. In the event of a family producing only sons, the eldest son's children can lay claim to the land of their father's mother, although their father himself cannot. Another option is to contribute consistently to the major life-cycle events in the lineage of one's father—such as weddings and funerals—regarded as adding "weight" (*polohe*) to the land and one's place on it, through which certain rights may be claimed. As a final option, a child can be adopted from the father's sister. The lineage affiliations of adopted children and those who adopt them become expansive. Land and children share certain forms of attention and care—the term *itawatan* "to look after," is used for both—and adopting a child from one's father's lineage is another way to add "weight" to one's standing within it. Any one of these can be trumped by a forcefully asserted claim based in matriliny and the *ulutubu* history to back it. My point is that there is both more and less to matriliny than a set of rules about inheritance or identity. Reducing matriliny to a "kinship system" obscures the dynamic relationships between people, their land, and their histories, all of which serve to constitute each other. Matriliny is one way among several possible ways to describe these relationships; "weight" could easily be another, describing as it does the shifting of lineage configurations due to a person's actions over the course of their lifetime.

At a land dispute in the Buhutu village of Duhumodawa in 1999, the mediators appeared to have all of this in mind. One invoked the need for "development" and asked disputants to think about the future, noting that land belongs "to our children, it's not ours." He enumerated the historical "times" (*huya* in coastal Suau dialects, *fuya* in the inland dialect spoken by the mediator) or epochs considered significant to the history of the province. He described the departure from the "old time" initiated by the "gathering together" of people from all over the province by missionaries and officials of the colonial administration, and proceeded from there to World War II and PNG's independence in 1975. He made the point that the various mobilities ushered in by each of these "times" made the land situation of the present day even more vexed. He reminded all present of the many ways people might have acquired land in the past, through bridewealth and other marriage-related payments or in exchange for pigs and shell valuables to meet other debts. He urged his disputants not to become preoccupied with trivial matters but to behave with dignity and "lift" the name of the Buhutu region. He appeared to be exhorting everyone to think as flexibly as they could about land tenure, because there was no longer—and had not been for a very long time—only one kind of relationship between a group of people and their land.

But his opening speech was mischievous, because when the disputes were actually under way, he and his co-mediator frequently invoked the little-used category of *sulu* to identify the disputants. He would in fact ask each disputant to name his or her *sulu* before hearing their arguments. The land mediators' appeal to *sulu* effectively removed the debate from the realm of the everyday, because most people generally pay little or no attention to *sulu* relations in their casual interactions with one another. In one dispute, the mediator had to repeat several times his assertion that the disputing parties were actually related, because they belonged to the same *sulu*, and therefore should share the contested land. Thus in the context of land mediations, a temporary respite from the topogenic identification of *ulutubu* actually forms part of the mediators' persuasive toolkit. And the persuasive force of *sulu* appears to rely explicitly on its having fallen out of everyday use as a form of reckoning relationships between people, across place and time. *Sulu* was, for land mediators twenty years ago, a means of stopping a dispute in its tracks, because this category of connection relies on the ironic capacity of removing debates about land from any association with land at all. To put it differently, land mediators on the Suau Coast can make explicit and ironic use of the fact that *sulu* as a relational knowledge practice has been, for nearly all practical purposes, forgotten.

The first dispute was brought by Bina,[7] acting in the capacity of *tanu-waga* for his lineage. He related some recent history of the lineage, wherein his great-grandmother, resident at Mahimahina, married a man from Magaya and relocated to live with him: so far, a standard virilocal move, which is the most common way for a matrilineage to become dispersed. The man's family at Magaya hosted a *mata'asi* competitive exchange feast, prompting the great-grandmother to seek pigs from her relatives back in Mahimahina. Her affines at Magaya repaid the pig debt with a piece of land called Bunalele Panepane that included valuable sago palms. This is where Bina was raised, and where his family made gardens and planted coconuts, another high-value tree in the arboricultural hierarchy and among those that signal ownership. When he reached adulthood, he and his family also began to plant oil palm— here is where the story shifts in its implications, as oil palm is not a traditional food-bearing tree but an introduced cash crop. Then Galuboi, a man originally from Magaya, came home after a stint working at a commercial oil palm plantation and also began planting the crop. Bina objected, and Galuboi's nephew damaged Bina's house and some of his oil palms in retaliation—this is also a method of "evicting" a resident on the land whose residency one is declaring to be illegitimate; the matter then went to the village court. But the village court cannot hear land claims, and so only the damage and reparations for it could be handled in that forum.[8] This was a new case, Bina insisted, to resolve the actual issue under dispute.

Bina's sister also spoke and pointed out that Bina was entitled to act as *tanuwaga* for the lineage because their great-grandmother had had no children.[9] This led to a discussion between her and the land mediators about how this ancestress had become obligated to her affines at Magaya in such a way that she had to supply pigs for their *mata'asi*. Bina reentered the conversation to propose that it was the substitution of land for pigs that was at the root of the problem, since the Magaya people ought to have settled the pig debt to their in-married affine correctly by repaying her family with further pigs rather than "mixing" such different forms of wealth. He went on to describe the boundaries of the land he was claiming at Bunalele Panepane, as he had walked them with his father's brothers from Magaya.

As the discussion unfolded, it became evident that neither of the land me-diators presiding thought this a particularly complex case. Bunalele Panepane, noted the first mediator, was a legitimate "block" for Bina to claim,[10] but not all of Magaya, which seemed to be the sticking point for Galuboi. Another issue for Galuboi was that the block where Bina had planted oil palm also contained the graves of people from the Magaya *ulutubu*, for which Bina was indeed at fault on several grounds. As graves along with fruiting trees signify long-term ownership of land by an *ulutubu*, planting oil palm on the same land consti-tuted something like an assertion of having removed the land permanently from Magaya. Notwithstanding Bina's transgression, the mediators noted, they could not ultimately tell Bina or Galuboi that the land belonged to either of them; instead, both would have to reach an agreement. The second mediator emphasized this point, noting how long the dispute had gone on already, and exhorted Galuboi and Bina to reach "one mind" through prayer. He seemed to persuade Galuboi, who conceded that he had tried to give his sister's son (that is, his heir through the matriline) some of the land at Bunalele Panepane whose ownership was under dispute. Having successfully implied that the real origin of the problem was his nephew's request for land, he said that he had nothing more to argue about.

The mediation then shifted to what I would term the "pastoral" mode of discourse that is observable not only in land mediations but also in village court hearings, informal *hadudulai*, and any meeting in which a figure of au-thority feels it is time to offer a set of moral or behavioral points for consider-ation—an example of this will also appear in chapter 6. The first mediator told his disputing parties, and everyone else present, that Bina's paternal uncles from Magaya had also contributed to the conflict. They ought, he observed, to have taken both Bina and Galuboi with them as they walked the boundaries of the land gifted to Bina's ancestress to make it clear what was being transferred to Bina (and what was not). "The people who came before us didn't know if the people to come after them would be few or many," the mediator said. "These days education has made us all very clever. If a mother gives birth to a baby boy, we know he'll marry a woman who is different from the family. But if she gives birth to a girl, then we know that she will be the 'boss' of the land. We should recognize that the children of our sisters will 'boss' the land. Our own children will not 'boss' because they are of a different kind." The English term "boss," which appeared throughout a discourse otherwise offered in the Buhutu dialect, seemed to punctuate his speech on purpose: he was speaking not only of owners but also of those who would direct the use of the land in the future, according to the principles of matriliny.

The moral-analytical framework was then taken up by the second media-tor, who said that "a woman's payment is land." This was not a statement about bridewealth, which takes the form primarily of pigs and secondarily of both garden and store-bought foods throughout the Suau Coast and its hinterland. His meaning instead seemed to indicate the movement of women in marriage and the division of land by their children that would be the outcome. I understood his statement in this way because of what he said next, addressing all the younger men present at the mediation: "At Gelemalaiya [the village he was from] I have a lot of sons-in-law, but we cannot work their land. Their children will look for land one day. If you get married in your own village, you must be of one mind and work together properly. You should marry a woman from your own place so that you'll hold onto the land. But if you marry someone from far away, there won't be any land for her. So remember that a woman's payment is land. Because business requires land and education requires foresight."

The overall impression gained from the speeches of the mediators was that the entire dispute should never have arisen in the first place—but they also offered an analysis of why it had occurred. They both referenced an increasingly pressing issue brought up by many of my Suau interlocutors, invoking the English phrase "population explosion" to describe it. The rise in the coastal population, and doubtless everywhere else in PNG, is easily observable; combined with the colonial legacy of villages concentrated on and near the coast, the problem of land scarcity has arisen for possibly the first time in Suau history. This problem, while serious in nature, will not necessarily write the epitaph for matriliny. Anthropologists working in other matrilineal contexts have demonstrated the elasticity and adaptability of the matrilineal ideal, whether ongoing ancestral engagement in the use of land may be reframed as "profit" (Pavanello 1995), for example, or the mode of inheritance persists even as households begin to appear more nucleated in form (Blackwood 1999). A number of Suau *ulutubu* have attempted to deal with the new pressure on land by reclaiming their ancestral ground in the mountains, from the era before the colonial administration relocated them. These historical territories are often difficult to reach, however, as they can only be accessed by long journeys on foot and are far removed from either road or sea connections to Alotau that are highly valued by the younger generations. Otherwise, families may agree to share land in a fairly improvised manner; however, these agreements will prove unstable over time, leading to land claims in the future staked on equally improvised arguments. Bina's attempt to claim all of Magaya because part of it had been granted to his great-grandmother was an example of precisely this kind of creativity around land claims, and the mediators' admonition that he could not do so was a warning of more such improper claims to come.

Three years earlier, I attended a land dispute at Leileiyafa wherein a land claim was staked by means of a connection through the patriline. The land mediators dismissed this out of hand. Although they cannot, again, actually award land to one party or another, they can reject nonsensical claims in the public forum of the mediation, which lends them a weight morally equivalent to telling a disputant they have no right to the land.[11] After the mediation, one of the successful disputants said to me in an astonished tone, "Those people tried to claim the land through their father. But the father is a completely different person." In common with the dispute of Bina and Galuboi, where the mediator explained that "our own children will not 'boss' because they are of a different kind," the man I spoke to in this case made a taxonomic distinction in who could and could not assert a claim. It is important to note that the matrilineal taxonomy in both instances was offered in relation to land claims, and I have not heard such a distinction drawn by Suau people in any other context. The fact that this taxonomy arises under the conditions of conflict over land is what matters. In these cases, matriliny appears not to distinguish heirs from nonheirs so much as land itself distinguishes people as either belonging to it or not. This formulation was originally offered by de Coppet (1985) in his discussion of land tenure for 'Are'are people in the Solomon Islands. In that context, he found, there are simultaneously available framings wherein people mediate relations between land as much as land mediates relations between people. The "arrow" of ownership for 'Are'are does not point invariably from people to land but, rather, can either work in that way or in the direction from land to people. Both of these ways of thinking about the relationship of people to land are present in the 'Are'are conceptual repertoire, and which one gets foregrounded is contingent upon the kind of claim being made.

As the case of Bina and Galuboi demonstrates, however, there is another factor to consider for the question of whether land is property, and, if so, who can own it. The capacity of land to generate money, as from a cash crop such as oil palm, lends it a novel and contentious set of legal, temporal, and moral dimensions. Land under cash crops can no longer be used for any other purpose, and oil palm in particular—unlike coconuts or cocoa—is grown as an input-intensive monoculture that degrades the soil on which it is cultivated. But as the most lucrative cash crop in Milne Bay, oil palm is now grown both on large commercial plantations and on family-owned blocks throughout the Sagarai Valley. Land disputes proliferate in its wake, and these are likely to intensify as the population grows, as land is needed both for home gardens and for income. This was one concern of the land mediators whose work I recorded twenty years ago; the other was that the increased pressure on land would cause people to seek land by means other than the matrilineal default: precisely why Matilda Pilacapio had brought me to Leilieyafa in the first place back in the mid-1990s.

Although Bina did not exactly attempt to do this in his bid for the land at Magaya, he did make the somewhat dubious claim that because his paternal uncles had given him the block at Bunalele Panepane, he thought perhaps he also had a maternal link of some kind through them and so would inherit the entire place. The land mediators disabused him of this notion—especially as he could not prove it—and refocused his claim on Bunalele Panepane alone through the pig debt incurred at the *mataʻasi*. While he accepted this correction, it was lost on nobody at the land mediation that had he successfully claimed all of Magaya, he would be in control of land that was planted extensively with oil palm. As Strathern (1999: 57) notes, "Money has become visible all the time, a medium whose enabling capacities cannot be hidden." Unlike land, the mediations of money differentiate people not by where they belong and the history of how that belonging came to be but by their ability to turn money into other resources. Money does not come with a history or a body of knowledge about that history: it exists only in the present.

This present is expressed by, among other things, the blithe disregard for "the matrilineal kinship" (in Matilda's phrasing) appearing in some land claims as land acquires new layers of potential monetary value, including the value of doing nothing at all with it, as I will discuss in the next chapter. But the present is also emergent in the desire of many Suau people to remind themselves and each other how things are "supposed" to work in their corner of PNG. This may appear in the sermons of land mediators and village court magistrates or in everyday conversations where people debate whether a particular action or way of conducting a relationship is *kastom* or not. Out of the picture almost entirely, in most of these debates both formal and informal, is law. Law cannot govern relationships not just because of the felt absence of the Papua New Guinean state: it cannot govern because, like money, it belongs to no place and no history as far as Suau people are concerned.

I will conclude with a brief comment on the relationship between law and matriliny, as two possible ways—among many—of determining the correct form and conduct of social relationships. Unlike, say, in India, where revisions to family and property law have threatened to force matrilineal peoples to discard their relational norms entirely (Jeffrey 2005), in Papua New Guinea this kind of social engineering has not been taken up by lawmakers. Arguably, the space carved out for customary law in the Constitution of Papua New Guinea is a deliberately ambiguous one: it allows not only for nonlegal forms of governing relationships but even—potentially—for any future attempts to coerce these relationships into conformity with a particular mold to be challenged on constitutional grounds.

Having said this, Suau people do sometimes attempt to make "landowners" appear in the form of individual, male persons with exclusive rights over land and disposal of its resources for the purposes of negotiating with foreign commercial interests. This phenomenon will appear in the next chapter and is a fairly common type of performance of the kind Papua New Guineans all over the country have found themselves engaging in when dealing with resource extractors who have no interest in finding out what land is in PNG and how it mediates relations between people (Toft 1997; Kirsch 2014; Jacka 2015). Meanwhile on the Suau Coast, matrilineal governance of land under the stewardship of *tanuwaga* continues when other interests have their backs turned, as it were. Those interests may be rapacious logging companies, well-meaning NGOs, or the PNG government itself, but as far as most Suau people are concerned, the state's back is turned as well: "There is no government here." The Suau present is characterized by tacking between attempts to comply with the presumed interests of others and the pursuit of their own interests, even when those lead to conflicts among themselves. It is in the negotiation of those conflicts that people encounter both the limits and the expansive potentials that still lie within their power to sort out what their relationships should be with each other and with the world they now find themselves in.

Notes

1. I also refer to the fact that, wishing to avoid mention of sorcery, Suau are more likely to refer to "customary sickness" or even "Suau sickness" when referring to illnesses inflicted by sorcery. Cf. Goddard 1998 for similar practices in an urban village court in a Port Moresby squatter settlement.
2. In fact, killings related to sorcery accusations are extremely rare in the Suau region, in common with most of Milne Bay where witchcraft and sorcery discourses are inflected with as much respect as fear (Lawrence 2015) and largely free from the vigilante violence that can follow on from sorcery accusations in other parts of PNG.
3. These days, Suau people along with members of other Milne Bay language groups also happily use disparaging language in reference to Trobrianders, known within the province as "the Japanese of Milne Bay"—as in, they think they are better than everyone else. But the insult contains more than a grain of grudging respect, because Trobriand Islanders are also widely seen as staunch holdouts for their own *kastom* in the face of the colonial experience, in stark contrast with their mainland neighbors.
4. That is to say, in cases where "lines" of any kind can be perceived in the first place. The 1960s ushered in a heated debate that questioned the existence of unilineal descent groups in parts of New Guinea, which until then were assumed by anthropologists to be a nearly universal characteristic of "tribal" social organization. See Lawrence (1984), Wagner (1974), and Barnes (1962) for key instances of this debate.
5. I have chosen to gloss *ulutubu* as "lineage" rather than "clan" because it better matches the distinction anthropologists traditionally draw between these two terms. Both connote a common identity and a certain degree of shared substance but are reckoned differently. A lineage is a group of people that can trace its descent more or less "genealogically" to a known ancestor, while a clan is a group of people who claim a common ancestry or substance but cannot necessarily demonstrate their precise relationships to one another or identify the ancestors through whom they are related. It is possible for a group to have both clans and lineages, as Suau do. "Clan" has, however, become the popular term in Papua New Guinea for referring to all forms of common "family" identity regardless of its origins.

6. The term *tanuwaga* is used by a neighboring language group to denote the "manager" (note the gloss) of a clan's seagoing canoes (Macintyre 1989: 160) in particular, but also all the clan's valuable resources in general. Another cognate term from Vanatinai/ Sudest Island, *tanuwagai*, is glossed by Lepowsky (1993: 129) simply as "owner."

7. I have substituted the names of the disputants' *sulu* totems for their actual names, given the sensitivity of the subject matter.

8. See Demian 2004a for a consideration of the assiduous distinctions Suau people maintain between litigating damage to property as opposed to disputing claims to property.

9. This is not a paradox; the ancestress in question will have been a classificatory rather than a lineal grandmother. All members of the second ascending and descending generations from Ego are called *tubu-*. All members of the third ascending and descending generations are called *waha-*. Both terms always take an "inalienable" possessive suffix; e.g., "my great-grandparent" would be *wahagu*. Bina used this term in reference to his ancestress, implying that she was at least three generations removed from him.

10. The English term "block," imported from Australian parlance for a parcel of land, is commonly used throughout PNG, especially for land that has been converted to use for cash cropping. In urban areas it may also refer to a neighborhood or an informal settlement on the periphery of a city or town. A "block" often has clearer ownership or tenancy boundaries than do larger areas of land held under customary tenure—but not always.

11. See Hukula (2019) for an extended discussion of other nonlegal forums in PNG where the moral assessment of behavior among disputing parties is what lends efficacy to these forums in the absence of, or even exceeding, the authority of a legal determination.

🎵 6
Times to Come
(in the Near Future)

A very great deal of this book has dealt with Suau histories, Suau memory practices, and how these continue to be felt in the Suau present, or the present in which this book was written in any event. This chapter deals, at last, with the ways in which a Suau sense of future might be drawn out of all those other temporalities. Whatever was abandoned during the missionary era to initiate new relationships, whatever then gave rise to a sense of abandonment by those relationships, there nonetheless remains a sense of potential in the act of waiting for whatever comes next.

This book may appear to have offered up a somewhat dreary catalog of relationships that never realized this potential: departed missionaries and other colonial actors, a withdrawn Papua New Guinean state, and, in this chapter, international donor agencies unable to make their intentions clear to their prospective Suau clients. All of this is unavoidably part of the process of ironic evaluation of relations of asymmetry, where the hospitality extended to others is not extended back because it was never recognized as hospitality to begin with. Through all these stories of endings and misbegotten beginnings, however, I hope to have shown that the techniques of social analysis that Suau people brought to each of these engagements remained consistent: the analysis, every time, has arisen from questions of how to use relationships with others to reflect on their own practices, and of how to use that reflexive knowledge to show their willingness to engage on a multitude of registers. A perception of futurity must also therefore come from this analytical technique, as the very act of extending hospitality anticipates a future relationship in some form. What form that might take is the subject of this chapter. I start, somewhat counterintuitively, with the social form that is felt by Suau people still to be holding them back—but also, how they use even the troubling aspects of their present world to speak about the world that they would like to inhabit instead.

The Threat of the Past

In 2008, during a return visit I made to Isuisu, there was a disturbance in the middle of the night. I heard voices, men shouting, and a gunshot. Then a man ran through the village shouting at people to wake up. It sounded like pot lids were being banged together. I stumbled out of my room and found other residents of the house—my host Baigayo and two of her daughters—turning up the wick of the kerosene lamp in the main room. Baigayo's husband Mamari had left the house, presumably to go restore peace in his capacity as local level government councillor. "Are you afraid?" Baigayo asked me with a smile. I said that I was. "Don't be afraid," she said, but we spent some time sitting there, saying very little and clutching pillows, until finally I went back to bed.

The next day there was a meeting of the entire village. Witches were abroad, we heard, and the only way to deal with the problem was to have a public forum to confront the events of the previous night. It was a tense atmosphere—"hot," as Mamari described it to me—with all the women sitting on one side of the beach and all the men on the other. One by one, people got up and related their version of what had happened. The story that emerged went something like this: up at the house of the Sundays, a prominent Isuisu family, a sound like the crying of a baby was heard. From there it had moved through the village. My friend Margaret Sunday said she had flashed her torch around but did not see anyone. Her older brother, an officer in the Papua New Guinea Defense Force, had then fired his rifle, which set off the alarm among a group of young men playing cards at another brother's house. This was the hue and cry we had heard during the night. The purpose of all the noise was to let the witch who was carrying her ghostly infant through the village know her presence had been detected and to ward her off. Mamari told me this kind of phenomenon is taken as a sign that someone was about to die, putting everyone on edge.

A recurring theme of people reporting on the previous night was that everyone could hear the sound of the baby crying but could not see who was making it, and it was this invisibility that was the hallmark of the witch. It also led to a debate on how she had accomplished her invisible sojourn through the village. A senior man stood up and quietly explained that a witch can send her spirit out in her sleep to conduct this kind of mischief, perhaps without even knowing it. A senior woman also stood and said that a witch can put leaves under her pillow and travel in her sleep—"To Australia, to America even"—which elicited laughter, but it was nervous laughter.

Once a narrative of the witch's movements had been established, several men got up to vent their anger that any woman in Isuisu should be playing tricks of this kind. There was a good deal of bluster and drama: younger men threatened variously to shoot the witch, to chop her to pieces, or to douse her in petrol and set her alight. I would have been more disturbed by these threats—actions that have actually been carried out in other parts of Papua New Guinea—had there been any recent history of this kind of violence on the Suau Coast, which there was not. David Kaisa, the village court magistrate, reminded everyone that courts and informal *hadudulai* for witchcraft and sorcery are the hardest of all to conduct, so it was in everyone's interests to stop the problem before it produced more court cases. Mamari said that if he heard anyone making an accusation of witchcraft against any named individual, he would fine them—the accuser, that is—and Eliot Sunday, the peace officer, also invoked a "law and order" theme, saying he did not want any further "*raskol* activity" in the village. A theme of general social disintegration was articulated by the next several speakers, as well as the reminder that accusations of witchcraft were almost as hazardous to the moral health of the village as the witchcraft itself. Later, Mamari clarified to me that if there was an accusation he would find a way to penalize every woman in the village, "because we don't know who it is." And there lay the crux of the problem: no one knew the identity of the witch, because she had acted invisibly and possibly even unconsciously.

Then the women began to stand up and speak. Some were as theatrically outraged as the men, waving their knives about and demanding of the witch presumed to be present whether she intended to sacrifice the village's children in the pursuit of her unholy agenda. Several adopted an indignant confessional or testimonial style, chastising themselves and their sisters for bearing the latent potential for witchcraft: "All of us women are witches!" Others were more conciliatory, suggesting that the women must sort out the problem among themselves and reminding the meeting that the majority of women in Isuisu were good Christians who would have nothing to do with old practices such as witchcraft. These women suggested that if everyone prayed together, the witch's heart would be moved to give up her witchcraft and behave like a proper human being.

In the event, this proposal was the one that could realistically be carried out. Following a stern reminder from Mamari that any actual woman accused of witchcraft was running the risk of finding herself in the village court (or worse), the pastor led the gathered village in a lengthy and fervent prayer. Following this, all the women of the village lined up shoulder to shoulder, and all the men moved down the line of women, shaking their hands. Most people treated this exercise with gravity, but some women appeared to find it amusing, barely suppressing laughter and exaggerating their handshaking when they saw I had my camera pointed in their direction. As the atmosphere of tension that had pervaded the meeting broke, the hilarity of the women and even some of the men was palpable. The better part of two hours had been spent venting very public fear and anger about the actions of a person who may or may not have been present. What could people do but laugh? The witch was knowable only by means of the mayhem she had caused; her identity and her actions were invisible, and only their effects felt upon the village at large.

Figure 6.1. Shaking hands after the witchcraft meeting, Isuisu. Photo by the author.

"But although others cannot see the witch," as Munn (1986: 232) has written of witchcraft on the Milne Bay island of Gawa, "the latter's own vision exceeds the ordinary." That is, ordinary human beings may see their own lives negated through the projected vision of the witch, a person for whom the positively valued relations to which most people aspire are but a mirror image of the power of negative action that is her stock in trade. In addition to inverting the moral order of the world, in which people nurture and support one another rather than causing illness and misfortune, the vision of witches inverts the temporal order, projecting a past many people have professed a wish to forget into the everyday lives of those in the present. Munn's "excess of the ordinary" is an excess of the normal state of personhood: witches can cause others to experience in their bodies what the witch perceives to be there. The fear and anger expressed at the village meeting, converted at the end into slightly hysterical relief, allowed everyone present to observe and gauge each other's bodily state. Like the resumption of ordinary temporality at the close of the funerary sequence, the mass *anto'i*—salutation or handshake—at the end of the meeting signaled the resumption of reinvigorated relations in the present. The specter of the past, manifested through the threat of witchcraft, had been lifted, at least for the time being.

Schram (2010) has noted of similar witchcraft meetings on Normanby Island that "confessional talk . . . functions as a collective epistemic practice by which people can presuppose the witchcraft that they cannot see. . . . Witchcraft thus becomes known as the inverse image of its confession" (2010: 735). In common with Suau and most if not all other Milne Bay societies, witchcraft for Auhelawa people on Normanby is held to be activated consciously or unconsciously by feelings of ill will: jealousy, resentment, and other grievances linked to perceived disparities in wealth and good fortune. The problem remains that neither witchcraft nor the feelings that animate it can be seen, and so confessional practices of the kind found at meetings across Milne Bay Province, from Normanby in the north to Suau in the south, bridge the visibility deficit in witchcraft discourses. Such meetings also seek to invert the danger of witchcraft, as Schram implies, through revelation of the negative sentiments that may have given rise to the witchcraft in the first place.

Revelation's efficacy as a technique works because it draws on multiple aesthetic resources available to people throughout Milne Bay Province. One might be described as indigenous: this is the value of "openness" (*so'e* in Suau), connoting positive flow, or being "out in the open" (*masalaha* in Suau, and compare Schram 2010: 737), where one's moral and affective states are available for others to see and assess. Another might be described as exogenous, although it has by now been so fully embraced in Milne Bay that its foreign origins are certainly debatable; I refer here to the confessional, testificatory, or revelatory modes of speech in Christian language practices as they have been adopted across the Pacific (Tomlinson 2009; Handman 2014b). The inversion implied by this speech register, of bringing the unknown interior state of a person outside to make it known, and the moral or spiritual inversion of the witch's malevolence that it is supposed to effect, run in analogous parallel to the temporal inversion implied by the eruption of witchcraft talk itself into everyday life. That is, to speak of witchcraft at all is to speak of the history to which witchcraft and its masculine counterpart, sorcery, belong and to which they were supposed to have been confined by the revelation of Christianity by James Chalmers to his Suau hosts. As I have discussed elsewhere (Demian 2006b and 2013), the modes in which the history of the Suau Coast are spoken of serve to emplace that history, to anchor it in time by means of anchoring it in space. Talk about witchcraft and sorcery, talk about *kastom*, and talk about other activities of the ancestors are all hazardous but vital, in that they bring the past into view in order to reassure people that it is, for the most part, behind them. Like the mortuary sequence described in chapter 2 and the permanent fixture in the landscape of mytho-historical persons in chapter 4, this kind of talk acts upon time in order to concentrate it and hold it in place, to prevent it from threatening the liveliness of those in the present or their aspirations for the future.

But as Andersen (2017) notes, one of the ironic functions of modernist narratives is that they always contain within them the specter of the incompletely released past. In her account of Papua New Guinean nursing students' fears of sorcerous attack while on their practicum rounds in rural areas, the threat of the past is very explicitly a past that dwells in particular places, in the particular kinds of relationships "still" conducted by rural (and by extension of the modernist narrative, less-educated) people. The past is also a place for these PNG cosmopolitans, and their affective experiences of remote villages are infused with

> a sort of temporal slippage in remote places that meant you could never be sure that ancestral *pasin* [a Tok Pisin alternative to *kastom*] was truly in the past. Because in many parts of PNG the practices classified as "pasin" or "kastom" were abandoned in performative ways at the time of conversion, they have a uniquely problematic status for Christians. Ancestral practices were not classified as ancestral because they were irrevocably in the past, left behind by the impersonal engine of historical progress, but because people had made a choice to repudiate them and become Christians. (Andersen 2017: 251)

Modernity, even when it is explicitly inculcated as a value in someone's education as a medical practitioner, is never a complete process; this is a feature of the modern constitution. The "nonmodern" must be continually held in check through practices such as Christian testimony and regular, as in daily, acts of worship.

Andersen's observations about the perpetual noncompletion of modernist projects are an important corrective, not only to the framework of modernism itself, which has been imported wholesale into the educational systems of countries like Papua New Guinea, but also to the notion that *any* temporal mode can completely deliver on its promises. Even when people engage in self-conscious or performative rejections of the past and the morally troubling practices emanating from it, they are bringing it into view, reminding themselves anew why it is so important to forget.

One Fine Day

During my earlier periods of fieldwork in Suau, I could not regard it as any coincidence that forgetting was cited to me as the culmination of two processes: the passage of time and the work of a funeral. While these would seem to be incommensurate, as the former is "cosmological" and the latter "sociological," they clearly are not perceived as differentiated in this way for the context I was working in—indeed, it may be that funeral work is ultimately necessary in order to *ensure* that time is reactivated as that process which sees people moving across the landscape, having children, making gardens and houses, and leaving behind trees, graves, roads, and other indicia of their presence in the world. When Battaglia asks "why mortuary practices everywhere tend to persist even after other forms of public ritual are all but forgotten" (Battaglia 1993: 437), she is not positing the timelessness of a type of institution in the face of "social change," or the "continuity thinking" against which Robbins (2007) has cautioned, but rather a recognition of the aspects of this institution that enables or encompasses change as a value proposition. Obviously, mortuary practices themselves change as well—for example, where there had once been up to six consecutive feasts in the Suau region, there is now only one. But what remains is that such practices in Milne Bay, not to mention many other Austronesian societies, are themselves technologies of forgetting.

Battaglia has argued for the reconsideration of this institutionalized forgetfulness as a constructive and generative, rather than amnesiac or otherwise truncating, process. This is highly consonant with what I have witnessed on the Suau Coast, where the stated goal of forgetting in mortuary practice is management of the pain of losing a member of one's family or wider social field. The goal is achieved through a refocusing or reorientation of the collective gaze to a redistributed configuration of relationships. In Battaglia's conceptualization, this sense of loss and the need to apprehend it stems from the absence of an object, in this case a person, but a person constituted as a relational node connecting other nodes, other people. "Forgetting" this absence enables these connections to be reestablished elsewhere; "memory" is the illusion of maintaining their former positions: "The fiction being constructed in commemoration is of a perduring connectivity. But it is a fiction constructed *against* the partibility and disconnectivity that is a fact of everyday social life" (1993: 432, emphasis in original).

Physical memorials (*he'ihe'inoi*) in Suau, such as coconut palms sprouted and planted on a gravesite, consolidate and anchor the memory of the dead to one place, preventing the dangers both of a mischievous wandering *yaluwa* and of unabating, perpetual grief. Memory is something fixed, immobile and immobilizing: forgetting, on the other hand, is what enables people and their relationships with one another to proceed into the future. It is a deliberate, necessary component of reproduction itself, because children do not fully re-place their parents—become their parents' *he'ihe'inoi*—until, paradoxically, the parents are "forgotten." Battaglia writes:

> Productive consequences derive not from the fact of a difference (substantive or spatiotemporal), not even from its manifestation, but from the orientation of manifest difference to what might be called *elementary fields of action*. . . . This orientation is achieved by way of recognizing and constituting an enduring purpose to separation. (1993: 438, emphasis in original)

The "elementary fields of action," as she conceives of them, are in the case of Suau temporality the ideological fields of movement and stasis. A difference has been produced between a past in which association with place was secondary to association with distant groups of people, and a present in which identity is formed primarily through association with named locations. The terms of separation, *huyahuya yai* (the times before) and *aho te* (the present day), are not indicative of an episodic temporal orientation so much as collective markers of ancestors, totems and institutions that have been fixed or concentrated in time, in opposition to living people, thriving lineages, and new economic roads. They are not necessarily forgotten because knowledge of them no longer exists (although this certainly is often the case) but because the knowledge no longer leads anywhere. It no longer creates connections between people that can be acted upon, the relationships whose care and nurture are generative of both space and time.

What does, then? The relationship of Suau people to the land they inhabit and depend upon has, over the turn of the recent century, become increasingly particular and arguably more contentious in the face of pressures such as oil palm, logging, and the population spike. Certain institutions may ensure the continuing redistribution of positive relationships even in the face of these economic, ecological, and demographic challenges. These could include the funeral process, the movement of people through marriage, education and employment, and their mobilization into groups of relatively novel categories of persons (especially "women" and "youth") through church activities.

Somewhat counterintuitively, the vigorous but selective forgetting engaged in by Suau people also guarantees the reproduction of relationships:

> In this part of the world where personhood is relationally *constituted* (not merely represented) in material exchanges ... and where selfhood is realized in relationality, what is lost and what is being commemorated is not a singular individual but rather the social connectivity, actual or possible, that the physical presence of a person allows. (Battaglia 1993: 432, emphasis in original)

If the wholesale discarding of practices during the colonial era by Suau people, ranging from dances to warfare, was agentive, it was an agency exercised in the interest of such social connectivity. It was also the mildly coercive agency of hospitality, the offering of one's home in order to—potentially—incorporate the other into one's category of homeliness, or at least to require a reciprocal offering. That the others in this case never intended to reciprocate the hospitality given them by Suau opened up the gap of irony, the knowledge, both painful and humorous, that the project of clearing away the past had been insufficient to capture and retain the attention of the other. The Suau project of eliciting relationships with planters, patrol officers, soldiers, and especially missionaries was largely a project of sacrifice, of a forgetting that would usher in a future of productive relations with foreigners. By the time I began work in this region in the 1990s, there was almost nothing left for them to forget and leave behind them—except for witchcraft and sorcery, the detritus of the past that Suau people feel they have never quite managed to clear away.

Techniques for locating oneself in time do change in response to such frustrated experiments in social innovation. The Suau Coast, during my period of acquaintance with it, has appeared to be holding time in abeyance—neither at the mercy of history nor entirely its master either, but rather existing in a state of poised alertness to what might come next. I cannot, with Miyazaki (2004), call this state of alertness a hopeful one. Although both he and Hage (2003) have done much to liberate the concept of hope from a merely optimistic affective mode, even showing how hope structurally carries with it a fear of failure into the future, I still find it too purposive or programmatic a stance vis-à-vis the future to describe what I have seen happening in Suau for nearly twenty years. Unlike Miyazaki's Fijian Methodist interlocutors, who "sought to introduce a prospective perspective to a present constantly invaded by retrospection" (2004: 120), Suau people do not appear to have developed comparable techniques or methods (to use Miyazaki's term) of acting as if they could act upon the future in spite of the frustrating tenacity of the past. Their encounter with the church as a structured and structuring institution was too brief by comparison with Fiji, their wider experience with the colonial project also too haphazard and piecemeal, and their own sensibilities for dealing with productive relationships too conducive to letting go of those deemed no longer productive. When forgetting is itself a fundamental technique for social reproduction, it is difficult to develop other techniques that require a commitment to the long term, either in prospect or retrospect.

But neither, as I hope I have made clear, are Suau people in a state of despair. The situation on the Suau Coast is more like what Street (2012) has described for the remnants of colonial infrastructure across Papua New Guinea—in the case of her particular focus, its hospitals. Modernism is not only a fetish encumbering the anthropology of Melanesia but also one built into the physical fabric of metropoles across the region, where the colonial era and its immediate aftermath saw the building, leaving behind, decaying, and rebuilding—but in diminished form—of the literal spaces of modernist "improvements" to the lives of Melanesian people. Street calls our attention to

> the importance of ruination as a process that is intrinsic to the lived experience of modernist planned space. Processes of renewal, construction, and reinvestment in the hospital as a space of improvement are as much a part of this process of ruination as the durable debris of colonial projects. I have therefore suggested that ruination be considered a dynamic process of shifting spatial inequalities (between "European" and "Native," "Private" and "Public," and "Western" and "Papua New Guinean") rather than a linear process of deterioration. The multiplicity of new building projects at Madang Hospital shows that the institution cannot simply be thought of as a static ruin. Instead, ruination is shown to be a dynamic ongoing process of simultaneous construction and disappointment. (2012: 54)

Many Papua New Guineans will feel the loss of the colonial era, with all its experiments in social engineering from the quixotic (a self-contained Christian society on a tiny island in the Coral Sea) to the pragmatic (hospitals originally built for a European patient base repurposed badly for a Papua New Guinean one), as an ironic one for some time to come. Because disappointment is never only disappointment: most Papua New Guineans of my acquaintance feel that things began to fall apart shortly after independence, yet they are perfectly cognizant at the same time that nothing built or otherwise "developed" during the colonial era was built with them in mind. This is the irony of history in many places in Papua New Guinea, not only on the Suau Coast.

Notwithstanding the experience of abjection that I argued for in chapter 3, there remains the potential to reassemble both a personal and a societal sense of the possible in the aftermath of such an experience. It is, however, a temporally constrained reassemblage, and one that holds not only time but also time's intelligibility at bay. The perspective of particular generations, and where they find themselves in relation to a place—literally—in history, is critical here. Le-Fevre (2013) has described the experience of Kanak youth in New Caledonia, who wait for an ever-imminent referendum that might make independence from France a reality at last, as one of inhabiting anticipation as a component of everyday life in the capital, Nouméa. "This generation has been shaped by anticipation—a pervasive and deeply held feeling that *something* is going to happen *soon* that will profoundly change what it means to be indigenous in New Caledonia" (2013: 216, emphasis in original). This anticipatory mode inspires young urban Kanaks to form voluntary associations, the form for which is provided by French law but the content of which is deeply Melanesian in that it creates a single identity through shared practices, some of which are drawn from New Caledonia's rural regions. Like Hukula's (2017) urban Papua New Guineans creating multiply emplaced relations of belonging, Kanak youth use French modes of association to assert new versions of indigeneity, grounded in a Kanak future that might, just possibly, no longer be French.

Here I find the "near future" perspective proposed by Guyer (2007) useful—her formulation is intended "to privilege emergent socialities rather than ideational forms. To ask what becomes 'near' when 'near' fades from collective consciousness is to ask about social distance and access as well as conceptual horizons. It is to invoke material and political urgencies as well as time-space schema" (2007: 410). Guyer's insistence on "emergent socialities" is key here, resonating with the sense of "Well, let's see what's next" that often pervades social life on the Suau Coast. Suau people, with their long but patchwork experience of colonial and postcolonial others, have become adept—perhaps too adept, in their estimation—at moving between social orders. The near future is not a cosmology, but a pre-cosmology or inter-cosmology, the gap of irony that people must occupy while they wait for the world to catch up with their expectations of it. For as Guyer crucially points out, the near future is the temporal register of both macroeconomic theory and evangelical Christianity, two cosmologies that arguably have had an outsized influence on Papua New Guinea as they have in other nations that are still, with a lack of irony so profound it is itself ironic, referred to as "emerging" or "developing." The projects of economic projection and religious prophecy, Guyer notes, both give rise to a futurity whose intelligibility is distanced from the quotidian activities of most people. Whether the good life has been promised in economic or spiritual terms, it is not coming any time soon. Guyer notes how "prophetic time" in evangelical Christianity is "a kind of hiatus, whose intelligibility is explicitly in abeyance" (2007: 414) because only God can reveal the commencement of the next epoch in history and thereby the meaning of events happening in the present moment. This idea, preached regularly from pulpits across the Suau Coast by pastors originating and trained throughout the country, also finds expression in the humble and oft-repeated Suau idiom *malaitom asubena*. Literally "tomorrow day," it is normally glossed by English-speaking Suau as "one fine day," a time when something of interest might happen that may be either positive or negative in nature. But the timing of that time, as it were, is entirely unknown to the speaker, who may indeed refer in the next breath to the fact that only God knows when the actions of people in the present will have their denouement in the future.

For the moment, people wait. Their waiting is by no means passive inaction, particularly among younger Suau, whose impatience for something to happen finds expression in the all-night homebrew drinking parties organized by young men and the massive population spike produced by young men and women alike, the responsibility for which falls disproportionately on the teen-aged girls who are taken out of school and marooned in the village to look after their children. The children are now legion, spilling out of the sides of the church on Sundays, trooping to their nearest underresourced primary school on weekdays, as older people struggle to recall either their names or their parentage when at one time these data would have been common knowledge to everyone. There are simply too many of them now, and too many of them the result of casual liaisons, for others to keep up. And it is not only keeping track of lineage information that produces disquiet among the older generations of Suau, but it is also the knowledge that the land on the Suau Coast needed to support them in the future, however abundant now, is nonetheless finite in nature. Or as one young woman whom I had known since she was herself a tiny girl chastised her mother at a village court hearing in 2015, "You have all these grandchildren, but you haven't set aside land for any of them! One fine day they will need land for their houses and gardens!" The elder generations are not exempt from the problems of future generations, but the time of efficacious action for any generation currently living on the Suau Coast is, as yet, unknown.

The Road to REDD+?

During a visit I made to Milne Bay in 2014, Alotau was abuzz with the news that pilot research was being done for a possible REDD+ (reducing emissions from deforestation and forest degradation)[1] project in the Suau hinterland, from Leileiyafa in the west to Modewa at the eastern end of the coast. It is arguable that this project, to be funded by a donor agency in Germany, represented the tail end of what Filer and Wood (2012: 673) have called "the moment of irrational exuberance" in the relationship between Papua New Guinea and the carbon trading market, which holds out the allure of a new exploitable resource—forest carbon—without the moral hazard of large extractive industries such as mining and logging. The "irrationality" in the picture refers to what might charitably be called a lack of congruence between official forestry policy in PNG, the country's commitments under the UN-REDD Programme of which it is a partner, the widespread political and media influence of large international logging interests, and any number of localized aspirations for economic and infrastructural improvements by any means necessary. As Filer and Wood observe, this incongruence also generates its own cyclical rhythm over time: "The popular demand for 'development' generates new forms of property in forest resources, these are 'corrupted' by the multiplication of con-tested claims to ownership and control, the claims are subjected to new forms of state regulation, but these fail to satisfy the original demand for develop-ment, and so the cycle starts again" (2012: 675). While PNG has probably by now seen the end of the most "irrational" period of unregulated voluntary carbon trading schemes of the kind described by Wood (2015), in which a carbon credit project was proposed for an area that mapped precisely onto a logging concession in PNG's Western Province, other local cycles of develop-ment continue to be generated by the reinvention of forest carbon as an object of commodifiable market value (Dalsgaard 2013). The heavily forested Suau Coast, early on the scene of missionization but late to practically every "devel-opment" party since then, suddenly appeared to be having its moment in the forest carbon spotlight.

In 2014 I was alerted to a one-day workshop for "landowners" being held at the Masurina Lodge, the oldest hotel in Alotau, by Nancy Sullivan, an an-thropologist who ran a social research consultancy in PNG and passed away tragically the following year. At this workshop, the consultant representing the German aid agency explained to an almost entirely male audience how the project might work. The next day, four-wheel drives and dinghies carrying survey teams headed down to the Suau Coast. I cadged a lift to Isuisu with the biological inventory team tasked with identifying the biodiversity value of the area. As they had explained to me the evening before at the Masurina Lodge, one of the factors affecting whether or not the project would go forward was the value placed on the number of species within the project region. In the global carbon trading market, to have trees and animals is not enough. It is not only forests in their capacity as carbon sequestration mechanisms that are to be protected by means of REDD+ initiatives, but biodiversity.

Also, as the pilot study researchers noted to me, the project would only work as a conservation scheme if the donor agency pays people more to leave their trees alone than the logging companies can pay them to cut the trees down. Additionally and somewhat perversely, to demonstrate this fact, peo-ple on the Suau Coast will have to show that they have been approached by such companies to prove that their forests are at risk for being logged. Taken together, these complications—or as Suau might say, "entanglements"—made me doubtful that the project would ever materialize. But there was an even more entangling factor: the issue of land ownership itself and its projection over time. Filer (2012) has warned that carbon trading and other "green economy" projects are dependent on very long-term agreements between those investing in carbon sequestration projects like REDD+ and customary landowners. These kinds of arrangements are something approaching a structural impossibility in PNG, where disputes over the same land boundaries are liable to crop up between different actors every time land and its resources are found to hold some form of market value. The German consultant who had presented the project at the Alotau workshop told me earnestly that they would need to deal with a single landowner per parcel of land; I told him he would never have a viable project if he insisted on dealing with ownership this way, as such a model of landownership does not exist in Suau or indeed anywhere else in PNG. I attempted briefly to explain the Suau relationship to land as I have outlined it here in chapter 4, and I warned him that many of the actual owners of the land his project is interested in would not be resident on that land, as their lineages would have been moved down to the coast or to Mullins Harbour by the colonial administration over the course of the twentieth century. He blinked in bafflement and said, "That would be as if I tried to claim land back in Poland where my family originally came from." I said, "Exactly. It wouldn't work for you, but that's how it works here. If you place a monetary value on the land, then you will find landowners coming out of the woodwork."

Once I had arrived in Isuisu, Mamari agreed that this was the likely outcome of land being given a monetary value by the REDD+ project, should it go forward. He told me the story of how, when the Irish telecommunications company Digicel began to install mobile base stations along the coast a year or two earlier, small pieces of mountaintop land that had previously been disregarded as having no value for gardening or any other use suddenly became prime real estate, and land disputes proliferated in their wake. So while by the time of my visit in 2014 I had a mobile phone signal in Isuisu—an unimaginable state of affairs just a few years earlier—this luxury had apparently come at the cost of bad blood between coastal *ulutubu* with hinterland origins and hence claims to land in the mountains. Herein lies one of the deepest entangling factors of REDD+: it relies on a potentially infinite projection of carbon ownership into the future, while land in Suau as elsewhere in PNG projects potentially infinite ownership into the past. Or as Dalsgaard has put it,

> REDD relies on this imaginary of potential (non-)action, where forest owners in the Global South will leave their trees alone in return for payments as long as the trees remain standing. REDD is thus a relationship construed as continuous, and the same trees and thus the same carbon will potentially be paid for again and again. For this reason, the ownership of the carbon is in this case termed "stewardship,"

and the local forest owners are paid to safeguard the carbon resource, which they no longer have undisputed ownership of. . . . At worst, the REDD scheme entails the controversial and counterintuitive situation where one can purchase the same carbon in perpetuity. (Dalsgaard 2013: 93)

It is hard to imagine a scenario in which Suau landowners, in full appreciation of this potential, would accept a permanent relinquishing of control over their forests. The flip side of REDD+'s potential, however, is contained in the "plus" symbol the acronym eventually acquired to indicate aspirations to go "beyond deforestation and forest degradation, and includes the role of conservation, sustainable management of forests and enhancement of forest carbon stocks" (UN-REDD.org). These aspirations may be read as a placeholder for the kind of continuous relationship alluded to by Dalsgaard, the idea that REDD+ creates a new, productive, and ongoing connection between the carbon-emitting countries of the "Global North" and the carbon-sequestering countries (if they are fortunate enough to be forested and biodiversity rich) of the "Global South." The connection depends, of course, on forested countries giving up control over their forests.

In Pascoe's (2018) critical intervention into what she terms the "REDD+ assemblage" in the Central Suau REDD+ Pilot Project, the implicit hierarchy of this relationship is made explicit through an analysis of how discourses of scale (the global, the national, the local) permeate the language used by every participant in the assemblage. These include the donor agencies, the national and provincial government offices, and the landowners on the Suau Coast trying to make sense of what exactly is being offered to them and what they are being asked to do in return. As Pascoe observes, this scalar language carries with it an implication of those at the level of "the local" having little control over the project, which instead circulates mostly at the level of the national and the international, leaving "locals" waiting—yet again, I am tempted to say—for the realization of any benefits to themselves. Referring to the smallest unit of local level government in PNG, the ward, she notes how

> the ward scale is constructed as the level where benefits should be distributed, which again bounds people at this scale and frames customary landowners as recipients, rather than decision-makers or active participants in REDD+. The emphasis on global environmental governance and national decisionmaking within the Central Suau REDD+ Pilot Project ignores the agency of local people and the role they play in governing their environments. (2018: 92)

The "environments" in question for Suau people are not just composed of trees, of course, but also stones, mountains, islands, rivers, caves, animals, ancestors, *kokome*, and all the histories and intentionalities that brought them into being. This environment that Suau people would very much like to govern for themselves is an expansive one, drawing in the interest of people from other places, and potentially inspiring them to stay.

Suau people know perfectly well by now that there is a cost to being connected, as the pervasive discussion of loss that I heard in the late 1990s suggested. Every new connection presents its own risks and its own apparent demand that some other valued area of everyday life be relinquished. Over the course of the twentieth century, giving up *kastom* in favor of new relationships with foreigners meant that when the foreigners left, people on the Suau Coast had neither the *kastom* nor the colonial infrastructure to show for their efforts. These days, such connections tend to be economic, such as the REDD+ initiative, but recently introduced connections of a technological and infrastructural nature still offer a beguiling combination of opportunity and jeopardy. The mobile telephony revolution introduced by Digicel, for example, presents its own particular challenges. People laud the convenience of calling dinghy operators and wholesalers in Alotau to stock their small canteens, and *wantoks* further afield to send remittances home, but they simultaneously worry about whom their young daughters and sons might be calling without their knowledge.

New possibilities continue to arise. Since the road was built as far as Leileiyafa, PMVs now leave daily from this once-isolated village to take people to Alotau via the burgeoning oil palm plantation "suburbs" in the Sagarai Valley, again a situation that was unimaginable when I first began fieldwork in this region in the 1990s. This road has been extended from Leileiyafa over the mountains to Fife Bay, a mere forty-minute walk from Isuisu and other villages at the western end of the coast. The completion of this road offers tremendous potential benefits to the area. But criminal gangs and, less ominously but just as problematically for parents, tearaway youth can also use roads. With the end of their former relative isolation, anything could travel along the road, from the Tok Pisin finally making linguistic inroads in Alotau to the viruses and bacteria that cause sexually transmitted infections. Connection is hazardous, to be sure—but disconnection, as I think my Suau friends have tried to make clear to me, is an even more parlous and undesirable state of affairs.

Times to Come: The Future of *Kastom* and the Future of a Relationship

Along with the potential of a road and the potential for land to hold a new kind of monetary value, an efflorescence in talk about *kastom* had arisen during my last periods of research on the Suau Coast. But this *kastom* talk took very particular forms on those more recent visits, mostly having to do with the governing of minor but significant actions that would keep people healthy and relationships benign. My host "sister" Marie explained that she had been discouraged from hanging an extra clothesline under her elder sister's unfinished new house because the presence of women's clothes would threaten the completion of the building work. "Because that's our *kastom*," she said, going on to elaborate that the men building it would lose the energy or will to finish the house if women entered the incomplete structure or even left their clothes there. Her account accorded with a much older description of canoe building I had been given years before, wherein women also could not touch either the unfinished canoe or the tools used to make it until it was complete—upon which the finished product of men's labor would be brushed with women's skirts to confer to the canoe the *gigiboli* ("heat" or "power") of women's bodies that would have been so dangerous prior to its completion. However, that earlier version of the hazards of women's clothing to incomplete construction projects had contained no reference to *kastom*.

But such references cropped up with a frequency that startled me on more recent visits. Baigayo explained why Marie's husband Kevin calls their son Joshua rather than Auswin, his given name: Auswin is the name of one of Kevin's affines, so he is obliged to practice *geba*, respectful name avoidance, which Baigayo attributed to *kastom*. Or on another occasion, when Sarah went with me to the compound of a family in mourning for a young kinswoman whose body had recently arrived from Alotau, she encouraged me to go in and cry but stopped short of actually entering the "mourning zone" herself because she had not cried yet and did not really intend to, and told me she needed to stay behind because of *kastom*. Indeed, I had been instructed to come and cry the day before by an older neighbor who said I would find the difference between Isuisu funerary *kastom* and Leileiyafa *kastom* interesting.

In point of fact, the differences in mortuary practices between these two places are minimal, or at least minimally discernible to the foreign ethnographer. But they form an important component in the rhetoric of distinctiveness that coastal and hinterland people draw between themselves, not only in the Suau region but also arguably throughout the Austronesian cultural complex. And perhaps it is no accident that *kastom* as an index of distinctiveness has also reemerged when Suau people are now contemplating new modes of connection to other parts of Papua New Guinea and beyond. If the *kastom* concept has always been, among other things, recognizing particular modes of differentiation between groups of people in Melanesia, it is tempting to suggest that my friends in Suau have begun to recast activities that did not used to fall under the *kastom* banner as now belonging to that category. The small, intimate, relationship-supporting actions I have been describing would more likely have been termed "respect" (*ha'atiti*) or simply "our way of living/inhabiting" (*ai*

Figure 6.2. Students at the Cameron Secondary School Cultural Show, Alotau. Photo by the author.

ema maoli; *ai ema babawa*) on my previous visits to Suau. It was specifically the things that had been *discarded* that were placed in the category of *kastom* in the 1990s—the songs and dances, styles of house and canoe building, the knowledge of gardening magic, the tattooing of women, and the spiritual and economic prowess of big men. These highly visible modes of Suau *kastom* now appear to have departed from everyday discourse altogether, possibly with the death of nearly the entire generation who could still speak about such practices from their own memory, and are only resurrected annually by students at the Cameron Secondary School Cultural Show in Alotau—sometimes with embellishments.

Suau people also now appear more comfortable—or perhaps resigned is the more appropriate word—in discussing the practices of the past that carry a more ambivalent moral value. On my 2014 visit, Baigayo spoke frankly to me of the prerogative of a husband to strike his wife once bridewealth had been paid, and claimed this prerogative as one arising from *kastom*, a connection I had never heard made before but one that appears to be gaining a disturbingly widespread currency throughout PNG (Macintyre 2011). I have documented village court cases from Leileiyafa in 1996–97 in which errant husbands were penalized for beating their wives. The contingent and often contested nature of what is and is not acceptable within a marital relationship is changing in Suau as it is everywhere else in the country (Cox and Macintyre 2014; Spark 2011), but again, the significance in the attribution of acceptable domestic violence to *kastom* accorded with the intimate rescaling and valuation that the category seems to have acquired.

But this conversation paled in comparison to the multiple discussions of *kastom* as the origin of sickness and death. Each illness endured by members of my host family, and each death in the village since my previous visit, was catalogued for me as a narrative of jealousy, the necessary precursor for an attack by means of sorcery, and *kastom*, the preferred gloss for such an attack that has remained constant from my first period of fieldwork onward. What has changed is, again, the moral evaluation of *kastom* appearing in this guise.

For sorcery is, after all, the artifact of the past that Suau people feel they have been unable to shed and possibly the thing that prevents their forming new relationships with others in the future, near or distant. All the talk about sorcery to which I have been subjected over the years also points not only to an orientation toward the world in general but also to an orientation toward what my Suau friends may have felt this anthropologist needed to know about them. And as I was reminded during my very first period of fieldwork in the 1990s, I will never know everything. One evening in Leileiyafa, my host Saunia said, apropos of nothing, "Next time your university sends someone to live here, make sure they send a man." Somewhat annoyed, I asked why. "So he can follow me around when I walk for very long distances, and so we can teach him about things we can't teach you about." Even more annoyed, I asked for an example of something I could not learn about. "Sorcery" was Saunia's one-word answer. And there the matter stayed. I had bumped right up against an internal knowledge partition, as anthropologists sometimes call the barriers between knowledge transmission and the structural distinction of the categories of persons who may access that knowledge, such as initiated and uninitiated, senior and junior, or men and women.

Losche (2001) records her own ambivalence with the secrecy discourses of the Abelam people with whom she has worked in the Sepik River region of Papua New Guinea. In particular, she notes the irony of some of her male colleagues' earnest belief in the capacity of senior Abelam men to reveal a complete cosmology to them in the face of her own certainty that the only secret knowledge is that there is no secret to reveal. Due to the competitive nature of political status in this as in most Papua New Guinean societies, and the "endless invention of secrets" to enhance the status of any given big man in Abelam, "there is unlikely to be, given the logic of this decentralized political system, one central man, or group of men, with a total, panoptic knowledge of the men's cults. . . . My own stance . . . became one of irony in the face of these masculine secrets, partly as the result of a sense of multiple outsiderness—as anthropologist and woman—watching the true believers and judging them naïve" (2001: 109). The "true believers," as Losche calls them, are the white men captivated by Abelam men's claims to secret knowledge. Such relations of captivation are not difficult to find throughout the anthropological literature, where internal knowledge partitions appear to exercise a peculiar hold on the imagination of anyone, of any gender, who regards themselves as able to access the totality of a given society's knowledge system and manner of forming relations with others in the world. Sometimes this totality is called a cosmology; at the moment in which this chapter is being written, it is *au courant* to call it an ontology. Like Losche, I am a skeptic in regard to claims of access to secret or otherwise totalizing knowledge of any society; also in common with her, my skepticism may largely be an acknowledgment of the temporal, professional, and other structural limits of the ethnographic relationship. Perhaps some anthropologists really have acquired a privileged access to a complete understanding of how their interlocutors conceive of the world. But I doubt it, and I am wholly committed to the partial understanding of the situations and societies anthropologists find ourselves in.

After all, "the field" is not a place just for the anthropologist to encounter but is a relationship the people hosting them are constantly negotiating. Which is why, for example, any philosophical claims made on behalf of a group of people are as ephemeral as the space of the relationship the anthropologist has sustained with them; it cannot endure in time if the relationship does not. *Kastom* referred to a particular, grand-narrative orientation to time and history when I first went to the Suau Coast in the mid-1990s. Twenty years later it refers to something else again, the near future of people's relationships with each other. And even my framing of the issue in this way is an outcome of the fact that I was the one to whom *kastom* was spoken about. Perhaps if, as Saunia wished, a man had been sent instead of me, Suau *kastom* would be revealed in the form of a complex of specialist magical knowledge.

Again, I doubt it, as male anthropologists who work in Milne Bay can find themselves as stymied by the enduring weight of the region's colonial relations as female ones are by our gender and the internal knowledge partitions attendant upon it. Rollason (2008) recounts his dismay at being positioned by interlocutors on the island of Panapompom as the latest manifestation of colonial judgment on their "wickedness" and lack of "development." Finding recourse in Wagner's notion of epochal time that I have also invoked in chapter 1, Rollason observes how ideally this temporal mode "is able to exploit the colonial rift between self and other, ironically, to unite them as moments in the other's time, granting them common ground in history, of a sort" (2008: 29). Rollason's "of a sort" here appears to be a throwaway remark, but in fact it is critical to the irony he identifies in the rift—or what I have called a gap—between what people all over Milne Bay may have thought the colonial other expected of them, what these others actually expected, and how Milne Bay peoples used those expectations to reflect on their own practices and inhabiting of the world. It was a relationship of a sort—until the colonials decided the relationship was no longer to the benefit of any interests in Europe, North America, or Australia, and they departed. Milne Bay societies and their colonial alters may once have occupied a common ground in history, but that history was never one they were allowed fully to own in mutuality with those alters.

Perpetual First Contact

The question remains, then, what future history might be written of this part of Papua New Guinea. I grew up reading science fiction and fantasy, two genres ideally suited to the imagination of a young person deeply curious about alternative ways of being in the world but as yet unaware that there was an entire academic discipline describing this curiosity. "Anthropology" did not enter my vocabulary until I was an undergraduate. Before that happened, I was entranced by stories such as Larry Niven's "Grammar Lesson" (1979), in which a well-intentioned human bartender is schooled by his alien clientele on his poor use of their language. The language has two possessive forms, described by Niven's characters as "intrinsic" and "extrinsic," where the intrinsic form refers to objects that are part of, say, the speaker's body.

I probably read that story in my early teens. A little over a decade later, I was endeavoring to learn a language that had precisely these two possessive forms plus a third, although the three possessives are normally designated as inalienable, alienable, and edible in scholarship on Milne Bay languages (Macintyre 1984; Demian 2021). The language was of course Suau, and learning that it had these three possessives was electrifying for me; the phenomenon had left the realm of fiction and entered real life. Nearly everything that science fiction writers dream up as features of alien social and cultural life tends already to exist in human ones. As a young science fiction reader, I thought I had encountered radical alterity in Niven's story. When I encountered it again as an ethnographer, the alterity of organizing a language in this way seemed suddenly less radical but all the more thrilling.

In the 1990s this insight suited the sensibilities of a novice fieldworker struggling with the romanticism that probably colors the beginning of most anthropologists' careers, whether we admit to it or not, and whose loss must mark the line between wanting to be an anthropologist and actually becoming one. It was a hard loss. In my mid-twenties I first went to Papua New Guinea dreaming of cargo cults, taro gardens, and the scene painted by one of my undergraduate lecturers: "I couldn't believe someone was paying me to sit under a palm tree on a beach in the Pacific!" Some of these things I got, including the tree and the beach. I also got malaria, the frustration and mild paranoia of learning a new language without formal instruction, and the irritation of being woken up at all hours of the night by village boys trying their luck.[2] Mostly, however, what I got was a relationship with people who had expectations of me that projected into a future far outstripping the blinkered perspective of my doctorate. Back in the 1990s this was, frankly, terrifying: my hosts in Leileiyafa and Isuisu could see a future that I could not. But they could do so because I had appeared at all, and in the context of Pacific sociality, making an appearance requires that some kind of relationship be recognized, although it may only be the provisional relationship of hospitality to begin with. It was the repeat visits that demonstrated a relationship to be cared for actually existed between us, even if a sufficient number of years had passed between two of those visits that some friends in Isuisu told me they assumed I had died in the Twin Towers on 11 September 2001. It made perfect sense: a lack of funding and the perpetual search for one's next job during the early years of an academic career were not sufficient to explain why I had not come back in such a long time. Only my speculative death, to clear me out of the way, was a satisfactory explanation.

In 2008 Mamari asked me with some resignation, "Melissa, u tawasola e ige'e?" (Are you getting married or not?) I replied with the most noncommittal word in my Suau vocabulary: "Iba'i!" which means roughly, "Who knows?" or "Beats me!" He accepted this nonanswer with his usual good grace. But I took his point. If I did not marry and have children, how would our friendship continue? It was a good question. In spite of the unparalleled privilege I enjoy in being able to visit their place while—as I am reminded continually—most of them will never see mine, there is no guarantee in the academic future that I will be able to return to Suau indefinitely. And the radical alterity cuts both ways: even if I had followed the "standard trajectory" of marriage and reproduction, I know perfectly well that children in the *dimdim* world tend not to feel that they have inherited all their parents' social obligations. Mamari, of course, did not know this when he asked his marriage question. So while he and his family may feel this book is a poor substitute for children, to me it is the most reliable form in which to generate an ongoing relation between my experiences of living with them and theirs of living with me. It is, in fact, the only way I have of making the intentions behind those many visits knowable to my hosts.

In a short essay on the philosophical underpinnings of critical anthropology, Hage (2014) offers up the notion that anthropology stands within a Renaissance tradition of regarding perspective (in art) and optics (in science) as a means of "touching the mystery of God." That is, new ways of seeing the world became new ways of thinking about the composition of the world, while yet laying no claim to being able to know the world in its totality. As with painting and physics, so in the much more recent disciplines of the social sciences: Hage suggests there is a "long tradition of an anthropology defined by a continual encounter with radical alterity: anthropology as a permanent state of first contact." First contact is the phrase most often used to indicate the historical encounters, normally in the context of colonial expansion, between Europeans and their alters—the crew of a ship being offered the invitation "Let's go up!" for example. First contact describes a situation in which the intentions of visitors and hosts are unknowable to each other. If I will claim any knowledge about the Suau Coast and its history, I might claim that what Suau people "really" feel they have lost was the project of perpetuating that state of first contact. First contact means resisting the impulse to believe that you can easily assimilate the differences of others to your own regime of value. This is the heart, I think, of the critical anthropology to which Hage is gesturing—and of course that project cuts both ways. "Oceania is vast, Oceania is expanding," Hau'ofa (1993: 16) reminded the reader to whom the sea of islands reaches out, requiring attention, connection, and care. "Oceania is hospitable and generous, Oceania is humanity rising from the depths of brine and regions of fire deeper still, Oceania is us."

And the question always is, when do we know we are confronting the exclusive "us" found in the pronouns of so many Oceanic languages, including Suau—"we but not you"—or the inclusive one—"all of us together"? First contact describes that vertiginous uncertainty of not knowing who "us" might include or exclude. The idea of first contact is also a popular one in science fiction, of course, itself a genre spawned in the colonial era, and one describing over and over the encounter between humans and their possible alters. Science fiction first-contact narratives can be terrifying or inspiring, magnifying as they do the attributes of an entire history of colonial contact events. And the irony of science fiction lies in precisely how nonfictional it fundamentally is; the radical alterity of an alien world can generally be found right here on this one, and the invasion tropes of so much filmic science fiction are of course lifted straight from the history of colonialism. This is also the underlying irony of a critical anthropology: however we might wish to hold the difference of others in our regard and make use of the creative potential of that difference, it will eventually collapse if we are actually holding the mutuality of regard in good faith and we are able to perceive the alien in ourselves. All of us together, then.

Perceiving the regard of the alien, anticipating it, and integrating it into a sense of who they have become has been a very long project on the Suau Coast. If the near future is all that is manageable now as a frame for action, this does not mean that it is the only future available to Suau people. The time of the colonial regard that they once endeavored to capture for themselves, the time of the near future in which they are now entangled in an attitude of expectation, and the time for which they wait, to be revealed (or not) in the course of the present century, is a question no anthropologist is in a position to answer. The future of the Suau Coast and its people is a vista that is only perceptible in the shared regard of Suau and the others who have come to them before, and who may one day come again.

Notes

1. The plus sign in REDD+ often causes confusion as to what it might stand for. Officially it indicates a suite of other benefits that ought to flow from these programs, to do with the long-term conservation and maintenance of forests. But even the agencies tasked with coming up with a standardized definition of REDD+ have consistently struggled to do so (Lee et al. 2018).
2. It was months before I worked out that this was formal courtship and not just the generic obnoxiousness of masculine youth. Some girls who had spent most of their lives in Alotau were visiting relatives in Leileiyafa, and they cut their visit short because of the incessant nocturnal visits of the local bachelors. "That's how these boys find a wife," one of them told me wearily, "but we're not used to it because we live in town." There are two popular techniques for waking up a girl or woman without waking her parents or guardians, which is the object of the endeavor. First you must work out which room of the house she is sleeping in. Then you can use a knife or slender stick to poke her through the floorboards of the house, if there is only the traditional pandanus sleeping mat between her and the floor. Alternatively, if she has been foolish enough to leave her window open, you can climb through the window and shine a torch in her face. It was a difficult decision to sacrifice cooling ventilation for an undisturbed night's sleep, but eventually the decision had to be made.

Conclusion
Measuring Time

"In Oceania," writes McDougall (2016: 29), "the spaces of hospitality are not houses, but beaches." She is referring to her own experience in the Solomon Islands, in an account that could—as her statement implies—refer to any number of Pacific contexts where the stranger is welcomed in an act of "irreducible ambivalence" (2016: 29) at the meeting of the sea and the land, its own kind of material and spatial ambivalence. The Suau Coast is one such context, where a long coastline with its heavily forested interior have hosted a series of visitors since at least the last third of the nineteenth century. Some of these visitors were passing through; others stayed for a time with the intention of changing the spiritual landscape; others stayed for another period with the intention of establishing a plantation economy; others were there to repel the military invasion that arrived in 1942; others still have come and gone to log tropical hardwoods, introduce new cash crops, attempt to trade in carbon credits, and gather ethnographic knowledge.

Each of these visitors has presumed upon the hospitality of Suau people, who have in turn extended it, time and again. In each case, they adopted a willingness to experiment with the new social orders represented by their guests, and to incorporate these social orders into their repertoire of connections to other people and other places. The consequences of their willingness have been manifold. Many guests on the Suau Coast never regarded themselves as guests, or Suau people as hosts; for this type of relationship to be recognized on both sides, an entire colonial project predicated on categorical asymmetry would never have been possible. That project was aimed at creating a context that would reproduce itself: whether a religious system, or an economic one, or a regime of law; and then, riding on the coattails of all of these, an independent state modeled after those of the former colonizers. To a degree, all of these efforts were successful, notwithstanding the disappointment in the Papua New Guinean state voiced nearly everywhere from the Australian media to the reports of international NGOs to the village meetings held throughout PNG. It is not the same kind of disappointment in each of these cases, however. No matter how international interests may regard the activities of a state that has existed for all of forty-five years, the disappointments of ordinary Papua New

Guineans have their own qualities and inflections. For Suau people, whose experiences with the world beyond their territory predate the nation of PNG by a century, that nation simply has never been able to measure up to what came before.

I invoke the idea of measurement for a reason. If irony is an effect of the gap between what was anticipated and what has happened instead, the very perception of a gap is a distancing, a comparison between terms. Consider Strathern's (2020) discussion of such comparisons as a temporal form, generated out of the delay in revelation implied in

> trying to describe a world where nothing present announces what it otherwise ("really") is, and where the idea that you learn by looking would strike people as extraordinary, for you wait on what the future will tell—an inscrutability as true of your state of relations with kin and friends as of anything else. Between an enactment and the interpretation of it, time must lapse; past events, including how persons impinge on one another, are "known" through their subsequent effects. (Your previous hospitality is measured by, exchanged with, their hospitality to yourself). (2020: 66)

Strathern's parenthetical comment is for my purposes the crux of the dilemma that has faced people on the Suau Coast for many decades now: if the hospitality they extended was never returned in the ways they anticipated, or returned in any way at all, how will they know who all those colonial agents "really" were or what they "really" wanted? What kind of history is so unfinished that it continues to intrude into the present with the effects of these unanswered extensions of friendship and kinship?

This book has been an attempt to describe such a history, and in that act of description, an attempt also to follow the lead of my Suau friends and interlocutors in how to do social analysis. My premise throughout, as noted in the introduction, has been that ironic reflection by Suau people on their own actions in the past is also an expression of what it means to have done a better job of analyzing their relationships with not-yet-known others than those others did. Suau people learned over the course of their pre-independence century of engagement with "the global"—in its manifestations through Christianity, the market economy, colonial administration, and a world war—to speak to others in terms those others would recognize. This ongoing effort of hospitable expansiveness has succeeded at some points and not so much at others: a cargo movement that appropriated the languages of prophecy and monarchy did not work out, whereas the steadfast and celebratory Suau claim to be among the first Christians in Papua has resulted in a secondary school named after the missionary who converted them and a road built by the descendant of another.

The comparison between successful and unsuccessful attempts by Suau people to occupy the new contexts offered to them over the course of this history also introduces gaps that are helpful to think about in terms of the Suau project of social analysis. Because while it may be obvious in retrospect where the analysis was faulty—one cannot declare oneself a prophet, at least not outside the context of the newer Pentecostal churches—the more interesting problems have arisen from those instances where it succeeded. Take the Suau claim to have forgotten *kastom*. Again, this could be read as a modernist narrative wherein the past is lost to us, and all that is authentically "ours" along with it, because we were hostages to historical-political processes over which we had no control. I continue to insist that it be regarded instead as an ironic one, because the discarding of *kastom* was deliberate, an outcome both of Suau analyses of what missionaries and other colonial agents wanted and of their willingness to act on those analyses. The irony here, again, is that what initially looked like a successful analysis turned out not to be one, in the longer term. Alternatively, one could say the analysis had its own temporariness built in, since nobody can predict the future, and the agents of the colonial endeavor also could not have foreseen how that entire project would itself come to an end in the decades following World War II.[1] Suau rhetoric about forgetting and loss may be a discourse of mourning among other things, but its nostalgia is not for the precolonial social order. Rather, it is oriented toward the proliferation of social orders that the colonial era appeared to introduce, and toward their varying durations, both long and short. The ability to act skillfully within these different social orders as well as their own is what Suau people lost when the missionaries, planters, and soldiers left, and the very seat of government itself then departed for another part of the province.

I take the concept of multiple social orders from Gershon's (2019) usage, wherein she notes a common theme running through a number of otherwise disparate ethnographic undertakings of the past decade or so. Having released themselves from the confines of both "society" and "culture" as organizing principles for the peoples they work with, ethnographers have instead turned to analyzing what Gershon refers to as "patterned, perduring, interwoven, and transportable repertoires of interactions that are available for reflexive explication" (2019: 405). The "reflexive explication" in her description is key, as it refers to the ways that people's own habits of social analysis become the techniques by which they make bids to move objects, signs, and themselves between social orders. Sometimes their bids fail, as when a cargo prophet has his nascent movement broken up by colonial administrators, or when an audacious young man is told his land claim cannot be made through the patriline. And those who would introduce new social orders can also make failed bids to do so, as for example when an international donor agency running a carbon credit scheme is consistently unable to make its intentions knowable to Suau people or to engage with what "landownership" on the Suau Coast actually entails (Pascoe 2019). Structural asymmetries persist in making some social orders more appealing than others.

Among whatever other reasons people are only incompletely able to make the move between social orders, or able to make social orders themselves mobile, I suggest that chief among them is an effort at reflexivity that falls short of the mark—again, this is about measurement, insofar as measurement supplies a metaphor for knowledge and relational practices aimed at bridging the gap of guest and host, ethnographer and research community. The task of reflexivity falls not only to anthropologists conscious of our own positionality but also to every population anthropologists have ever worked with, which have practiced reflexivity in multiple ways. When an ethnography succeeds at its job, the success has been one of mutual reflexive explications: the ability of anthropologists and their hosts to make a relational bid in terms that are both intelligible and acceptable to each other. But any success of this kind will also only ever be partial and also temporary in nature, as a consequence of where the parties to the ethnographic relationship are located in their own life trajectories, and in the broader histories informing these subject positions.

Gershon in fact takes her cue for the way people do this from the Melanesian ethnographic record and its theoretical interventions. In her discussion of the way people may bring one social order to the fore in their assertions of who they are and whose interests they have in mind, she writes:

> For people familiar with Melanesian notions of personhood and relationality, I am describing an analogous engagement with social orders. Just as in a moment of exchange, Melanesian social actors are choosing to foreground one relationship or one way of being related while letting others fade into the background (but not vanish entirely); so it is also with social orders. Actors will foreground some social orders while the traces of other social orders remain present but retreat into the surroundings. (Gershon 2019: 415)

This is how, for example, a Suau person may make an assertion along the lines of "We've forgotten all about those old funerary practices" and then describe in exquisite detail how they were once observed. It is also how Schram's (2018) interlocutors in the neighboring Milne Bay group of Auhelawa speakers are able to talk about their own relationship to *kastom* in terms of both space—entered into, as if it were a room—and volume—in that one can observe either a little of it or a lot. These are terms of measurement and also of movement, and they indicate how not only Suau but people all over Milne Bay Province are engaged in reflecting on their histories of moving between the social orders that have been available to them since the earliest days of missionization.

Why talk about people's historical consciousness in this way—as a process of moving between social orders in order to measure them against each other? I find it useful because of the way it enables a conversation about distances that people imagine in time and space, of the kind that have appeared throughout this book, without leaning too hard on the terms of a modernist division between opposed categories of experience that must then be kept conceptually separate. The labor involved in that strategy forces the use of terms such as "hybridization," "syncretism," "mixing" (I have been guilty of this one myself), and other awkward ways of talking about combining things that were artificially designated as separate in the first place. Instead, what Suau people appear to be doing is backgrounding some relationships, seen as belonging to a particular version of the past or leading to nothing fruitful, while foregrounding others that appear to offer more potential, more liveliness, for the present and for the near future.

That people on the Suau Coast *do* sometimes talk about their histories in terms of a profound break has served as my signal to keep in view whom they are talking to when they do this, and in what context. This is another way to view the comparisons that Suau people make between social orders—in the form of nostalgia for the missionary era, say, or fear that witchcraft continues to intrude into the present from the ancestral past—by reframing statements about time as statements about relationships, and how intentionality is (or was presumed to be) formed in the process of recognizing those relationships. Even more than they are *about* relationships, people's comparative or measuring statements are what *constitute* those relationships, because they already have in mind an entire set of interests, known or guessed or hoped for, on the part of their interlocutors. This is an effect of addressivity, not just for Suau people or Papua New Guineans in general but for all speakers in any of the social orders we may be inhabiting at any given moment. "We are in dialogue with our predecessors, and addressivity refers to this historical aspect of utterances as well as to the present speaker-listener relationship. Whether we are considering the second or third person in addressivity, the utterance is shaped by others" (Morson 2006: 55), as the concept is articulated in some of the linguistic scholarship developed out of Bakhtin's original formulation of it. For my purposes, the addressivity of Suau assertions about history and memory is a prompt to ask which relationships have informed these assertions, both past and present. Addressing a missionary is different from addressing a village court magistrate or addressing an anthropologist, but each of these social moments carries with it the weight of those other experiences that are not immediately foregrounded. They are, nevertheless, present in how people present their own experiences to each other.

There are other ways to frame what people are doing in these moments. Moutu (2007) has observed, in a meditation on how acts of collection and

acting collectively produce particular social orders of their own, a need to recognize "the place of time that is lurking within the alternating sequence of
loss and projection" (2007: 97) in the ways that people reconstitute their social
worlds in the wake of dramatic change. Loss in some of the cases Moutu describes is an outcome of violent, catastrophic, and *brief* events: a tsunami on
PNG's northwest coast, a well-orchestrated robbery of its National Museum
and Art Gallery in Port Moresby. In these cases, the "projection" following
loss seems self-evident: the loss is material and visible across the landscape,
in smashed exhibition cabinets, and on the bodies of people caught up in
these events. These effects must be reckoned with immediately, and people
are forced to reconfigure their lives in the wake of such losses—there is no
other choice. But note Moutu's attention to the "alternating sequence" in which
experiences of loss and experiences of projection and reconstitution seem to
present themselves. The implication here is that any temporality is possible for
this sequence to take place, whether in the sudden shock of disaster or in the
gradual proliferation of available social orders over the course of a century,
and that both loss and reconstitution will continue to alternate. In so doing,
the sequence can constitute its own temporality, and yet another social order
within which people can experiment with new social forms.

One of the implications Moutu draws out from this temporality is to note
that "the way in which collectivities enact their way of life is structured within
a particular nexus of relations which allow people involved to define themselves differently in different moments" (2007: 108). Here I see his analytical
project as congruent with Gershon's, in that both are aiming for an anthropology that recognizes not only its own reflexive moments but also those acts of
reflexivity made by any person or group of people who wish to discover who
they might become in the context of a new social order. Another way to put
this is that I am inspired by the interventions of Gershon, Moutu, and other
anthropologists asking who people become when they shift their attention and
redirect their actions among multiple social orders, and in so doing reconstitute each social order through a perceived or asserted loss of others.

I use this inspiration, and that of my Suau friends, to call for some discarding of old practices of our own. Along with culture and society, I am keen for
anthropologists to remove or at least downgrade the status of identity in our
conceptual repertoire, at least insofar as it has been used—usually although
not always in political contexts—to refer to any sort of positionality that remains constant regardless of who is speaking to whom, out of what kind of
historical consciousness, and with what kind of future relationship in mind.
If I learned anything over the course of nearly twenty years as an intermittent
guest on the Suau Coast, it was that neither my hosts' sense of themselves
as "a people" nor my own positioning as an ethnographer was ever entirely
under our control: there were too many social orders both they and I were

negotiating for this ever to be the case. And when I later added a new area of research to my own collection of social orders by doing work in an urban context elsewhere in PNG, my own identity as a researcher was still not mine to assert: for my new friends and interlocutors in the city of Lae, I was not so much an American national or a member of staff at a Scottish university, as I was a "Milne Bay woman" in need of reeducating in the ways of the rest of the country (Demian 2021).

Which brings me back to the image of the beach with which I opened, taken from the work of McDougall. The beach is the place of disembarkation, contact (whether first, second, or recurring), extending hospitality, and rendering the unknown knowable—perhaps. I also want to retain McDougall's attention to ambivalence, and the way that hospitable overtures can produce effects that reverberate for a century or more. Not all those effects, as they are compared by people in the present day to the way they speak about the past, have been as welcome as were the first missionaries to arrive on the Suau Coast, walking ashore armed with nothing but enthusiasm for introducing a new social order and an absolute conviction of its appeal to others. Ambivalence came later: in the ways that wage labor and war reshaped the coast, in the unruliness of a burgeoning population and its youthful disregard for the good things the elders would like to see retained from the past and carried into the future.

Do they want this because being "Suau" will otherwise be lost to them for good? I do not think this is quite the issue, since who is and is not Suau has never been a stable proposition to begin with, as I have been illustrating in one way or another for the whole of this book. My disquiet with the idea of identity stems from my very earliest work on the Suau Coast, as a guest in the village of Leileiyafa, where nobody could tell me in any definitive way who they were. This turned out to be, in my own historical consciousness as an ethnographer, the most important thing I needed to know about where I was, and who was extending their hospitality even in the space of ambivalence around who any of us were in that encounter. The encounters themselves then became multiple in nature, and they produced different knowledge as my interlocutors and I got older, underwent significant changes in our lives, and understood different things about each other as a consequence, every time we met again on the beach as the hull of the dinghy carrying this ethnographer ground against the coral sand. On each of the occasions that I have returned to the Suau Coast I have encountered people in the midst of exploring what new kinds of relationships could become available to them through the social orders of church, work, law, education, and anything else that might appear on the horizon and stop with them for a time.

The work on this book was concluded in 2020, a year of pandemic-induced crisis and all manner of other uncertainties and constraints on anyone's perception of what the future could hold. Completing the book under these conditions has itself carried the irony of writing about history and memory, when writing itself is a future-oriented activity—but the future seems very parlous indeed right now, both where I write in Scotland and in PNG where so many friends are. A great deal has been lost during this year. I take heart in the proposition, made implicitly by people on the Suau Coast and more explicitly by the work of my colleagues, that loss always contains the potential for other actions, other assemblages of people and their intentions for one another. In this particular case, however, the action no longer belongs to me. I have said enough about what I think Suau people were telling me on the subject of who they were, and how who they were changed in the space of repeated extensions of hospitality over the course of two decades. Anything more on the subject cannot be said by this ethnographer, or in this book: that work is theirs to continue.

Note

1. It is of course debatable whether the colonial era ever really ended in terms of PNG's relationship with Australia, as commentators on the Manus Island Regional Processing Centre have noted (Rooney 2013; Wallis and Dalsgaard 2016).

References

Abel, Cecil. 1969. "The Impact of Charles Abel." In *The History of Melanesia*, edited by K. S. Inglis, 265–82. Canberra: Australian National University Press.

Abel, Charles W. 1898. *New Guinea Mission Kwato District Annual Report.* Council for World Mission/London Missionary Society archives, Papua Reports, Box 1.

———. 1902. *Savage Life in New Guinea.* London: London Missionary Society.

Abel, Chris. 2013. *Ta Alina Suau (Let's Speak Suau): A Dictionary and Grammar, and Nostalgic Appreciation of the Suau Language in the Milne Bay Province, Papua New Guinea.* Alotau: Independent imprint.

Abel, Russell W. 1934. *Charles W. Abel of Kwato: Forty Years in Dark Papua.* New York: Fleming H. Revell Company.

Andersen, Barbara. 2017. "Learning to Believe in Papua New Guinea." In *Pentecostalism and Witchcraft: Spiritual Warfare in Africa and Melanesia*, edited by Knut Rio, Michelle MacCarthy, and Ruy Blanes, 235–55. Cham: Palgrave Macmillan.

Anere, David Lusa. 1979. "Pig Exchange in Suau in the Milne Bay Province." *Oral History* 8: 54–89. Port Moresby: Institute of Papua New Guinea Studies.

Arens, W. 1979. *The Man-Eating Myth: Anthropology and Anthropophagy.* Oxford: Oxford University Press.

Armstrong, W. A. 1921. *Report on Suau-Tawala.* Port Moresby: Territory of Papua Anthropology Report No. 1.

Astuti, Rita. 1995. *People of the Sea: Identity and Descent among the Vezo of Madagascar.* Cambridge: Cambridge University Press.

Balderson, John. 1970. *Patrol Report no. 1–69/70, Suau Census Division, Milne Bay District.* Port Moresby: National Archives of Papua New Guinea.

Barker, John. 2013. "Anthropology and the Politics of Christianity in Papua New Guinea." In *Christian Politics in Oceania*, edited by Matt Tomlinson and Debra McDougall, 146–70. New York: Berghahn Books.

Barnes, J. A. 1962. "African Models in the New Guinea Highlands." *Man* 62(1/2): 5–9.

Battaglia, Debbora. 1985. "'We Feed Our Father': Paternal Nurture among the Sabarl of Papua New Guinea." *American Ethnologist* 12(3): 427–41.

———. 1990. *On the Bones of the Serpent: Person, Memory, and Mortality in Sabarl Island Society.* Chicago: University of Chicago Press.

———. 1992. "The Body in the Gift: Memory and Forgetting in Sabarl Mortuary Exchange." *American Ethnologist* 19: 3–18.

———. 1993. "At Play in the Fields (and Borders) of the Imaginary: Melanesian Transformations of Forgetting." *Cultural Anthropology* 8: 430–42.

———. 1995. "On Practical Nostaglia: Self-Prospecting among Urban Trobrianders." In *Rhetorics of Self-Making*, edited by Debbora Battaglia, 77–96. Berkeley: University of California Press.

———. 2005. "'For Those Who Are Not Afraid of the Future': Raëlian Clonehood in the Public Sphere." In *E.T. Culture: Anthropology in Outerspaces*, edited by Debbora Battaglia, 149–79. Durham, NC: Duke University Press.

Bellwood, Peter, James J. Fox, and Darrell Tryon (eds.). 2006. *The Austronesians: Historical and Comparative Perspectives*. Canberra: ANU Press.

Beran, Harry. 1996. *Mutuaga: A Nineteenth-Century New Guinea Master Carver*. Wollongong: University of Wollongong Press.

Bercovitch, Eytan. 1994. "The Agent in the Gift: Hidden Exchange in Inner New Guinea." *Cultural Anthropology* 9(4): 498–536.

Berliner, David. 2020. *Losing Culture: Nostalgia, Heritage, and Our Accelerated Times*. Translated by Dominic Horsfall. New Brunswick, NJ: Rutgers University Press.

Biersack, Aletta. 1982. "Ginger Gardens for the Ginger Woman: Rites and Passages in a Melanesian Society." *Man* 17(2): 239–58.

———. 1999. "The Mount Kare Python and His Gold: Totemism and Ecology in the Papua New Guinea Highlands." *American Anthropologist* 101(1): 68–87.

Bissell, William Cunningham. 2005. "Engaging Colonial Nostalgia." *Cultural Anthropology* 20(2): 215–48.

Black, C. F. 2011. *The Land Is the Source of the Law: A Dialogic Encounter with Indigenous Jurisprudence*. Abingdon: Routledge.

Blackwood, Evelyn. 1999. "Big Houses and Small Houses: Doing Matriliny in West Sumatra." *Ethnos* 64(1): 32–56.

Bolyanatz, Alexander. 1996. "Musings on Matriliny: Understandings and Social Relations among the Sursurunga of New Ireland." In *Gender, Kinship, Power: A Comparative and Interdisciplinary History*, edited by Mary Jo Maynes, Ann Waltner, Birgitte Soland, and Ulrike Strasser, 81–97. New York: Routledge.

Bovensiepen, Judith. 2009. "Spiritual Landscapes of Life and Death in the Central Highlands of East Timor." *Anthropological Forum* 19(3): 323–38.

———. 2014. "Installing the Insider 'Outside': House Reconstruction and the Transformation of Binary Ideologies in Independent Timor-Leste." *American Ethnologist* 41(2): 290–304.

Brenner, Suzanne. 1998. *The Domestication of Desire: Women, Wealth, and Modernity in Java*. Princeton, NJ: Princeton University Press.

Burridge, Kenelm O. L. 1978. "Introduction: Missionary Occasions." In *Mission, Church and Sect in Oceania*, edited by James A. Boutilier, Daniel T. Hughes, and Sharon W. Tiffany, 1–30. Ann Arbor: University of Michigan Press.

Chalmers, James. 1884. *Annual Report*. Council for World Mission/London Missionary Society archives, Papua New Guinea, Reports 1882–1898 Box 1.

———. n.d. *Notes for Lizzie*. Council for World Mission/London Missionary Society archives, Papua New Guinea, Papua Personal Box 1.

Chowning, Ann. 1989. "Death and Kinship in Molima." In *Death Rituals and Life in the Societies of the Kula Ring*, edited by Frederick H. Damon and Roy Wagner, 97–129. DeKalb: Northern Illinois University Press.

Clay, Brenda Johnson. 1977. *Pinikindu: Maternal Nurture, Paternal Substance*. Chicago: University of Chicago Press.

Colson, Elizabeth. 1980. "The Resilience of Matrilineality: Gwembe and Plateau Tonga Adaptations." In *The Versatility of Kinship*, edited by Linda S. Cordell and Stephen Beckerman, 359–74. New York: Academic Press.

Cooper, Russell E. 1970. *Suau Texts: Stories, Interviews, Reports and Songs of the Suau People*. Marion, IN: Marion College.

———. 1975. "Coastal Suau: A Preliminary Study of Internal Relationships." In *Studies in Languages of Central and South-East Papua*, edited by T. E. Dutton, 227–278. Pacific Linguistics Series C No. 29. Canberra: Australian National University.

Coupaye, Ludovic. 2013. *Growing Artefacts, Displaying Relationships: Yams, Art and Technology amongst the Nyamikum Abelam of Papua New Guinea*. New York: Berghahn Books.

Cox, John. 2018. *Fast Money Schemes: Hope and Deception in Papua New Guinea*. Bloomington: Indiana University Press.

Cox, John, and Martha Macintyre. 2014. "Christian Marriage, Money Scams, and Melanesian Social Imaginaries." *Oceania* 84(2): 138–57.

Dalsgaard, Steffen. 2013. "The Commensurability of Carbon: Making Value and Money of Climate Change." *Hau: Journal of Ethnographic Theory* 3(1): 80–98.

Dalsgaard, Steffen, and Marianne Pedersen. 2015. "The Portable Sawmill and Other Challenges to REDD+ in Papua New Guinea." *Asia Pacific Viewpoint* 56(1): 128–39.

Dalton, Doug. 2004. "Cargo and Cult: The Mimetic Critique of Capitalist Culture." In *Cargo, Cult and Culture Critique*, edited by Holger Jebens, 187–208. Honolulu: University of Hawai'i Press.

Damon, Frederick H., and Roy Wagner (eds.). 1989. *Death Rituals and Life in the Societies of the Kula Ring*. DeKalb: Northern Illinois University Press.

de Coppet, Daniel. 1985. ". . . Land Owns People." In *Contexts and Levels: Anthropological Essays on Hierarchy*, edited by R. H. Barnes, Daniel de Coppet, and R. J. Parkin, 78–90. JASO Occasional Papers, 4. Oxford: JASO.

Delaney, Carol. 1986. "The Meaning of Paternity and the Virgin Birth Debate." *Man* (N.S.) 21(3): 494–513.

Demian, Melissa. 2000. "Longing for Completion: Toward an Aesthetics of Work in Suau." *Oceania* 71(2): 94–109.

———. 2003. "Custom in the Courtroom, Law in the Village: Legal Transformations in Papua New Guinea." *Journal of the Royal Anthropological Institute* 9(1): 97–115.

———. 2004a. "Disputing Damage versus Disputing Ownership in Suau." In *Rationales of Ownership: Transactions and Claims to Ownership in Contemporary Papua New Guinea*, edited by Lawrence Kalinoe and James Leach, 27–41. Wantage: Sean Kingston Publishing.

———. 2004b. "Transactions in Rights, Transactions in Children: A View of Adoption from Papua New Guinea." In *Cross-Cultural Approaches to Adoption*, edited by Fiona Bowie, 97–110. London: Routledge.

———. 2006a. "'Emptiness' and Complementarity in Suau Reproductive Strategies." In *Population, Reproduction and Fertility in Melanesia*, edited by Stanley J. Ulijaszek, 136–58. New York: Berghahn Books.

———. 2006b. "Reflecting on Loss in Papua New Guinea." *Ethnos* 71(4): 507–32.

———. 2007. "'Land Doesn't Come from Your Mother, She Didn't Make It with Her Hands': Challenging Matriliny in Papua New Guinea." In *Feminist Perspectives on Land Law*, edited by Hilary Lim and Anne Bottomley, 155–70. London: Routledge-Cavendish.

———. 2011. "'Hybrid Custom' and Legal Description in Papua New Guinea." In *Recasting Anthropological Knowledge: Inspiration and Social Science*, edited by Jeanette Edwards and Maja Petrović-Šteger, 49–69. Cambridge: Cambridge University Press.

———. 2013. "When We Were in Darkness: The Hazards of Knowing History on the Suau Coast." In *Melanesia: Art and Encounter*, edited by Nicholas Thomas, Lissant Bolton, Elizabeth Bonshek, Julie Adams, and Ben Burt, 32–38. London: British Museum Press.

———. 2014. "Overcoming Operational Constraints in Papua New Guinea's Remote Rural Village Courts: A Case Study." *In Brief* 2014/52. State, Society and Governance in Melanesia, Australian National University.

———. 2015. "Dislocating Custom." *PoLAR: Political and Legal Anthropology Review* 38(1): 91–107.

———. 2021. "The Problem of the Semi-alienable Anthropologist." In *Unequal Lives: Gender, Race and Class in the Western Pacific*, edited by Nicholas Bainton, Debra McDougall, John Cox, and Kalissa Alexeyeff, 109–129. Canberra: ANU Press.

Derrida, Jacques. 2000. *Of Hospitality*. Translated by Rachel Bowlby. Stanford, CA: Stanford University Press.

Diaz, Vicente M. 2011. "Voyaging for Anti-Colonial Recovery: Austronesian Seafaring, Archipelagic Rethinking, and the Re-mapping of Indigeneity." *Pacific Asia Inquiry* 2(1): 21–32.

Dinnen, Sinclair, and John Braithwaite. 2009. "Reinventing Policing through the Prism of the Colonial Kiap." *Policing and Society* 19(2): 161–73.

Douglas, Bronwen. 2001. "Encounters with the Enemy? Academic Readings of Missionary Narratives on Melanesians." *Comparative Studies in Society and History* 43(1): 37–64.

Englund, Harri, and James Leach. 2000. Ethnography and the Meta-Narratives of Modernity. *Current Anthropology* 41(2): 225–48.

Eriksen, Annelin. 2006. "Expected and Unexpected Cultural Heroes: Reflections on Gender and Agency of Conjuncture on Ambrym, Vanuatu." *Anthropological Theory* 6(2): 227–247.

Fabian, Johannes. 1983. *Time and the Other: How Anthropology Makes Its Object*. New York: Columbia University Press.

Fann, K. T. 1970. *Peirce's Theory of Abduction*. The Hague: Martinus Nijhoff.

Filer, Colin. 2012. "Why Green Grabs Don't Work in Papua New Guinea." *Journal of Peasant Studies* 39(2): 599–617.

Filer, Colin, and Michael Wood. 2012. "The Creation and Dissolution of Private Property in Forest Carbon: A Case Study from Papua New Guinea." *Human Ecology* 40(5): 665–77.

Fitzpatrick, Peter. 1980. *Law and State in Papua New Guinea*. London: Academic Press.

Ferguson, James. 1999. *Expectations of Modernity: Myths and Meanings of Urban Life on the Zambian Copperbelt*. Berkeley: University of California Press.

Fernandez, James W., and Mary Taylor Huber. 2001. "Irony, Practice, and the Moral Imagination." In *Irony in Action: Anthropology, Practice, and the Moral Imagination*, edited by James W. Fernandez and Mary Taylor Huber, 261–64. Chicago: University of Chicago Press.

Foster, Robert J. 1992. "Commoditization and the Emergence of *Kastam* as a Cultural Category: a New Ireland Case in Comparative Perspective." *Oceania* 62(4): 284–94.

———. 2002. *Materializing the Nation: Commodities, Consumption, and Media in Papua New Guinea*. Bloomington: Indiana University Press.

Fox, James J. 1997. "Place and Landscape in Comparative Austronesian Perspective." In *The Poetic Power of Place: Comparative Perspectives on Austronesian Ideas of Locality*, edited by James J. Fox, 1–21. Canberra: Australian National University.

Freud, Sigmund. 1950. *Collected Papers*. Vol. 5: *Miscellaneous Papers, 1888–1938*. Edited by James Strachey. London: Hogarth Press and Institute of Psycho-Analysis.

Gell, Alfred. 1998. *Art and Agency: An Anthropological Theory*. Oxford: Oxford University Press.

Gershon, Ilana. 2007. "Viewing Diasporas from the Pacific: What Pacific Ethnographies Offer Pacific Diaspora Studies." *Contemporary Pacific* 19(2): 474–502.

———. 2019. "Porous Social Orders." *American Ethnologist* 46(4): 404–16.

Gerritsen, Rolf. 1982. "The Politics of Ambition: Damuni, from Micronationalism to a Pressure Group." In *Micronationalist Movements in Papua New Guinea*, edited by R. J. May, 301–26. Political and Social Change Monograph No. 1. Canberra: Australian National University.

Gewertz, Deborah B., and Frederick K. Errington. 1991. *Twisted Histories, Altered Contexts: Representing the Chambri in a World System*. Cambridge: Cambridge University Press.

Gillison, Gillian. 1980. "Images of Nature in Gimi Thought." In *Nature, Culture and Gender*, edited by Carol MacCormack and Marilyn Strathern, 143–73. Cambridge: Cambridge University Press.

Goddard, Michael. 1998. "Off the Record: Village Court Praxis and the Politics of Settlement Life in Port Moresby, Papua New Guinea." *Canberra Anthropology* 21(1): 41–62.

———. 2009. *Substantial Justice: An Anthropology of Village Courts in Papua New Guinea*. New York: Berghahn Books.

Gordon, Robert. 1983. "The Decline of the Kiapdom and the Resurgence of 'Tribal Fighting' in Enga." *Oceania* 53(3): 205–23.

Gough, Kathleen. 1961. "The Modern Disintegration of Matrilineal Descent Groups." In *Matrilineal Kinship*, edited by David M. Schneider and Kathleen Gough, 631–52. Berkeley: University of California Press.

Greenhouse, Carol. 1996. *A Moment's Notice: Time Politics across Cultures*. Ithaca, NY: Cornell University Press.

Gregory, C. A. 1982. *Gifts and Commodities*. London: Academic Press.

Grosart, Ian. 1982. "Nationalism and Micronationalism: The Tolai Case." In *Micronationalist Movements in Papua New Guinea*, edited by R. J. May, 139–75. Political and Social Change Monograph No. 1. Canberra: Australian National University.

Guo, Pei-yi. 2003. "'Island Builders': Landscape and Historicity among the Langalanga, Solomon Islands." In *Landscape, Memory and History: Anthropological Perspectives*, edited by Pamela J. Stewart and Andrew Strathern, 189–209. London: Pluto Press.

Guyer, Jane I. 2007. "Prophecy and the Near Future: Thoughts on Macroeconomic, Evangelical, and Punctuated Time." *American Ethnologist* 34(3): 409–21.

Haddon, Alfred C. 1894. The Ethnography of British New Guinea. *Science Progress* 2(8): 83–95.

Hage, Ghassan. 2003. *Against Paranoid Nationalism: Searching for Hope in a Shrinking Society*. Annandale: Pluto Press Australia.

———. 2014. "Critical Anthropology as a Permanent State of First Contact." Fieldsights: Theorizing the Contemporary, *Cultural Anthropology* Online, 13 January. Retrieved 12 February 2021 from https://culanth.org/fieldsights/critical-anthropology-as-a-permanent-state-of-first-contact.

Handman, Courtney. 2014a. "The Future of Christian Critique: Lost Tribes Discourses in Papua New Guinean Publics." In *Pacific Futures: Projects, Politics and Interests*, edited by Will Rollason, 114–32. New York: Berghahn Books.

———. 2014b. "Becoming the Body of Christ: Sacrificing the Speaking Subject in the Making of the Colonial Lutheran Church in New Guinea." *Current Anthropology* 55(S10): S205–S215.

Harrison, Simon. 2000. "From Prestige Goods to Legacies: Property and the Objectification of Culture in Melanesia." *Comparative Studies in Society and History* 42(3): 662–79.

Hau'ofa, Epeli. 1993. "Our Sea of Islands." In *A New Oceania: Rediscovering Our Sea of Islands*, 2–16. Suva: University of the South Pacific.

High, Holly. 2011. "Melancholia and Anthropology." *American Ethnologist* 38(2): 217–33.

Hirsch, Eric. 2004. "Techniques of Vision: Photography, Disco and Renderings of Present Perceptions in Highland Papua." *Journal of the Royal Anthropological Institute* 10(1): 19–39.

Hukula, Fiona. 2017. "Kinship and Relatedness in Urban Papua New Guinea." *Journal de la Société des Océanistes* 144–45: 159–70.

———. 2019. "Morality and a Mosbi Market." *Oceania* 89(2): 168–81.

Jacka, Jerry. 2015. *Alchemy in the Rain Forest: Politics, Ecology, and Resilience in a New Guinea Mining Area*. Durham, NC: Duke University Press.

Jebens, Holger. 2006. *Pathways to Heaven: Contesting Mainline and Fundamentalist Christianity in Papua New Guinea*. New York: Berghahn Books.

Jeffrey, Robin. 2005. "Legacies of Matriliny: The Place of Women and the 'Kerala Model.'" *Pacific Affairs* 77(4): 647–64.

Jessep, Owen, and John Luluaki. 1994. *Principles of Family Law in Papua New Guinea*. 2nd ed. Waigani: University of Papua New Guinea Press.

Jolly, Margaret. 1994. *Women of the Place: Kastom, Colonialism and Gender in Vanuatu*. Chur: Harwood Academic Publishers.

Jones, Ernest. 1955. *The Life and Work of Sigmund Freud*. Vol. 2: *1901–1919: Years of Maturity*. New York: Basic Books.

Jorgensen, Dan. 2005. "Third Wave Evangelism and the Politics of the Global in Papua New Guinea: Spiritual Warfare and the Recreation of Place in Telefolmin." *Oceania* 75(4): 444–61.

Kahn, Miriam. 1986. *Always Hungry, Never Greedy: Food and the Expression of Gender in a Melanesian Society*. Prospect Heights, IL: Waveland Press.

———. 1990. "Stone-Faced Ancestors: The Spatial Anchoring of Myth in Wamira, Papua New Guinea." *Ethnology* 29(1): 51–66.

———. 1996. "Your Place and Mine: Sharing Emotional Landscapes in Wamira, Papua New Guinea." In *Senses of Place*, edited by Steven Feld and Keith H. Basso, 167–96. Santa Fe, NM: School of American Research Press.

Kaʻili, Tēvita O. 2005. "Tauhi Vā: Nurturing Tongan Sociospatial Ties in Maui and Beyond." *Contemporary Pacific* 17(1): 83–114.

Kaniku, John Wills Teloti. 1975. *The Epic of Tauhau*. Port Moresby: Institute of Papua New Guinea Studies.

Kelly, John D. 1999. "Time and the Global: Against the Homogeneous, Empty Communities in Contemporary Social Theory." In *Globalization and Identity: Dialectics of Flow and Closure*, edited by Birgit Meyer and Peter Geschiere, 239–71. Oxford: Blackwell.

Kirsch, Stuart. 2001. "Lost Worlds: Environmental Disaster, 'Culture Loss,' and the Law." *Current Anthropology* 42(2): 167–98.

———. 2004a. "Keeping the Network in View: Compensation Claims, Property and Social Relations in Melanesia." In *Rationales of Ownership: Transactions and Claims to Ownership in Contemporary Papua New Guinea*, edited by Lawrence Kalinoe and James Leach, 79–89. Wantage: Sean Kingston Publishing.

———. 2004b. "Changing Views of Place and Time along the Ok Tedi." In *Mining and Indigenous Lifeworlds in Australia and Papua New Guinea*, edited by Alan Rumsey and James Weiner, 182–207. Wantage: Sean Kingston Publishing.

———. 2014. *Mining Capitalism: The Relationship between Corporations and Their Critics*. Berkeley: University of California Press.

Knauft, Bruce M. 2002. *Exchanging the Past: A Rainforest World of Before and After*. Chicago: University of Chicago Press.

———. 2019. "Finding the Good: Reactive Modernity among the Gebusi, in the Pacific, and Elsewhere." *Australian Journal of Anthropology* 30(1): 84–103.

Kristeva, Julia. 1982. *Powers of Horror: An Essay on Abjection*. Translated by Leon S. Roudiez. New York: Columbia University Press.

Küchler, Susanne. 1993. "Landscape as Memory: The Mapping of Process and Its Representation in a Melanesian Society." In *Landscape: Politics and Perspectives*, edited by Barbara Bender, 85–106. Oxford: Berg.

———. 1999. "The Place of Memory." In *The Art of Forgetting*, edited by Adrian Forty and Susanne Küchler, 53–73. Oxford: Berg.

Latour, Bruno. 1993. *We Have Never Been Modern*. Translated by Catherine Porter. Cambridge, MA: Harvard University Press.

Lattas, Andrew. 1992. "Skin, Personhood and Redemption: The Double Self in West New Britain Cargo Cults." *Oceania* 63(1): 27–54.

———. 1996. "Memory, Forgetting and the New Tribes Mission in West New Britain." *Oceania* 66(4): 286–304.

———. 2000. "Telephones, Cameras and Technology in West New Britain Cargo Cults." *Oceania* 70(4): 325–44.

Latukefu, Sione. 1978. "The Impact of South Sea Islands Missionaries on Melanesia." In *Mission, Church and Sect in Oceania*, edited by James A. Boutilier, Daniel T. Hughes, and Sharon W. Tiffany, 91–108. Ann Arbor: University of Michigan Press.

Lawrence, Peter. 1969. "The State versus Stateless Societies in Papua and New Guinea." In *Fashion of Law in New Guinea*, edited by B.J. Brown, 15–37. Sydney: Butterworths.

———. 1984. *The Garia*. Manchester: Manchester University Press.

Lawrence, Salmah Eva-Lina. 2015. "Witchcraft, Sorcery, Violence: Matrilineal and Decolonial Reflections." In *Talking It Through: Responses to Sorcery and Witchcraft Beliefs and Practices in Melanesia*, edited by Miranda Forsyth, 55–73. Canberra: ANU Press.

Lee, Donna, Margaret Skutsch, and Marieke Sandker. 2018. *Challenges with Measurement and Accounting of the Plus in REDD+*. San Francisco: Climate and Land Use Alliance.

LeFevre, Tate A. 2013. "Turning Niches into Handles: Kanak Youth, Associations and the Construction of an Indigenous Counter-public Sphere." *Settler Colonial Studies* 3(2): 214–29.

Lepowsky, Maria. 1983. "Sudest Island and the Louisiade Archipelago in Massim Exchange." In *The Kula: New Perspectives on Massim Exchange*, edited by Jerry W. Leach and Edmund Leach. Cambridge: Cambridge University Press.

———. 1993. *Fruit of the Motherland: Gender in an Egalitarian Society*. New York: Columbia University Press.

Lévi-Strauss, Claude. 1964. *Totemism*. Translated by Rodney Needham. London: Merlin Press.

Levine, Nancy E. 1987. "Fathers and Sons: Kinship Value and Validation in Tibetan Polyandry." *Man* (N.S.) 22(2): 267–86.

Lindstrom, Lamont. 1993. *Cargo Cult: Strange Stories of Desire from Melanesia and Beyond*. Honolulu: University of Hawai'i Press.

Lindstrom, Lamont, and Geoffrey M. White. 1989. "War Stories." In *The Pacific Theater: Island Representations of World War II*, edited by Lamont Lindstrom and Geoffrey M. White, 3–40. Honolulu: University of Hawai'i Press.

LiPuma, Edward. 2000. *Encompassing Others: The Magic of Modernity in Melanesia*. Ann Arbor: University of Michigan Press.

Losche, Diane. 2001. "What Makes the Anthropologist Laugh? The Abelam, Irony, and Me." In *Irony in Action: Anthropology, Practice, and the Moral Imagination*, edited by James W. Fernandez and Mary Taylor Huber, 103–17. Chicago: University of Chicago Press.

Lynch, John, Malcom Ross, and Terry Crowley. 2002. *The Oceanic Languages*. London: Routledge.

MacGillivray, John. 1852. *Narrative of the Voyage of H.M.S.* Rattlesnake. Vol. 1. London: T. & W. Boone. Reproduced at Project Gutenberg Australia, http://gutenberg.net.au/ebooks/e00031.html.

Macintyre, Martha. 1984. "The Problem of the Semi-Alienable Pig." *Canberra Anthropology* 7(1–2): 109–22.

———. 1989. "The Triumph of the *Susu*: Mortuary Exchanges on Tubetube." In *Death Rituals and Life in the Societies of the Kula Ring*, edited by Frederick H. Damon and Roy Wagner, 133–52. DeKalb: Northern Illinois University Press.

———. 2011. "Money Changes Everything: Papua New Guinean Women in the Modern Economy." In *Managing Modernity in the Western Pacific*, edited by Mary Patterson and Martha Macintyre, 90–120. St. Lucia: University of Queensland Press.

Māhina, ʻOkusitino. 1999. "Theory and Practice in Anthropology: Pacific Anthropology and Pacific Islanders." *Social Analysis* 43(2): 41–69.

Malinowski, Bronisław. 1984 [1922]. *Argonauts of the Western Pacific*. Long Grove, IL: Waveland Press.

———. 1972 [1926]. *Crime and Custom in Savage Society*. Totowa, NJ: Littlefield, Adams & Co.

———. 1967. *A Diary in the Strict Sense of the Term*. London: Athlone Press.

Mallett, Shelley. 1998. "Living Death: Understanding Respect and Respectful Understanding on Nuaʻata, Papua New Guinea." *Canberra Anthropology* 21(1): 1–24.

———. 2003. *Conceiving Cultures: Reproducing People and Places on Nuakata, Papua New Guinea*. Ann Arbor: University of Michigan Press.

Marshall, Ruth. 2016. "Destroying Arguments and Captivating Thoughts: Spiritual Warfare Prayer as Global Praxis." *Journal of Religious and Political Practice* 2(1): 92–113.

Martin, Keir. 2013. *The Death of the Big Men and the Rise of the Big Shots: Custom and Conflict in East New Britain*. New York: Berghahn Books.

Massey, Doreen. 2005. *For Space*. London: SAGE.

McDougall, Debra. 2003. "Fellowship and Citizenship as Models of National Community: United Church Women's Fellowship in Ranongga, Solomon Islands." *Oceania* 74(1–2): 61–80.

———. 2016. *Engaging with Strangers: Love and Violence in the Rural Solomon Islands*. New York: Berghahn Books.

McDowell, Nancy. 1985. "Past and Future: The Nature of Episodic Time in Bun." In *History and Ethnohistory in Papua New Guinea*, edited by Deborah Gewertz and Edward Schieffelin, 26–39. Sydney: Oceania Monograph No. 28.

———. 1988. "A Note on Cargo Cults and Cultural Constructions of Change." *Pacific Studies* 11(2): 121–34.

McKaughan, Daniel J. 2008. "From Ugly Duckling to Swan: C. S. Peirce, Abduction, and the Pursuit of Scientific Theories." *Transactions of the Charles S. Peirce Society* 44(3): 446–68.

McKinnon, Susan. 2001. "The Economies in Kinship and the Paternity of Culture: Origin Stories in Kinship Theory." In *Relative Values: Reconfiguring Kinship Studies*, edited by Sarah Franklin and Susan McKinnon, 277–301. Durham, NC: Duke University Press.

Mead, Margaret. 1956. *New Lives for Old: Cultural Transformation—Manus, 1928–1953*. London: Gollancz.

Melville, Herman. 1847. *Typee, or, A Narrative of a Four Months Residence among the Natives of the Marquesas Islands, or, A Peep at Polynesian Life*. London: John Murray.

Merry, Sally Engle. 1990. *Getting Justice and Getting Even: Legal Consciousness among Working-Class Americans*. Chicago: University of Chicago Press.

Minnegal, Monica. 2009. "The Time Is Right: Waiting, Reciprocity and Sociality." In *Waiting*, edited by Ghassan Hage, 89–96. Melbourne: Melbourne University Press.

Miyazaki, Hirokazu. 2004. *The Method of Hope: Anthropology, Philosophy, and Fijian Knowledge*. Stanford: Stanford University Press.

Morson, Gary S. 2006. "Addressivity." In *Encyclopedia of Language and Linguistics*, 2nd ed., edited by Keith Brown, 55–58. Amsterdam: Elsevier Ltd.

Moutu, Andrew. 2007. "Collection as a Way of Being." In *Thinking through Things: Theorising Artefacts Ethnographically*, edited by Amiria Henare, Martin Holbraad, and Sari Wastell, 93–112. London: Routledge.

Munn, Nancy. 1986. *The Fame of Gawa: A Symbolic Study of Value Transformation in a Massim (Papua New Guinea) Society*. Cambridge: Cambridge University Press.

———. 1990. "Constructing Regional Worlds in Experience: Kula Exchange, Witchcraft and Gawan Local Events." *Man* (N.S.) 25: 1–17.

Na'puti, Tiara R., and Michael Lujan Bevacqua. 2015. "Militarization and Resistance from Guåhan: Protecting and Defending Pågat." *American Quarterly* 67(3): 837–58.

Niiniluoto, Ilkka. 1999. "Defending Abduction." *Philosophy of Science* 66: S436–S451.

Niven, Larry. 1979. "Grammar Lesson." In *Convergent Series*, collected stories of Larry Niven, 153–57. New York: Del Rey/Ballantine Books.

Oram, Nigel D. 1976. *Colonial Town to Melanesian City: Port Moresby 1884–1974*. Canberra: Australian National University Press.

Özyürek, Esra. 2006. *Nostalgia for the Modern: State Secularism and Everyday Politics in Turkey*. Durham, NC: Duke University Press.

Paliwala, Abdul. 1982. "Law and Order in the Village: The Village Courts." In *Law and Social Change in Papua New Guinea*, edited by D. Weisbrot, A. Paliwala, and A. Sawyerr, 191–217. Sydney: Butterworths.

Pascoe, Sophie. 2018. "Interrogating Scale in the REDD+ Assemblage in Papua New Guinea." *Geoforum* 96: 87–96.

———. 2019. *Storytelling REDD+: Ontological Intersections and Inequalities between Global Environmental Governance and Local Lives in Papua New Guinea*. PhD diss., University of Melbourne.

Pavanello, Mariano. 1995. "The Work of the Ancestors and the Profit of the Living: Some Nzema Economic Ideas." *Africa* 65(1): 36–57.

Petersen, Glenn. 1982. "Ponapean Matriliny: Production, Exchange, and the Ties That Bind." *American Ethnologist* 9(1): 129–44.

Pietz, William. 1985. "The Problem of the Fetish, I." *RES: Anthropology and Aesthetics* 9(1): 5–17.

Piot, Charles. 2010. *Nostalgia for the Future: West Africa after the Cold War*. Chicago: University of Chicago Press.

Poewe, Karla O. 1981. "Matrilineal Ideology: Male-Female Dynamics in Luapula, Zambia." In *The Versatility of Kinship*, edited by Linda S. Cordell and Stephen Beckerman, 333–57. New York: Academic Press.

Prendergast, Patricia Ann. 1968. *A History of the London Missionary Society in British New Guinea, 1871–1901*. PhD diss., University of Hawai'i.

Richards, Audrey. 1950. "Some Types of Family Structure amongst the Central Bantu." In *African Systems of Kinship and Marriage*, edited by A. R. Radcliffe-Brown and Daryll Forde, 207–51. Oxford: Oxford University Press.

Riseman, Noah. 2012. *Defending Whose Country? Indigenous Soldiers in the Pacific War*. Lincoln: University of Nebraska Press.

Robbins, Joel. 2004a. *Becoming Sinners: Christianity and Moral Torment in a Papua New Guinea Society*. Berkeley: University of California Press.

———. 2004b. "The Globalization of Pentecostal and Charismatic Christianity." *Annual Review of Anthropology* 33: 117–43.

———. 2007. "Continuity Thinking and the Problem of Christian Culture." *Current Anthropology* 48(1): 5–38.

———. 2009. "Recognition, Reciprocity, and Justice: Melanesian Reflections on the Rights of Relationships." In *Mirrors of Justice: Law and Power in the Post-Cold War Era*, edited by Kamari Maxine Clarke and Mark Goodale, 171–90. Cambridge: Cambridge University Press.

Rodman, Margaret C. 1992. "Empowering Place: Multilocality and Multivocality." *American Anthropologist* 94(3): 640–56.

Rollason, Will. 2008. "Counterparts: Clothing, Value and the Sites of Otherness in Panapompom Ethnographic Encounters." *Anthropological Forum* 18(1): 17–35.

Rooney, Michelle Nayahamui. 2013. "Negotiating Asylum and Settlement in PNG: Who Has Snookered Whom?" ANU DevPolicy Blog, 29 July. Retrieved 12 February 2021 from https://devpolicy.org/negotiating-asylum-and-settlement-in-png-who-has-sno okered-whom-20130729/.

———. 2017a "'There's Nothing Better than Land': A Migrant Group's Strategies for Accessing Informal Settlement Land in Port Moresby." In *Kastom, Property and Ideology: Land Transformations in Melanesia*, edited by Siobhan McDonnell, Matthew G. Allen and Colin Filer, 111–43. Canberra: ANU Press.

———. 2017b. *Nogat Mani: Social Safety Nets for Tufi Migrants of ATS Settlement, Moresby, Papua New Guinea*. PhD diss., Australian National University.

Rousseau, Benedicta, and John P. Taylor. 2012. "*Kastom Ekonomi* and the Subject of Self-Reliance: Differentiating Development in Vanuatu." In *Differentiating Development: Beyond an Anthropology of Critique*, edited by Soumhya Venkatesan and Thomas Yarrow, 169–86. New York: Berghahn Books.

Ryser, Rudolph Carl, Dina Gilio-Whitaker, and Heidi G. Bruce. 2017. "Fourth World Theory and Methods of Inquiry." In *Handbook of Research on Theoretical Perspectives on Indigenous Knowledge Systems in Developing Countries*, edited by Patrick Ngulube, 50–84. Hershey: IGI Global.

Sahlins, Marshall. 1992. "The Economics of Develop-Man in the Pacific." *RES: Anthropology and Aesthetics* 21(1): 12–25.

———. 1993. "Goodbye to *Tristes Tropes*: Ethnography in the Context of Modern World History." *Journal of Modern History* 65(1): 1–25.

Scaglion, Richard. 1990. "Legal Adaptation in a Papua New Guinea Village Court." *Ethnology* 29(1): 17–33.

Schieffelin, Edward L. 1976. *The Sorrow of the Lonely and the Burning of the Dancers*. New York: St. Martin's Press.

Schieffelin, Edward L., and Robert Crittenden, eds. 1991. *Like People You See in a Dream: First Contact in Six Papua Societies*. Stanford, CA: Stanford University Press.

Schram, Ryan. 2007. "*Sit, Cook, Eat, Full Stop*: Religion and the Rejection of Ritual in Auhelawa (Papua New Guinea)." *Oceania* 77(2): 172–90.

———. 2010. "Witches' Wealth: Witchcraft, Confession and Christian Personhood in Auhelawa, Papua New Guinea." *Journal of the Royal Anthropological Institute* 16(4): 726–42.

———. 2018. *Harvests, Feasts, and Graves: Postcultural Consciousness in Contemporary Papua New Guinea*. Ithaca, NY: Cornell University Press.

Scott, Michael W. 2007. "Neither 'New Melanesian History' Nor 'New Melanesian Ethnography'": Recovering Emplaced Matrilineages in Southeast Solomon Islands. *Oceania* 77(3): 337–54.

Seligman, Charles G. 1910. *The Melanesians of British New Guinea*. Cambridge: Cambridge University Press.

Sillitoe, Paul. 2000. *Social Change in Melanesia: Development and History*. Cambridge: Cambridge University Press.

Simpson, Audra. 2007. "On Ethnographic Refusal: Indigeneity, 'Voice' and Colonial Citizenship." *Junctures* 9: 67–80.

Sinclair, James. 1984. *Kiap: Australia's Patrol Officers in Papua New Guinea*. Bathurst, NSW: Robert Brown & Associates.

Slotta, James. 2012. "Dialect, Trope, and Enregisterment in a Melanesian Speech Community." *Language & Communication* 32(1): 1–13.

Smith, Linda Tuhiwai. 2008. "On Tricky Ground: Researching the Native in the Age of Uncertainty." In *The Landscape of Qualitative Research*, edited by Norman K. Denzin and Yvonna S. Lincoln, 113–43. London: SAGE.

———. 2012. *Decolonizing Methodologies: Research and Indigenous Peoples*. 2nd ed. London: Zed Books.

Smith, Rachel E. 2018. "Changing Standards of Living: The Paradoxes of Building a Good Life in Rural Vanuatu." In *The Quest for the Good Life in Precarious Times: Ethnographic Perspectives on the Domestic Moral Economy*, edited by Chris Gregory and Jon Altman, 33–55. Canberra: ANU Press.

Spark, Ceridwen. 2011. "Gender Trouble in Town: Educated Women Eluding Male Domination, Gender Violence and Marriage in PNG." *Asia Pacific Journal of Anthropology* 12(2): 164–79.

Stocking, George. 1992. *The Ethnographer's Magic and Other Essays in the History of Anthropology*. Madison: University of Wisconsin Press.

Strathern, Marilyn. 1972. *Official and Unofficial Courts: Legal Assumptions and Expectations in a Highlands Community*. New Guinea Research Bulletin no. 47. Canberra: ANU New Guinea Research Unit.

———. 1984. "The Social Meanings of Localism." In *Locality and Rurality: Economy and Society in Rural Regions*, edited by Tony Bradley and Philip Lowe, 181–97. Norwich: Geo Books.

———. 1985. "Discovering 'Social Control.'" *Journal of Law and Society* 12(2): 111–34.

———. 1992. "The Decomposition of an Event." *Cultural Anthropology* 7(2): 244–54.

———. 1999. *Property, Substance and Effect: Anthropological Essays on Persons and Things*. London: Athlone Press.

———. 2020. *Relations: An Anthropological Account*. Durham, NC: Duke University Press.

Street, Alice. 2012. "Affective Infrastructure: Hospital Landscapes of Hope and Failure." *Space and Culture* 15(1): 44–56.

Strong, Thomas. 2006. "Land and Life: Some Terrains of Sovereignty in the Eastern Highlands of Papua New Guinea." *Suomen Antropologi* 3–4: 37–52.

Sykes, Karen. 2001. "Paying a School Fee Is a Father's Duty: Critical Citizenship in Central New Ireland." *American Ethnologist* 28(1): 5–31.

Teaiwa, Katerina Martina. 2014. *Consuming Ocean Island: Stories of People and Phosphate from Banaba*. Bloomington: Indiana University Press.

Teaiwa, Teresia K. 1999. "Reading Paul Gauguin's *Noa Noa* with Epeli Hau'ofa's *Kisses in the Nederends*: Militourism, Feminism, and the 'Polynesian' Body." In *Inside Out: Literature, Cultural Politics, and Identity in the New Pacific*, edited by Vilsoni Hereniko and Rob Wilson, 249–63. Lanham, MD: Rowman & Littlefield.

———. 2006. "On Analogies: Rethinking the Pacific in a Global Context." *Contemporary Pacific* 18(1): 71–87.

Tengan, Ty P. Kāwika. 2005. "Unsettling Ethnography: Tales of an 'Ōiwi in the Anthropological Slot." *Anthropological Forum* 15(3): 247–56.

Tilley, Christopher. 1994. *A Phenomenology of Landscape: Places, Paths and Monuments*. Oxford: Berg.

Toft, Susan (ed.). 1997. *Compensation for Resource Development in Papua New Guinea*. Canberra: Resource Management in Asia and the Pacific, Australian National University/Law Reform Commission of Papua New Guinea Monograph No. 6.

Tomlinson, Matt. 2009. "Efficacy, Truth, and Silence: Language Ideologies in Fijian Christian Conversions." *Comparative Studies in Society and History* 51(1): 64–90.

Toren, Christina. 1995. "Seeing the Ancestral Sites: Transformations in Fijian Notions of the Land." In *The Anthropology of Landscape: Perspectives on Place and Space*, edited by Eric Hirsch and Michael O'Hanlon, 163–83. Oxford: Oxford University Press.

Tsing, Anna Lowenhaupt. 1993. *In the Realm of the Diamond Queen: Marginality in an Out-of-the-Way Place*. Princeton, NJ: Princeton University Press.

Tuwere, Ilaitia S. 2002. *Vanua: Towards a Fijian Theology of Place*. Suva: Institute of Pacific Studies, University of the South Pacific.

Wagner, Roy. 1974. "Are There Social Groups in the New Guinea Highlands?" In *Frontiers of Anthropology: An Introduction to Anthropological Thinking*, edited by Murray J. Leaf, 95–122. New York: Van Nostrand.

———. 1981. *The Invention of Culture*. Chicago: University of Chicago Press.

———. 1986. *Symbols That Stand for Themselves*. Chicago: University of Chicago Press.

———. 1989. "Conclusion: The Exchange Context of the Kula." In *Death Rituals and Life in the Societies of the Kula Ring*, edited by Frederick H. Damon and Roy Wagner, 254–74. DeKalb: Northern Illinois University Press.

Wallis, Joanne, and Steffen Dalsgaard. 2016. "Money, Manipulation and Misunderstanding on Manus Island." *Journal of Pacific History* 51(3): 301–29.

Weiner, Annette. 1976. *Women of Value, Men of Renown: New Perspectives in Trobriand Exchange*. Austin: University of Texas Press.

West, Paige. 2006. *Conservation Is Our Government Now: The Politics of Ecology in Papua New Guinea*. Durham, NC: Duke University Press.

———. 2016. *Dispossession and the Environment: Rhetoric and Inequality in Papua New Guinea*. New York: Columbia University Press.

Westermark, George D. 1986. "Court Is an Arrow: Legal Pluralism in Papua New Guinea." *Ethnology* 25(2): 131–49.

Wetherell, David. 1996. *Charles Abel and the Kwato Mission of Papua New Guinea 1891– 1975*. Melbourne: Melbourne University Press.

Williams, F. E. 1933. *Depopulation of the Suau District*. Port Moresby: Territory of Papua Anthropology Report No. 13.

Wood, Michael. 2015. "Representational Excess in Recent Attempts to Acquire Forest Carbon in the Kamula Doso Area, Western Province, Papua New Guinea." In *Tropical Forests of Oceania: Anthropological Perspectives*, edited by Joshua A. Bell, Paige West, and Colin Filer, 211–36. Canberra: ANU Press.

Worsley, Peter. 1957. *The Trumpet Shall Sound: A Study of "Cargo" Cults in Melanesia*. London: MacGibbon and Kee.

Young, Michael. 1971. *Fighting with Food: Leadership, Values and Social Control in a Massim Society*. Cambridge: Cambridge University Press.

———. 1981a. "Oil Palm for Milne Bay? A Social Feasibility Study of a Proposed Oil Palm Project in Milne Bay Province." Port Moresby: PNG Institute of Applied Social and Economic Research.

———. 1981b. Notebook ANUA 553/11, University Archives, Menzies Library, Australian National University.

———. 1983a. "The Massim: An Introduction." *Journal of Pacific History* 18(1): 3–10.

———. 1983b. "The Theme of the Resentful Hero: Stasis and Mobility in Goodenough Mythology." In *The Kula: New Perspectives on Massim Exchange*, edited by Jerry W. Leach and Edmund Leach, 383–94. Cambridge: Cambridge University Press.

———. 1984. "The Hunting of the Snark in Nidula: Ruminations on Pig Love." *Canberra Anthropology* 7(1–2): 123–44.

———. 1989. "Suffer the Children: Wesleyans in the D'Entrecasteaux." In *Family and Gender in the Pacific: Domestic Contradictions and the Colonial Impact*, edited by Margaret Jolly and Martha Macintyre, 108–34. Cambridge: Cambridge University Press.

———. 1994. "From Riches to Rags: Dismantling Hierarchy in Kalauna." *History and Anthropology* 7(1–4): 263–27.

Index

Milton Keynes UK
Ingram Content Group UK Ltd.
UKHW022010131223
434314UK00012B/623

9 781805 391364